WITHDRAWN
HARVARD LIBRARY
WITHDRAWN

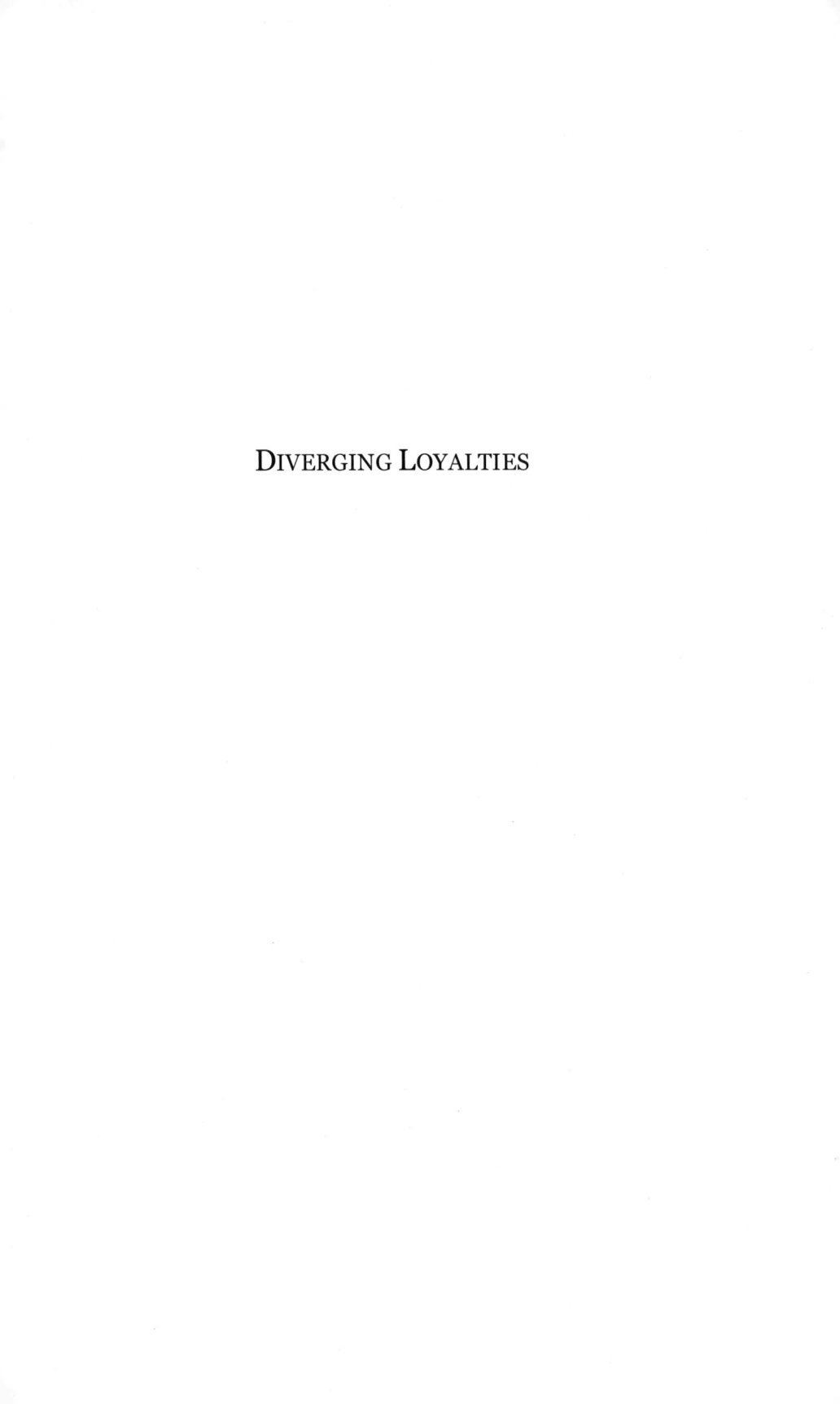

DIVERGING LOYALTIES

MERCER
UNIVERSITY PRESS

Endowed by
TOM WATSON BROWN
and
THE WATSON-BROWN FOUNDATION, INC.

DIVERGING LOYALTIES

BAPTISTS IN MIDDLE GEORGIA DURING THE CIVIL WAR

Bruce T. Gourley

MERCER UNIVERSITY PRESS
MACON, GEORGIA

MUP/H833

© 2011 Mercer University Press
1400 Coleman Avenue
Macon, Georgia 31207
All rights reserved
First Edition

Books published by Mercer University Press are printed on acid-free paper that meets the requirements of American National Standard for Information Sciences—Permanence of Paper for Printed Library Materials.

Mercer University Press is a member of Green Press Initiative (greenpressinitiative.org), a nonprofit organization working to help publishers and printers increase their use of recycled paper and decrease their use of fiber derived from endangered forests. This book is printed on recycled paper.
Library of Congress Cataloging-in-Publication Data

Gourley, Bruce T.
Diverging loyalties : Baptists in middle Georgia during the Civil War / Bruce T. Gourley. -- 1st ed.
p. cm.
Includes bibliographical references and index.
ISBN 978-0-88146-258-6 (hardcover : alk. paper)
1. Baptists—Georgia—History--19th century. 2. United States—History—Civil War, 1861-1865—Religious aspects. 3. United States—Church history—19th century. I. Title.
BX6248.G4G68 2011
286'.175809034—dc23
2011024536

CONTENTS

Acknowledgments / vii

Preface / ix

Introduction / 1

1. "A Frowning Providence" / 16

2. Church and State Revisited / 51

3. A Fleeting Hope: Southern Baptist Army Missions / 83

4. Baptist Soldiers: From Church to Battlefield / 134

5. Personal Morality and Spirituality: Patterns in

Race and Gender / 158

6. Local Church Responses / 199

Conclusion / 239

Works Cited / 245

Appendices / 257

Index / 265

The James N. Griffith Series in Baptist Studies

This series on Baptist life and thought explores and investigates Baptist history, offers analyses of Baptist theologies, provides studies in hymnody, and examines the role of Baptists in societies and cultures around the world. The series also includes classics of Baptist literature, letters, diaries, and other writings.

—Walter B. Shurden, Series Editor

ACKNOWLEDGMENTS

The writing of this volume has been aided by many people, most notably: Kenneth Noe, Draughon Professor of Southern History at Auburn University, who immersed me in the study of the American Civil War, shepherded me through my doctoral studies, and guided my dissertation work; Wayne Flynt, professor emeritus and former Distinguished University Professor of Auburn University's history department, whose insight into Southern religion compelled me to re-examine the faith of a region I grew up in before moving westward; the Auburn History Department at large, who equipped me with a solid historical foundation and modeled a friendliness and openness for which I remain most appreciative; Walter "Buddy" Shurden, currently minister at large for Mercer University and formerly the chair of Mercer's Robert's Department of Christianity and executive director of the Center for Baptist Studies, who (many years after having me as a college student, and not his top student, admittedly) encouraged me to pursue doctoral work, and then supported me immensely in the midst of the dissertation process and provided invaluable mentorship while I worked as his associate for several years within the Center for Baptist Studies; and the special collections department of Mercer University's Jack Tarver Library, where I spent countless research hours and where Susan Broome, Arlette Copeland, Robert Gardner, and Laura Botts demonstrated much patience with me and provided ongoing valuable assistance and feedback.

Also, I wish to acknowledge the patience and support of my wife Debra, especially in the latter stages of this work when we became parents. And while Elizabeth (now five) did not understand why her daddy frequently seemed to have a laptop computer attached to him while he was at home, she provided the occasion for many much-needed breaks. She also learned a love of books from a very early age, for which her daddy is very pleased.

Preface

The story of religion and the American Civil War is both beguilingly simple and surprisingly complex. C. C. Goen in *Broken Churches, Broken Nation: Denominational Schisms and the Coming of the Civil War* (1985) sketched the broad portrait of antebellum regional tensions over the issue of slavery specifically reflected in the splintering of religious denominations North and South, as portending a national bloodbath. Mark Noll in *The Civil War as Theological Crisis* (2006) later explored the theological tensions undergirding religious divisions North and South, demonstrating that differing views of scriptural interpretation and competing understandings of God's providence clouded national discourse, posited conflicting views of humanity, and ultimately clashed on the battlefield.

Meanwhile, since the 1997 publication of a collection of essays titled *Religion and the American Civil War* (edited by Randall M. Miller, Harry S. Stout, and Charles Reagan Wilson), historians have honed in upon a variety of religiously themed nuances that took place upon the stage of the Civil War beneath broadly accepted canopies represented by authors such as Goen and Noll.

My own interest in the subject of Baptists and the Civil War arose as I pursued a doctorate in History at Auburn University, under the tutelage of Civil War historian Kenneth Noe and Southern Religion historian Wayne Flynt. Delving into the unfolding stories of religion and the war on local and regional levels, I searched for primary material of enough depth and breadth to enable a meaningful examination of Baptist voices of the era, a search that in time led to Middle Georgia, due both to available primary materials and proximity. Assuming that dissenting Baptist voices in the Deep South during the Civil War would be few and far between, I was surprised to discover a rich complexity of voices, attitudes, and ideologies emanating from the ground levels of public Baptist faith: local churches, regional associations, personal journals, and a locally published Baptist newspaper (the *Christian Index*). From these ground-level sources evolved this volume, an examination of religion and the Civil War era that reveals Baptists in this region of the Deep South harbored a plurality of diverging motivations and agendas that betrayed pretences of unanimity underneath the banner of the Confederacy.

The larger story of Baptists during the Civil War, of course, is broader than that of either Middle Georgia or the whole of the South. For readers interested in exploring the broader story, I recommend *Baptists and the American Civil War: In Their Own Words* (www.civilwarbaptists.com), a digital project that explores the Baptist experience—South and North, white and black—in a daily journal format.

INTRODUCTION

Looking backward, Samuel Boykin, prominent nineteenth-century Baptist historian and editor of the Macon-based *Christian Index* during the Civil War, dismissed any Georgia Baptist opposition to the Confederacy in his 1881 *History of the Baptist Denomination of Georgia*. Following a lengthy recounting of the fervent nationalism of the 1861 Southern Baptist Convention meeting in Savannah, as well as the Georgia Baptist Convention of the same year, Boykin devoted two sentences to the collective voices of Georgia Baptists: "An examination of the minutes of our various Associations makes it evident that the Baptists of the State were intensely interested in the war, thoroughly loyal to the Confederate cause and abundant in prayers for the success of the Confederate cause." Advocating Lost Cause themes, Boykin, in short, echoed Southern apologists of his era. Yet his post-war nationalistic rhetoric signaled a departure from his war-time criticism that many Baptist individuals and churches were insufficiently patriotic.[1]

In the decades following, Southern historians of the twentieth century continued to turn to strong post-war rhetoric such as Boykin's and likewise concluded that the churches of the South wholeheartedly supported the Confederacy. In the 1950s, James Silver declared that "the Church was the most powerful organization

---

[1] Samuel Boykin, *History of the Baptist Denomination of Georgia*, 2 vols. (Atlanta: Jas. P. Harrison, 1881) 1:225–35. Edward A. Pollard institutionalized the term Lost Cause in his *The Lost Cause: A New Southern History of the War of the Confederates*, published in 1866. Jubal A. Early, former lieutenant general of the Confederate States of America, is credited with popularizing the Lost Cause in a series of articles written in the 1870s for the Southern Historical Society, an organization founded in 1868 to advance Southern interpretations of the Civil War. In short, the Lost Cause advocated that a virtuous South, defending states rights and the benign institution of slavery, suffered inevitable loss to superior military forces. This interpretation remained popular well into the twentieth century.

influencing the lives of men and women in the South in the days before and during the Confederacy." Three decades later and at the forefront of a revival of scholarly interest in religion and the Civil War, David B. Chesebrough examined a small sampling of Southern Baptist source material during the war—selected sermons, associational minutes, state meetings and national meetings—and concluded that Southern Baptists, like other denominations in the South, were indeed unified and enthusiastic in support of the Confederacy as "primary instigators in promoting sectionalism and justifying war." Maintaining that war might never have happened without the influence of the clergy and churches, Chesebrough further described the nexus of the Southern Baptist mindset during the Civil War era as "cultural tunnel-vision and ardent nationalism mixed with religious passion."[2]

Other forays in recent decades into understanding the larger dynamic of Baptists in the larger South during the Civil War have resulted in a nuanced understanding of Baptists during the war years against the background of the largely unchallenged theme of overwhelming loyalty to the Confederacy. While Daniel Stowell concluded "the vast majority of Baptists in the South supported the Confederacy from the beginning to the end of its brief existence," Paul Harvey suggests prior theological commitments constrained some Baptist attitudes toward the war. In a study of white Southern Baptist ministers, Harvey traced the rise of white supremacy among ministers during the Civil War era and noted a correlation in increased political activity, contrasted with a pre-war reticence toward political activity because of widespread Baptist support of the separation of church and state. Martin Lyndon McMahone further qualified Harvey's conclusions in arguing that Baptists in the Civil

---

[2] James W. Silver, *Confederate Morale and Church Propaganda* (New York: W. W. Norton, 1957) 93; David B. Chesebrough, "A Holy War: The Defense and Support of the Confederacy by Southern Baptists," *American Baptist Quarterly* 17/1 (March 1987): 17–31. Chesebrough examined eleven associational meetings, eight state meetings, five sermons, two national meetings, and no local church records.

War era were willing to allow the state to recognize Christianity if no preference were shown for a specific denomination.[3]

In a broader sense, Baptists have been included in recent studies of Southern evangelicals of the nineteenth century as related to the war. Randy Sparks and Jean Friedman analyzed evangelicals in Mississippi and the Eastern seaboard, respectively, discovering nuanced racial and gender patterns in the era during which Southern evangelicals transitioned from outsiders to insiders. C. C. Goen echoes the theme of Southern evangelicals coming of age, arguing that in the years immediately prior to the war, the leading clergy of Baptists, Methodists, and Presbyterians alike further agitated a regional hysteria that played a decisive role in bringing about secession and war. Mark Noll points to 1860 as the time when religion in American public life reached a zenith as evangelical Protestants, touting individualistic interpretations of scripture that reinforced Southern slave culture, became the "nation's most influential cultural force." Yet even as white evangelicals extrapolated the Old Testament story of Ham following the Genesis flood to produce the "Myth of Ham" narrative in order to justify Southern social structures, Sylvester Johnson points out that African Americans also appropriated the Ham narrative as a point of ethnic insertion, and hence biblical legitimacy.[4]

---

[3] Daniel W. Stowell, "The Ways of Providence: Baptist Nationalism and Dissent in the Civil War," *Baptist History & Heritage* 32/3,4 (July/October 1997): 8; Paul Harvey, "'Yankee Faith' and Southern Redemption: White Southern Baptist Ministers, 1850–1890," in *Religion and the American Civil War*, ed. Randall M. Miller (New York: Oxford University Press, 1998) 167–86; Paul Harvey, *Redeeming the South: Religious Cultures and Racial Identities among Southern Baptists, 1865–1925* (Chapel Hill: University of North Carolina Press, 1997); Martin L. McMahone, "Liberty More than Separation: The Multiple Streams of Baptist Thought on Church-State Issues, 1830–1900" (Ph.D. dissertation, Baylor University, 2001).

[4] Randy J. Sparks in *On Jordan's Stormy Banks: Evangelicalism in Mississippi 1773–1876* (Athens: University of Georgia Press, 1994); Jean E. Friedman, in *The Enclosed Garden: Women and Community in the American South, 1830–1900* (Chapel Hill: University of North Carolina Press, 1985); C. C. Goen, *Broken Churches, Broken Nation* (Macon GA: Mercer University Press, 1985) 65; Mark A. Noll, *The*

Theologically, the public role of providence in the faith and politics of Southern evangelicals of the Civil War era has received treatment from Noll and Nicholas Guyatt, who argue that proclamations of God's providence upon the Confederacy ultimately transcended the spiritual dimension and succumbed to Enlightenment philosophies and political agendas.[5]

The personal faiths of Southern soldiers of the Civil War era have been examined from a number of angles. Mark Wetherington estimates that only one-third of Georgians attended church during the Civil War era, and Kurt Berends argues that Southern ministers viewed a converted army as critical to sectional victory. Expectations of army revivals notwithstanding, Reid Mitchell concludes that Confederate religion affected only surface change in the lives of individual soldiers. In contrast, Steven Woodworth portrays soldiers' faith as genuine and individualistic, yet affirmative of prior religious and sectional convictions, rather than transformative. Drew Gilpin Faust offers a somewhat similar conclusion, identifying revivalist religion in the camps as a coping mechanism more than a tool for producing individual transformation. Confederate chaplains, on the other hand, according to Paul Harvey, found spiritual upliftment in the service of the Confederacy, later in their lives pointing to their war-time ministry as a high point of their Christian experience.[6]

Civil War as a Theological Crisis (Chapel Hill: University of North Carolina Press, 2006) 29.

[5] Noll, *Theological Crisis*, 94; Nicholas Guyatt, *Providence and the Invention of the United States* (Cambridge University Press, 2007); Sylvester A. Johnson, *The Myth of Ham in Nineteenth-Century American Christianity* (New York: St. Martin's Press, 2004).

[6] Mark V. Wetherington, *Plain Folk's Fight: The Civil War and Reconstruction in Piney Woods Georgia* (Chapel Hill: University of North Carolina Press, 2006); Kurt O. Berends, "'Wholesome Reading Purifies and Elevates the Man': The Religious Military Press in the Confederacy," in *Religion and the American Civil War*, ed. Randall M. Miller (New York and Oxford: Oxford University Press, 1998) 131–66; Reid Mitchell, "Christian Soldiers?: Perfecting the Confederacy," in Randall M. Miller, Harry S. Stout, Charles Reagan Wilson, *Religion and the American Civil War* (New York: Oxford University Press, 1998) 308; Steven E. Woodworth, *While God Is Marching On: The Religious World of the Civil War Soldiers* (Lawrence: University

Studies of Baptists subsumed within the larger context of Southern evangelicalism offer useful insights. But "any true in-depth study of [Baptist Civil War era] material must be done state by state and not of the South in general," Baptist historian Jesse C. Fletcher noted in a 1997 essay titled "The Effect of the Civil War on Southern Baptist Churches." Fletcher, noting the "scantiness of wartime and immediate postwar recounting" of Baptist source material, recognized that local collections were imperative for "the study of the impact of the war" within a given region. At the time, he singled out the archives of the Virginia Baptist Historical Society as the best collection available.[7]

This sub-state, regional study of Baptists in the South, utilizing at its core the extensive collection of local Baptist records in Mercer University's Special Collections, burrows down to the ground level of Baptist life in Middle Georgia. This ground level narrative reveals a religious people struggling to sort through political, theological, cultural, gender, and racial issues that belie semblances of surface unity. Prior denominational theological and polity commitments experienced complex transformations, while gender and racial patterns among Southern evangelicals, as identified by historians, did not summarily apply to Baptists. In short, Baptists in Middle Georgia responded to the war and Confederacy in patterns both similar and different than their contemporaries in the South at large, while also exhibiting significant internal diversity.

With Bibb County as the hub, Middle Georgia, for purposes of this study, is bounded by Newton, Morgan, and Greene counties to the north, Dooly and Telfair counties to the south, Washington County to the east, and Upson County to the west. The included counties are based on Baptist association boundaries. Five counties border Bibb: Crawford, Jones, Houston, Monroe, and Twiggs. Eight

---

Press of Kansas, 2001); Drew Gilpin Faust, "Christian Soldiers: The Meaning of Revivalism in the Confederate Army," *Journal of Southern History* 53/1 (February 1987): 63–90; Harvey, "'Yankee Faith' and Southern Redemption," 172.

[7] Jesse C. Fletcher, "Effect of the Civil War on Southern Baptist Churches," in *Baptist History & Heritage*, 32/3–4 (July/October 1997): 33.

Baptist associations are within or overlap these six counties. The churches of these eight associations are spread over a total of the 27 counties that comprise Middle Georgia (see Appendix A).[8]

Diversity characterized Baptist life in antebellum Georgia, expressed in theological and missionary differences. In addition to the Southern Baptist-affiliated Georgia Baptist Convention, statewide Baptist groupings included Free Will, Primitive (Old-Line), Primitive (Absoluter), Cherokee, Independent, Two Seed, and Duck River Baptists. Regionally, Baptists in Georgia were further divided into associations, each usually consisting of like-minded churches located in multiple adjoining counties, and each typically a member of one statewide Baptist organization as noted above. No African-American Baptist associations existed until after the war. In the antebellum era, African Americans and whites commonly attended church together in segregated facilities controlled by whites.[9]

---

[8] In addition to the qualifications of including churches in Bibb County or one of the five counties touching Bibb, the eight Georgia Baptist associations included in this study are represented by available records, and do not contain churches below Dooly, Wilcox, or Telfair counties, an area that is clearly South Georgia. The first requirement is self-explanatory. The second is necessitated by the sometimes-odd geographical boundaries of Baptist associations, often the result of splits among churches and/or long distances between churches, which cross regional designations in Georgia.

[9] Regarding the early history of Baptists in Georgia, including statewide and associational groupings and the establishment of African-American congregations in Savannah during the first half of the nineteenth century, an excellent primary source is Boykin, *History of the Baptist Denomination of Georgia*, vol. 1. Theological differences among Baptists typically focused on the issue of Predestination and Free Will, while missionary differences revolved around organizational philosophy. Missionary Baptists followed the practice of cooperating for mission efforts through external organizations, while Primitive Baptists believed mission work should be left to each local congregation directly. Boykin explores both of these issues. No one volume offers a comprehensive history of all Baptist groups in Georgia during the nineteenth century. A bibliography of Baptists in Georgia, including early primary sources and more recent scholarship, is available online at http://tarver.mercer.edu/archives/subjects.php. As tallied from associational indexes located in the Georgia Baptist Collection, Special Collections, Jack Tarver Library, Mercer University, Macon, Georgia, a total of eighty-three Baptist associations existed in Georgia prior to the Civil War.

Baptist associations of the nineteenth century were voluntary organizations comprised of like-minded Baptist churches existing within certain geographical boundaries. Some Baptist associations, such as the Georgia Association, the original Baptist association in Georgia that once covered much of the state, changed notably in terms of geographical boundaries as new associations were birthed. The Georgia Association in 1860 defied a simple geographical designation. Shaped somewhat like a bent finger pointing east, the association ran roughly north to south through the central-eastern portion of the state, touching the South Carolina border on its northernmost boundary.[10]

Now well established in Middle Georgia, Baptist associations on the eve of the Civil War represented the theological and missions diversity among Baptists, the differences arising from shared roots in the antebellum era. Primitive Baptists claimed the oldest association in the region, the Ocmulgee Primitive, founded in 1810. Stretching northward from Bibb, the anti-missions body of churches claimed members in Baldwin, Butts, Jasper, Jones, Monroe, Newton, and Putnam counties. Originally a missionary body, mission sentiments gradually changed among member congregations and the Ocmulgee in 1834 joined the Primitive Baptists. Nonetheless, the breaking point of cooperation with missionary Baptists in this instance was one of doctrine pertaining to church members. The split from missionary Baptists followed criticism of the association's practice of "the very new doctrine" of "the removal of membership by majority only."[11]

Ranging opposite of the Ocmulgee Primitive and only four years junior, the Ebenezer Association, the oldest Georgia Baptist

---

[10] See Robert G. Gardner, Charles O. Walker, J. R. Huddlestun, Waldo P. Harris III, *A History of the Georgia Baptist Association, 1784–1984* (Atlanta: Georgia Historical Society, 1996). The volume's dust jacket includes a map of the Georgia Baptist Association.

[11] Ibid., 111–12. For a number of years, pro-mission and anti-mission forces coexisted within the Ocmulgee Association. Declining to roughly one-third its former membership in the decade following the shift to Primitive Baptists, the Ocmulgee never recovered.

(missionary) body, was formed in Middle Georgia in 1814. Member churches in Laurens, Montgomery, Pulaski, Telfair, Twiggs, and Wilkinson were clustered immediately southeast of Bibb. Against the backdrop of the initial rise of anti-missions sentiment in Georgia, two associations were birthed in the 1820s. In 1824, one year before debates over the subject of missions began within the body, the Ocmulgee Association released fourteen of its churches to join six new congregations in the formation of the Flint River Association. In addition, the Ebenezer Association released two ministers to assist in the formation of the Flint River body. Extending north of Bibb County as did the Ocmulgee, the two overlapped in Butts and Monroe counties, with Flint River also claiming churches in Clayton, Fayette, Henry, Pike, and Spalding counties. Following a trajectory opposite that of the Ocmulgee, Flint River for the remainder of the decade and through the 1830s effectively existed as an anti-missions organization, largely refusing to relate with missionary associations. Internally during that time, the subject of missions remained a contentious topic, reflective of growing divisions statewide. By 1840, Flint River finally sided with missionary Baptists on a permanent basis.[12]

Meanwhile, the second Baptist association founded in Middle Georgia during the 1820s, the Echeconnee Association, was a Primitive Baptist body that overlapped Flint River in Monroe County but also encompassed Bibb, Crawford, Houston, Upson, and Taylor counties. Against the larger backdrop of missions controversy between Primitive and Georgia Baptist associations and churches, the Echeconnee Association in 1852 found itself at odds with other Primitive Baptists in accepting Masons as members.[13]

The divisions in Baptist life were evident when seven missionary-minded churches from the Flint River and Ocmulgee associations met in February 1834 to establish the Central Association.

---

[12] Ibid., 111, 137; minutes, Flint River Baptist Association, 1824–1860, Special Collections, Jack Tarver Library, Mercer University, Macon GA.

[13] John G. Crowley, *Primitive Baptists of the Wiregrass South, 1815 to the Present* (Gainesville: University Press of Florida, 1998) 51.

When the Central sought to establish formal relations with the Georgia Association in fall 1834, the oldest association in the state deferred while discussing relations with the now anti-missions Ocmulgee Association. Upon deciding to maintain ties with the Ocmulgee, the Georgia Association then welcomed the Central as a partner missionary association. That decision in turn provoked the Ocmulgee to distance itself from the Georgia Association, and the Flint River promptly followed suit. Despite the inauspicious beginning, the Central Association would become the dominant Middle Georgia association by the Civil War era. Comprised of churches in Baldwin, Bibb, Butts, Greene, Henry, Jasper, Jones, Morgan, Newton, and Putnam counties, the addition of the large and prominent First Baptist Church of Christ in Macon, Georgia, cemented the Central as the foremost regional body of Baptists in Middle Georgia.[14]

While missionary and anti-missionary forces continued to jockey for position among Middle Georgia associations, three additional associations took shape between 1836 and 1838. Seeking to staunch the flow of missionary churches to the anti-missions camp, missionary Baptists called for a July 1836 meeting of Georgia ministers to discuss the divisions. Held in the Middle Georgia town of Forsyth, anti-mission Baptists refused to attend, convinced that missionary Baptists were seeking to gain the upper hand. On the heels of the failed Forsyth meeting, the missionary Ebenezer Association split, with seven churches departing to form the Primitive Ebenezer Association in 1836. In response, the Ocmulgee Primitive Association, continuing a pattern of severing relations with missionary Baptists, dropped ties with the Ebenezer Association the following year. Sharing roughly the same geographical boundaries as

---

[14] Gardner, et al., *A History of the Georgia Baptist Association*, 114; minutes, Central Baptist Association, 1860, Special Collections, Jack Tarver Library, Mercer University, Macon GA.

the Ebenezer, the Primitive Ebenezer encompassed Baldwin, Jones, Pulaski, Washington, and Wilkinson counties by the Civil War era.[15]

Counterbalancing the Ebenezer Primitive Baptist Association, the missionary Rehoboth Baptist Association was founded in 1838 and included churches in Bibb, Crawford, Dooly, Houston, Macon, Monroe, Pike, and Upson. That same year, the Primitive Old School Original Towaliga Association, overlapping the Rehoboth, was also formed by churches in Butts, Clayton, Henry, Jasper, Monroe, Pike, Spalding, and Upson.

With the formation of the last two associations, the geographical stage was set for the following two decades leading up to the Civil War. Organizationally, Flint River's solid alignment with the missionary camp in 1840 cemented denominational alignments in the region. Collectively, the eight associations comprised churches located in twenty-seven counties, with Bibb as the center of a cluster that trended roughly from the north/northwest to the south/southeast of Bibb. In short, of the eight associations, by 1860 four were Southern Baptist organizations affiliated with the Georgia Baptist Convention, while the remaining four were Primitive Baptist organizations.

The available records from churches within the eight associations, associational records, the *Christian Index*, and writings of individual Baptists from Middle Georgia provide the nucleus of the primary sources. From these sources, this study examines the diversity that characterized the voices of Baptists and Baptist communities in Middle Georgia as pertaining to the Civil War era.

Chapter 1 examines the theological tensions brought about by the Civil War. On 27 January 1861 in Middle Georgia, Ebenezer W. Warren, pastor of Macon's First Baptist Church, epitomized the prominent place of evangelical clergy in the secession debate as he delivered the sermon "Scriptural Vindication of Slavery," before a

---

[15] James R. Mathis, *The Making of the Primitive Baptists: A Cultural and Intellectual History of the Antimission Movement, 1800–1840* (New York: Routledge, 2004) 115.

standing-room-only crowd. Two weeks following the beginning of hostilities, twenty Middle Georgia Baptist pastors joined other Baptists from around the state in support of the Confederacy and affirmation of the righteousness of the new nation. During the first summer of war, Julia Stanford from Forsyth confided in her diary a trust in God's favor upon the South. Well into the war, Samuel Boykin, from his newspaper office in Macon, led a chorus of individual voices in affirmation of God's providential hand upon the South. Meanwhile, collective voices of Baptist associations reinforced Warren, Boykin, and others in publicly pronouncing inevitable Southern victory predicated on the providence of God. Yet in the second half of war, disagreements over and refinement of the concept of Providence and its relation to human will increasingly occupied Baptists as the outcome of the war grew more doubtful.

Chapter 2 examines the war-time transformation of a central tenet of historical Baptist faith, the separation of church and state. John Brinsfield's analysis of Civil War chaplains uncovered relatively few of the Baptist persuasion, and the experience of Middle Georgia Baptists indicates that the shortage of chaplains stemmed from a refusal to accept government funding of chaplain salaries, the stance consistent with long-standing Baptist aversion to the joining of church and state. At the same time, and somewhat surprisingly, Baptist congregations in Middle Georgia evidenced little enthusiasm in terms of direct support of army chaplains and missionaries, much to Samuel Boykin's displeasure. Among instances of Baptist clergy ministering within the ranks, Boykin and others hoped that resulting revivals in the second half of the war would lead to personal commitments for God as well as victory for the Confederacy. Finally, despite aversion to government-sponsored chaplains, Baptists in Middle Georgia quickly embraced church-state collaboration on a number of other fronts during the war years, including matters related to the Sabbath and government-appointed days of fasting and prayer. Sabbath issues proved especially difficult as Baptists displayed a lack of consistency concerning the issue of church-state separation.[16]

Elaborating upon the theme of army missions, chapter 3 analyzes the changing narrative of missions as the war progressed. Disrupting established foreign and home mission fields, the war in turn presented a new opportunity for Baptists in Middle Georgia: army missions. While many Baptists in Middle Georgia eventually came to view the conversion of soldiers as critical to Southern victory, spiritual conversion of soldiers was widely understood to be more important than temporal battlefield successes. The narratives of the transition among Baptists to the cause of army missions varied greatly among different associations and churches, widely framed in the context of spiritual gain. Benjamin Murrow, missionary to Native Americans, left the reservations for army missions, his personal influence impacting Rehoboth Baptist's mission efforts. Flint River Baptists switched to army missions without offering criticisms of camp life, while Central Baptists' focus on soldiers took place alongside acknowledgments of grave sin among troops. Diversity characterized the manner in which army missions were carried out, while home-front observers debated the effectiveness of Baptist efforts. While mission efforts sometimes contributed to revivals, Samuel Boykin and others questioned the sincerity of converts. For Baptists in Middle Georgia, the defeats at Gettysburg and Vicksburg in summer 1863 lent greater urgency to spiritual conversion among soldiers; yet Northern victory in 1865 brought army missions to an abrupt end, leaving the mission-minded scrambling to find new venues to direct their mission efforts.[17]

---

[16] John W. Brinsfield, William C. Davis, Benedict Maryniak, and James I. Robertson, Jr., eds., *Faith in the Fight: Civil War Chaplains* (Mechanicsburg PA: Stackpole Books, 2003); Mitchell, "Christian Soldiers?: Perfecting the Confederacy," 308.

[17] Wetherington, *Plain Folk's Fight*; Berends, "Wholesome Reading," 131–66; Drew Gilpin Faust, *This Republic of Suffering: Death and the American Civil War* (New York: Alfred A. Knopf, 2008).

Chapter 4 moves beyond army missions and the camps at large and examines the lives of Civil War soldiers who departed local churches and the Baptists' Mercer University to fight for the Confederacy. Few active ministers joined the ranks, but young Baptist laymen from churches large and small left home and hearth and marched northward or westward to fight for the preservation of the South. Baptists among the Twiggs County Volunteers reflected James McPherson's conclusion that defense of homeland and a sense of duty motivated soldiers to march off to war. Yet personal views of the war varied among soldiers. Second Lieutenant Edwin Davis, captured at Vicksburg then released, remained upbeat even during the fall of Atlanta, while fellow soldier Alva Spencer, survivor of Gettysburg, alternated between hope and discouragement from 1862 onward. Like other soldiers, Baptists expressed anxiety for family and friends back home, as well as a longing for normalcy. While battles and injuries claimed the lives and limbs of some Baptists, their congregations expressed great concern regarding physical death and spiritual conversion. Nonetheless, churches kept few records of soldier-sons, and soldier diaries reflected little of the Baptistness of individuals. In the end, Baptist soldiers in the field often stood outwardly apart from their faith family, their public identify that of warrior rather than denominational devotee. Trajectories of personal spirituality proved difficult to ascertain, and congregations displayed little inclination to formally celebrate the return of soldier-sons following Southern defeat.[18]

Focusing again on the home-front, chapter 5 addresses patterns of race and gender. Defending slavery as righteous in an effort to frame the morality of war, white Baptists joined other white Southerners in embracing the Myth of Ham narrative. Yet Baptist minister A. C. Dayton feared that young, white Baptists were not fully committed to a slave society, and Baptists in Middle Georgia at large struggled over the question of the humanity of slaves. Church

---

[18] James W. McPherson, *For Cause and Comrades: Why Men Fought in the Civil War* (New York: Oxford University Press, 1997).

discipline in theory affected all equally and implied both racial and gender equality on a spiritual level. The narrative of Baptists in Middle Georgia indicates that church members took discipline seriously, voluntarily (at least among whites, who had the option of resisting) submitting to measures meted out by their spiritual peers. Specific instances of discipline cases broken down by race and gender reveal patterns that at points deviate and in other instances reinforce prior studies of Southern evangelicals of the era by Randy Sparks and Jean Friedman. In addition, patterns of participation in congregational life during and after the war varied along racial and gender lines. While the narrative of women reflected a significant degree of uniformity among congregations, the story of African-American members in the months following Southern defeat traversed divergent paths.[19]

The final chapter addresses the over-encompassing subject of nationalism at the local church level. In short, Baptist congregations in Middle Georgia did not respond to the Confederacy and Civil War in a uniform manner. Boykin in particular criticized rural Baptists for a lack of patriotism, an observation that took place against the backdrop of a growing divide among urban, modernistic evangelical churches and rural, traditional congregations immediately preceding the war, as identified by Randy Sparks and Samuel Hill. Many were the external criticisms of pastors in Middle Georgia who, with few exceptions, ignored repeated calls to abandon pulpit for service in the army as chaplains and missionaries. Other patterns among Middle Georgia Baptists revealed internal fault lines, as local congregations responded to the war and the Confederacy in one of three identifiable ways: nationalistic expressions, spiritual concerns, or silence. Within these variances, sub-patterns are examined, including correlations

---

[19] Johnson, *The Myth of Ham*; Bertram Wyatt-Brown, *Southern Honor: Ethics and Behavior in the Old South* (New York: Oxford University Press, 1982); Randy J. Sparks in *On Jordan's Stormy Banks*; Jean E. Friedman, in *The Enclosed Garden*.

with associational affiliation, the impact of the *Christian Index*, and the number of congregational deaths.[20]

In short, while Baptist soldiers in Middle Georgia joined their fellow Southerners in fighting for the Confederacy, Baptists living in Middle Georgia were transformed by both the politics and the battles of the war. The war-time transformation found expression within church walls, denominational life, and individuals, in some instances creating friction among Baptists of Middle Georgia and evidencing new patterns of behavior and thought not evident prior to the war.

---

[20] Sparks, *On Jordan's Stormy Banks*, 78–114; Samuel S. Hill, ed., *Encyclopedia of Religion in the South* (Macon GA: Mercer University Press, 1984) 293–97.

CHAPTER 1

"A FROWNING PROVIDENCE"

Contemplating the twin disasters of Gettysburg and Vicksburg in summer 1863, Samuel Boykin, editor of Georgia Baptists' *Christian Index*, probed the foundations of his faith and that of his readers. Perhaps many Southerners, expecting their prayers to force God to come to the rescue of the South, had become their own foils by not living righteously, Boykin surmised. Yet if the war served as a punishment from God designed to effect righteousness among his people, why did immorality remain rampant? And if God intended the war to be a blessing rather than a curse, praying for peace would instead invoke heavenly wrath. Struggling to make sense of new realities, Boykin concluded, "good and evil are strangely commingled in this world of ours." Later, in spring 1865, with the Confederacy in tatters, Boykin conceded the human prism of God's will. "In our bereavements we have seen a frowning providence hiding a smiling face," the editor acknowledged, "and in our victories we have read the favor God extends to a righteous cause."[1]

As editor of the South's largest Christian newspaper in terms of circulation, Boykin's words carried significant weight among Baptists in Georgia. His office in Macon, the newspaperman's influence was particularly felt in Middle Georgia, the region of his birth. Born in 1829 in Milledgeville, Georgia, to the son of a wealthy planter banker, the young Samuel went to Pennsylvania and Connecticut for his education. He returned to Georgia and graduated from the state university in 1851. After spending a year traveling overseas, he came home, converted to Christianity, joined a Baptist church, and was

---

[1] Samuel Boykin, "The Moral Effects of the War," *Christian Index*, 21 August 1863, 2; Samuel Boykin, "Lessons of War—No. 1," *Christian Index*, 30 March 1865, 2.

almost immediately licensed to preach in 1852. Despite abundant opportunities for preaching, Boykin turned to journalism rather than pastoral ministry, a transition facilitated by both his education and family wealth. Settling in Macon and becoming active as a layman in the First Baptist Church, Boykin was hired as editor of the *Christian Index* in 1859. Two years later he purchased the paper from the financially struggling Georgia Baptist Convention. As a condition of the purchase, Boykin agreed to retain the publication as a voice of Georgia Baptists. Under Boykin's ownership, *Index* circulation increased noticeably, reflecting his attentiveness to his constituency. Although he received ministerial ordination in 1861, Boykin remained a writer for the remainder of his career. In addition to owning and editing the *Index* until 1865, in the ensuing years he wrote and edited Baptist children's literature and authored an exhaustive history of Baptists in Georgia, titled *History of the Baptist Denomination in Georgia*.[2]

Boykin represented a denomination transitioning from outsiders to insider status and wealth in antebellum Georgia. Baptist views before and during the Civil War era followed a journey of hardship, perseverance and other-world certainty. Beginning in earnest in the middle of the eighteenth century, Baptist migration southward established evangelical outposts on the Southern frontier. By sheer numbers, they quickly became a force to be reckoned with in Virginia. Some, yet restless, pushed onward into the Deep South, spilling over into Georgia and present-day Alabama in the post-Revolutionary era. Enduring the daily dangers of the wilderness, the

---

[2] William Cathcart, *The Baptist Encyclopedia*, 2 vols. (Philadelphia: Louis H. Everts, 1881) 1:123–24; Jack U. Harwell, *An Old Friend with New Credentials: A History of the Christian Index* (Atlanta: Georgia Baptist Convention, 1972) 86–97; Samuel Boykin, *History of the Baptist Denomination of Georgia*, 2 vols. (Atlanta: Jas. P. Harrison, 1881). Boykin did serve as pastor of the Second Baptist Church in Macon for one year, 1872–1873.

Baptist pioneers, buttressed by a Calvinistic theology of providence, found comfort in the heavenly world that awaited the faithful.[3]

Yet while providence flourished in the soil of Southern Baptist life, the certainty of God's anointing failed to prevent them and other Southern evangelicals from parting ways with their Northern counterparts between 1837 and 1845. Southern Presbyterians and Methodists preceded Baptists in creating separate regional entities, with all three denominations splitting over questions related to the issue of slavery in church life. C. C. Goen argues that slavery-induced denominational schisms "riveted the attention of the whole nation" and signaled the end of national unity. With leaders of the nation's largest denominations unable or unwilling "to reconcile their differences over the moral issue posed by slavery" it became "difficult to believe that the sectional conflict was by any means repressible."[4]

As the political antagonism between North and South deepened, Southern evangelicals increasingly defended the slave culture of their region even as the role of religion in national public life grew. Southern church leaders insisted that slavery was ordained by God, yet also presented slavery as a civil institution beyond the realm of religious action, thus entangling (white) Southern rights with the will of God. Goen argues that prominent clergy of all three leading Protestant denominations helped sustain "an atmosphere of

---

[3] See William L. Lumpkin, *Baptist History in the South: Tracing through the Separates the Influence of the Great Awakening, 1754–1787* (St. John IN: Larry Harrison, 1995). This volume is the definitive work on the early migration and settlement of Baptists in Virginia and the Southern frontier. Although the early Separate Baptists in the South, so labeled because they separated from traditional Baptists in embracing the revivalism of the early eighteenth century, downplayed Calvinistic doctrine; by the last two decades of the century, Calvinistic orthodoxy became more and more of a concern (133–34).

[4] C. C. Goen, *Broken Churches, Broken Nation* (Macon GA: Mercer University Press, 1985) 65. See also Mitchell Snay, *Gospel of Disunion: Religion and Separatism in the Antebellum South* (New York: Cambridge University Press, 1993). Snay argues that Southern evangelical identification with culture impeded development of a perception of slavery as immoral.

excitement that approached hysteria," in turn playing a critical and decisive role in effecting secession and the formation of the Confederate States of America. Mark Noll offers a broader context for the influence of Southern clergy, arguing that the influence of religion in American public life reached a zenith in 1860. Evangelical Protestants, believing the truth of the Bible as interpreted by their own individual interpretations, "constituted the nation's most influential cultural force." Thus Southern clergy clutched the Bible and preached slavery, their rhetoric spurred on by Northern clergy's biblical opposition to slavery.[5]

For white Baptists in Middle Georgia, Southern secession confirmed and reinforced widespread confidence that God's providential hand rested firmly upon Southern Baptists and the Southern states. Secession vindicated the formation of the Southern Baptist Convention over the issue of slavery, and in turn Baptists extended the providential blessings of God upon the Confederacy and reiterated slavery as God's will for African Americans.

From the pulpit, for example, Ebenezer W. Warren, pastor of the First Baptist Church of Christ in Macon, Georgia, explained God's relationship to the South and slavery in the wake of the state's secession. Facing pews filled with eager listeners on 27 January 1861, Warren preached a sermon titled "Scriptural Vindication of Slavery" that offered justification for Southern secession as well. Slavery, Warren insisted, comprised the root of the sectional conflict. Following a reading from Ephesians 5:5-8, he declared that "slavery forms a vital element of the Divine Revelation to man. Its institution, regulation, and perpetuity, constitute a part of the many books of the Bible." He continued: "Both Christianity and Slavery are from Heaven; both are blessings to humanity; both are to be perpetuated to

---

[5] Goen, *Broken Churches, Broken Nation*, 170–71; Mark A. Noll, *The Civil War as a Theological Crisis* (Chapel Hill: University of North Carolina Press, 2006) 29; Drew Gilpin Faust, *Creation of Confederate Nationalism: Ideology and Identity in the Civil War South* (Baton Rogue: Louisiana State University Press, 1988). Faust argues that Southern clergy provided the "central foundation" of Southern nationalism (22, 23).

the end of time.... Slavery is right; and because the condition of the slaves affords them all those privileges that would prove substantial blessings to them; and, too, because their Maker has decreed their bondage, and has given them, as a race, capacities and aspirations suited alone to this condition in life." In the following weeks, against the backdrop of the formation of the Confederate nation, both the *Macon Telegraph* and *Christian Index* reprinted Warren's sermon verbatim.[6]

While secession affirmed the Baptist denominational split of 1845, the ensuing declaration of hostilities and early battles of the Civil War seemed to reveal the favorable hand of God for all to see. Two weeks after the firing upon Fort Sumter, at least 20 Baptists from Middle Georgia, from a total of 104 statewide, attended the annual meeting of the Georgia Baptist Convention. War was upon their minds, a conflict understood as the will of God. As one of the first orders of business, Nathaniel M. Crawford, president of Mercer University and son of former United States Secretary of the Treasury William H. Crawford, motioned that a committee be appointed to report on the "condition of the Country." The motion passed, and the following morning, delegates listened to the "Report of the Committee on the present political crisis." The statement declared that "Almighty God" had thus far "blessed our arms and our policy" and the committee expressed confidence "that God will deliver us from all the power of our enemies and restore peace to our country."[7]

With the pronouncements of the GBC yet reverberating, Samuel Boykin, from his editorial office in Macon, quickly moved to assure the Baptist public that the South was on the side of God in its war against the North. In early June, he offered biblical support for the war under the guise of 1 Timothy 1:18. The "object" of the war was "good—to save the soul and bless the world." The "end" was also

---

[6] *Christian Index*, 13 February 1861, 3; *Macon Telegraph*, 7 February 1861.

[7] *Christian Index*, 8 May 1861, 2; minutes, Georgia Baptist Convention, 1861, 3–6, 28, Special Collections, Jack Tarver Library, Mercer University, Macon GA. For more on N. H. Crawford, see Boykin, *History of the Baptist Denomination in Georgia*, 1:154–57.

"good—life, peace, joy, eternal rest." A month later, the editor asked, "How do we know that we are right?" This time the answers were anything but spiritual: the spirit of the American Revolution, the aggression of the North and the right of the Southern states to self-defense provided enough of a rationale for Southerners to "confidently look up to the God of nations and invoke His aid in our struggle for the right."[8]

The two-pronged approach to underscoring God's alliance with the South resonated with Baptists. A biblical defense appealed to the theology of a Calvinistic-influenced denomination well-versed in God's providence. The concurrent theme of Southern righteousness appropriated God's will for the nation. Baptists in the South seemingly stood in unison. Victory at Manassas evidenced the dual apologetic. Julia Stanford, a young Baptist living in Forsyth, did not need theological training to understand the significance of Manassas as related to God's providence. "I am a firm believer in our overruling all wise and omnipotent God," Stanford declared. As to Manassas, "this has truly been a day of thanksgiving to God for the kindness bestowed upon our soldiers and for the victory at Manassas.... Truly the Lord is our God and our God is the Lord.... I today felt this was a Sabbath."[9]

In the weeks following the South's initial victory at Manassas, four elder Georgia Baptist ministers, all currently or formerly Middle Georgians, joined the *Index* as editorial voices. Adiel Sherwood, arguably the most prominent Baptist in the entire state and one of the best known in the nation during the first half of the nineteenth century, had taken a lead in both the formation of the Georgia Baptist Convention and Mercer University. Former *Index* editor Joseph S. Baker had long and ardently defended slavery among Baptists. Long-time pastor Charles D. Mallary had also worked as an area evangelist.

---

[8] "War a Good Warfare," *Christian Index*, 5 June 1861, 2; "The Present War: How Do We Know We Are Right?" *Christian Index*, 10 July 1861, 2.

[9] Julia A. Stanford, diary, Spencer King Papers, Special Collections, Jack Tarver Library, Mercer University, Macon GA, 18 July, 21 July.

Now retired, he continued to serve as a Mercer trustee. Finally, former pastor of First Baptist in Macon and acting editor of the *Index*, Sylvanus Landrum, the only Southern-born member of the informal editorial board, was now in his second year as pastor of First Baptist Church, Savannah.[10]

---

[10] *Christian Index*, 31 July 1861; Harwell, *An Old Friend with New Credentials*, 86–93. In 1827, as pastor of Eatonton Baptist Church in Eatonton, Sherwood's preaching helped bring about the greatest Baptist revival in Georgia up until that time. In addition to pastoring the Eatonton church, from the 1820s through the Civil War years Sherwood pastored numerous other congregations in Middle Georgia. However notable Sherwood's activities as a pastor in Middle Georgia, his service in a denominational capacity, both within and without the state of Georgia, became his most visible contribution to Baptist life. In short, when Boykin chose Adiel Sherwood to contribute to the collective voice of the *Index* during the troubled years of war, he chose not only perhaps the most prominent Baptist in the state, but also one of the most recognized Baptist leaders on the continent. See Cathcart, *The Baptist Encyclopedia*, 1055–56. For more information on Adiel Sherwood's early and important role in Georgia Baptist life, see Jarrett Burch, *Adiel Sherwood: Baptist Antebellum Pioneer in Georgia* (Macon GA: Mercer University Press, 2003). Born in Liberty County GA in 1798, Joseph S. Baker, a Yale-educated, Columbian college graduate was a Presbyterian farmer, businessman, and doctor before converting to the Baptist faith in 1831. He first became a preacher in Virginia and then a newspaper publisher in Columbus, Georgia. He served as editor of the *Index* from 1843–1849, covering the separation of Baptists in the North and South, and the subsequent formation of the Southern Baptist Convention. An ardent defender of slavery, Baker took exception to Northern abolitionists who sought to purchase the freedom of escaped Southern slaves. "There is not a Christian slave, in any of our colored Baptist churches in the South," he editorialized in 1848, "who would not vote to excommunicate a member that should attempt to run away from his or her master; so much purer are the Christian morals of Southern slaves, than are the morals of fanatical freemen of the North!" During the war, Boykin served as an evangelist among the soldiers. Minutes, Georgia Baptist Convention, 1845, Special Collections, Jack Tarver Library, Mercer University, Macon GA; *Christian Index*, 16 May 1845, 23 May 1845, 20 January 1848, 16 November 1848; Cathcart, *The Baptist Encyclopedia*, 1:61. Younger than Sherwood and Baker, Charles Dutton Mallary was born in West Poultney, Vermont, in 1801. In 1830, he moved to Georgia and assumed the pastorate of First Baptist Church in Augusta, and in 1834 moved to Middle Georgia to pastor the First Baptist Church of Milledgeville. Resigning from the pastorate, he worked as an agent of Mercer University from 1837 to 1840, afterwards returning to pastor in various Middle Georgia churches, serve as

Together with Boykin, the four prominent Baptists confidently assured the Baptist public of God's providential hand upon the Confederacy. "The victory at Manassas," according to one editorial, "suggests the victory of Gideon over the Midianites [sic].... In each case a large and well appointed army, vastly superior in numbers, suddenly became panic-stricken, and fled in utter and hopeless confusion. God was the author of the rout of the Midianites, and he is no less the author of the victory at Manassas."[11]

---

acting evangelist for the Central Baptist Association, and serve on the board of trustees of Mercer University. Retiring in 1852 due to declining health, he lived out his remaining years on a farm he owned near Albany. He would die in 1864 before the war ended. Cathcart, *The Baptist Encyclopedia*, 2:741–43; minutes, Georgia Baptist Convention, 1864, Special Collections, Jack Tarver Library, Mercer University, Macon GA; report, Mercer University Board of Trustees, 1866, Special Collections, Jack Tarver Library, Mercer University, Macon GA. The youngest of the four, Sylvanua Landrum was born in Oglethorpe County GA in 1820 and was educated at Mason Academy in Virginia and Mercer University. Unlike the others, Landrum had spent his entire life in the South, with his ministerial experiences confined to the state of Georgia. From 1849 to 1859, he pastored First Baptist Macon, and also served as chairman of the Georgia Baptist Convention's *Index* committee during the paper's move from Penfield to Macon, and he briefly served as acting editor of the *Index* for three months in 1857. His editorial voice during the war spoke from the context of a more pragmatic understanding of the conflict. When Savannah fell to Union control, Landrum demonstrated his commitment to spiritual matters above temporal issues when he refused to close the doors of the church, choosing instead to preach to Union soldiers during the occupation. Under his leadership, First Baptist Savannah "was the only white Baptist church on the coast line from Baltimore to Texas which did not close at all during the conflict." Cathcart, *The Baptist Encyclopedia*, 2:669–70; minutes, Georgia Baptist Convention, 1856–1857, Special Collections, Jack Tarver Library, Mercer University, Macon GA; Samuel Boykin, *History of the Baptist Denomination in Georgia*, 1:231; Harwell, *An Old Friend with New Credentials*, 86. Boykin and Harwell disagreed on Landrum's tenure as acting editor of the *Index* in 1857. Boykin notes that Landrum served for two months, while Harwell lists the assignment as a three-month arrangement.

[11] "God Crowns the Battle," *Christian Index*, 21 August 1861, 2. Like many editorials written by Boykin, Sherwood, Baker, Mallary, and Landrum, the article is unsigned. As chief editor, Boykin doubtlessly wrote the bulk of unsigned editorials.

Yet just as God's chosen people of the Old Testament had at times grumbled despite Yahweh's blessings, even before the celebration of Manassas subsided some Baptists voiced complaints regarding weather conditions on the home-front, concern about food supplies, and inflationary pressures. Chiding such unbelief, Boykin insisted that "Providence rules." Had God "not led our generals, protected our soldiers, fought our battles, crowned us with victory? It may be that these long and heavy rains of summer were necessary upon such a protracted drought in spring.... It may be that Providence designs to shorten the crop, and thereby increase the demand, raise the price, and open our ports," the editor suggested.[12]

Despite such assurances, some Baptists felt compelled to acknowledge that God's will, originating in the heavenly realms, might also confound the expectations of his people on earth. Confidence in the Southern armies did not negate the mysterious ways of God. Discerning and claiming the future for Baptists in the South in the name of God proved early on to be an overarching theme of Baptists in Middle Georgia during the war years. In September 1861, for example, Boykin began a systematic apologetic for the Christian South as he attempted to answer the question, "What shall we do?" Drawing back from the immediate war news, he surveyed the larger series of events precipitating the moment's crisis. The first task involved establishing the righteousness of the South in the midst of evil times. The sins of the South had brought war upon God's people, and the North served as God's instrument of wrath. The events befallen the South were in accordance with God's plan and designed to lead his people to repentance. Win or lose, the war

---

[12] "Thoughts on Current Events," *Christian Index*, 21 August 1861, 3. Lewis O. Saum, *The Popular Mood of Pre-Civil War America* (Westport CT: Greenwood Press, 1980) 3–26, identifies two distinct views of Providence during the antebellum and Civil War era. Editors of religious publications, when addressing the general public, posited Providence as future-oriented, framing it in terms of manifest destiny. But when speaking on a personal level to soldiers, the same editors positioned Providence as that which had protected and provided the individual in the past. The *Index* follows this general pattern.

originated from the hand of a God willing to rip apart nations in order to love his chosen people. Spiritual gain ultimately trumped battlefield victories, effected by trust in God. Early the following year, the *Index* editor warned that the "the iron hand of despotism may crush out every spark of life, but it will not compel us to surrender," acknowledging that only by trusting in God could the South achieve victory. Without that trust, "like Pharaoh's host, we will be utterly destroyed."[13]

Baptists of the Central Baptist Association, which included Samuel Boykin's home church of First Baptist Macon, seemingly echoed Boykin's hesitation in asserting too certain a knowledge of God's will. Meeting at Bethel Baptist Church in Jasper County in late August 1861, Central Baptists, pondering "the present state of the country, fully recognize the hand of Almighty God," vowed to "humbly bow before Him, and patiently wait for his will to be done in all our borders." Separately, they offered praise to God "for the victories given by Him to our arms." Although Central Association churches counted more black members than whites (1415 to 1327), the utterances were those of white members only. African-American members, nearly all slaves, were neither present nor represented in the crafting of the statements, their presence deemed unnecessary, their voices unwanted, as was the case in all Baptist associations in Middle Georgia prior to and during the Civil War.[14]

Yet while Boykin and the Central Baptist Association took a somewhat measured approach in late summer 1861 by publicly asserting the primacy of spirituality and humility, other Baptists in Middle Georgia were not so hesitant in affirming confidence that God's providence assured military victory. Meeting at Traveler's Rest

---

[13] "What Shall We Do?" *Christian Index*, 3 September 1861, 2; "Thoughts; For Citizen and Soldier," *Christian Index*, 18 February 1862, 3.

[14] Minutes, Central Baptist Association, 1861, 11–14, Special Collections, Jack Tarver Library, Mercer University, Macon GA. Typical of Baptist associations in the South of this era, the voices of African Americans are silent in associational records. No known records of black congregations or associations in Middle Georgia exist prior to the war.

Baptist Church in Macon County on 14 September, white Baptists of the Rehoboth Baptist Association expressed certainty of God's will as it pertained to the South. "We honestly believe," they proclaimed, "that in this great struggle for all that is dear to us as a people, we have the approving smiles of Him who rules at his will the destinies of nations...and His sure protection to our friends and relatives upon the tented field."[15]

Other Baptists expressed confidence in the Confederacy and voiced hope that God's hand would effect Southern victory. Baptists of the Flint River Association, meeting 22 September at the Shiloah Baptist Church in Monroe County, "heartily" endorsed "separation from the North and the formation of the Southern Confederacy." Pledging themselves to the "defence and support" of the Confederacy, they credited the summer's military successes to God and "sincerely and earnestly pray that He will guide us in all our efforts and sustain us in all our righteous purposes to a successful and triumphant determination of this war." While stopping short of the unmitigated certainly of Rehoboth Baptists, Flint River Baptists clearly believed God was on the side of the "righteous" South.[16]

One of the four Primitive Baptist associations also echoed similar themes in September, voicing confidence in God's hand upon the South and pledging support for the Confederacy, "a country highly favored of the Lord." Declaring before "nations of the earth" that "the Government of our Southern Confederacy has our confidence and esteem," Baptists of the Ocmulgee Baptist Association pledged to sustain their country with "united hearts and hands."[17]

Self-declared corporate assurance in God's will for the South, however, did not preclude personal agony over the loss of loved ones. A tiny congregation in Middle Georgia, Lebanon Baptist

---

[15] Minutes, Rehoboth Baptist Association, 1861, 2–3, Special Collections, Jack Tarver Library, Mercer University, Macon GA.

[16] Minutes, Flint River Baptist Association, 1861, 4–12, Special Collections, Jack Tarver Library, Mercer University, Macon GA.

[17] Minutes, Ocmulgee Baptist Association, 1861, 8, Special Collections, Jack Tarver Library, Mercer University, Macon GA.

Church in Crawford County, mourned over the loss of a soldier member and his father in October 1861. Despite publicly affirming and accepting the providence of Almighty God, the death of young Owen M. McAfee and his father A. J. McAfee proved a bitter pill to swallow:

> Whereas, it has been the pleasure of the alwise dispenser of events, to cut down by the relentless hand of death, away from home & most of his family connexion, in the service of his country at Yorktown, Va. on the 11th Sept. 1861 our much beloved brother & esteemed friend Owen M. McAfee, aged 25 years, in prime of life & at an hour, when the energies of his mind were absorbed in the cause of the Liberty & Independence of his country & the protection of the helpless & defenseless women & children of the same.

Even more tragic was the fact that the young McAfee's death had followed that of his father, a "kind and devoted" family man and "kind and benevolent" and "unassuming" deacon of the church who exhibited an "exemplary walk" as a Christian. The resolution assured family and friends that McAfee died a noble death as a soldier in the 6th Georgia Infantry, in service of home and country. Months later, on 3 June 1862, the death of young McAfee at Yorktown still haunted the Lebanon congregation, as members "devoted a short time to prayer for our soldiers in the tented field whom we suppose to be now engaged in battle at Yorktown, Va."[18]

Baptists' refuge in God's providence during the early months of war ultimately reflected larger patterns among Southern evangelicals and the nation at large. Evangelical clergy South and North appropriated God's will in staking out moral high grounds and predicting victory. Labeling providence's transformation as a "crisis,"

---

[18] Minutes, Lebanon Baptist Church, Crawford County, 1861–1862, Special Collections, Jack Tarver Library, Mercer University, Macon GA, microfilm reel 638; minutes, Rehoboth Baptist Association, 1862, 16, Special Collections, Jack Tarver Library, Mercer University, Macon GA; National Park Service Civil War Soldiers and Sailors System, http://www.itd.nps.gov/cwss/ (accessed 14 June 2011).

Noll concludes that the problem was rooted in "trust in providence so narrowly defined by the republican, covenantal, commonsensical, Enlightenment, and—above all—nationalistic categories that Protestant evangelicals had so boldly appropriated with such galvanizing effects in the early decades of the nineteenth century." Nicholas Guyatt goes a step further, arguing that by the Civil War era, providence, appropriated from Europe and first introduced in the New World in the early days of colonial America, had a longstanding history as a decidedly non-monolithic tool for achieving political ends expedient to a given time and purpose. Thus the members of Lebanon Baptist agonized over the death of the McAfees, yet at the same time deemed battlefield sacrifices honorable and remained confident in the Southern concept of providence.[19]

Unwavering confidence in the providence of God, at least on the part of some Baptists, continued into 1862, as the war dragged on beyond the expectations of many. In April of that year, J. H. Stockton declared that "No other spot upon the whole earth has ever been favored with the goodness of God, as the people who compose the Southern States." One month later, Ebenezer Warren assured Baptists that Southern victory was inevitable, because God favored the South. And in June, Samuel Boykin renounced any sign of wavering or hesitation on the part of the South. He adamantly averred that a God of righteousness would bring triumph because of the rightness of the Southern cause, writing that "We battle for the *principles of constitutional government*; for the *legitimate privileges of State*; for the *sacred rights of freemen*; for *liberty of conscience*; for the *defence of our homes, our loved ones, and our property*."[20]

---

[19] Noll, *Theological Crisis*, 94; Nicholas Guyatt, *Providence and the Invention of the United States* (Cambridge University Press, 2007).

[20] Rev. J. H. Stockton, "To the 'Lord's Host' Throughout the Confederacy," *Christian Index*, 22 April 1862, 1; E. W. Warren, "Sabbath Evening Reflections: Improvement of Troubled Times," *Christian Index*, 20 May 1862, 1; "Informal Chat," *Christian Index*, 3 June 1862, 2. Stockton, a pastor in the Georgia Association, is best remembered for his role in an 1870 associational resolution

The assurance of victory thus remained despite growing doubts about the South's wartime capabilities. In the face of the coming of fall and winter, one Baptist warned that an enlarged and energized Union army could overrun portions of the South and force residents to flee further inward. Admitting the superiority of the North in numbers, wealth and munitions, as well as noting the discipline within Union ranks, the writer allowed that the South's "superior generals and brave soldiers may be overcome by the mere weight of numbers." Nonetheless, the disadvantaged South boasted the ultimate weapon. "What then is our dependence? THE ALMIGHTY AND EVER BLESSED GOD."[21]

Yet while some Baptists in 1862 resolutely affirmed God's providential hand upon the South with no qualifiers, others repositioned God's favoritism as contingent upon Southern morals. While the responsibility for victory remained in God's hands, the responsibility of earning God's favor through proper behavior fell upon the Confederacy. Baptists were not alone, in the face of national upheaval, in turning their attention to personal morals. Refusing to recognize slavery as a sin in the early war years, Southern evangelicals at large focused instead on behavioral sins such as drinking and gambling, a reflection of the legacy of antebellum social reform efforts that fostered evangelical piety.[22]

In Middle Georgia, Samuel Boykin slowly developed a Southern interpretation of providence hedged by evangelical piety. In March 1862, he admonished his fellow Baptists and Southerners at large to renounce the sins of Sabbath-breaking, profanity, gambling, extortion

---

opposing Mercer University's relocation from Penfield to Macon. See B. D. Ragsdale, *Story of Georgia Baptists* (Atlanta: Foote and Davis, 1932) 208–209.

[21] "What May Be Before Us," *Christian Index*, 21 October 1862, 2.

[22] See Michael P. Young, *Bearing Witness against Sin: The Evangelical Birth of the American Social Movement* (Chicago: University of Chicago Press, 2006); Charles Reagan Wilson and Mark Silk, eds., *Religion and Public Life in the White South* (Lexington: University Press of Kentucky, 2005); and Edward R. Crowther, *Southern Evangelicals and the Coming of the Civil War* (Lewiston: Edwin Mellen Press, 2000).

and drunkenness in the camps before asking God to save the South. The following month a Baptist who only identified himself as "Paulus" declared in the *Index* that God's providence hinged on sins national and personal, and he warned pastors to proclaim the message of individual as well as national repentance.[23]

Rising to the surface in 1862 as a primary concern, observance of the Sabbath became a barometer of God's now-uncertain attitude toward the South. One Baptist that spring, observing empty pews, judged that the South was no more religious at that time than it had been prior to the war. To the contrary, the opposite seemed "true in many parts of our land. The God who delivered our forefathers from bondage, and gave to them the goodly land which we have inherited, has been ignored by many, and the homage which is His due has been rendered to Caesar!"[24]

To be sure, a few Baptist associations in Middle Georgia, meeting during late summer and early fall, still insisted upon a providence unaffected by personal piety and Sabbath attendance. Flint River Baptists, although "afflicted" and "sad" over the deaths of family members, stood alone in affirming God's unconditional favor upon the Confederacy. "We believe the good Lord is with our Southern Confederacy, and will enable us eventually to throw off the yoke of oppression, repel our enemies, and take our place among the family of nations, a free and independent people." Offering no recognition of sins national or personal, nor related punishments from the hand of God, Flint River Baptists pledged to support the military effort and offer weekly "special prayer for our suffering country." In a similar fashion, Ocmulgee Association Baptists reaffirmed their faith in the "just cause" of the Confederacy favored by the "God of hosts," avoiding the subject of national and personal morality.[25]

---

[23] "A Skeleton of a Fast Day Address," *Christian Index*, 18 March 1862, 1; "A Word to Pastors and Churches," Paulous, *Christian Index*, 1 April 1862, 1.

[24] "Read and Ponder," *Christian Index*, 8 April 1862, 1.

[25] Minutes, Flint River Baptist Association, 1862, 4, Special Collections, Jack Tarver Library, Mercer University, Macon GA; minutes, Ocmulgee Baptist

In contrast, however, Baptists of the Ebenezer Association acknowledged and accepted "chastisements from the Lord" and accepted the South's punishment fully as God's will. The absence of any direct statement concerning God's providence upon the Confederacy marked the meeting of Central Baptists, although concern for Sabbath observances surfaced. Gathered at Madison Church in Morgan County, Central Baptists thanked General Robert E. Lee for "ordaining that all drills, parades and reviews, except for the purpose of inspection, shall be dispensed with in the Army on the Holy Sabbath, so that our soldiers may attend divine worship."[26]

While 1862 led some Baptists in Middle Georgia to qualify the nature of God's providence, the following year witnessed Baptist struggles to understand the divide that separated God's providence from human actions. Samuel Boykin's probing questions, and his puzzlement over good and evil coexisting in the Confederacy in the week's following Gettysburg and Vicksburg, were the results of a theological struggle that began months earlier.

The tension inherent in the dual Baptist heritage of Calvinism and Arminianism was on full display by January 1863. As the national conflict dragged on month after month, and as God's people continued to be chastised by their loving Deity, many struggled to understand why war and punishment seemingly knew no end. "Why is the war prolonged?" Boykin asked, searching the mind of God and examining the morals of men. Concluding that sinfulness and worldliness plagued the South and bore responsibility for the punishment meted upon the nation, Boykin declared, "People of the Confederate States, if ye would end this war so unconscionably protracted, ye must do so by appeasing the wrath of Heaven!" Appeasement required "the reformation of public and prevalent

---

Association, 1862, 12, Special Collections, Jack Tarver Library, Mercer University, Macon GA.

[26] Minutes, Ebenezer Baptist Association, 1862, 8, Special Collections, Jack Tarver Library, Mercer University, Macon GA; minutes, Central Baptist Association, 1862, 10, Special Collections, Jack Tarver Library, Mercer University, Macon GA.

iniquities" and necessitated the forsaking of evil and the living of honorable lives. Personal morality, in short, remained the sole source of national woes, as determined by white Southerners. Yet unwilling to cede the nation's ultimate destiny to the actions of men, Boykin ultimately affirmed providence as the eventual determiner of victory.[27]

By late spring, however, at least one Baptist abandoned entirely the language of providence in urging white Southerners to renew the fight for their freedoms. The future of the Confederacy, according to a minister referred to only as "a warm-hearted pastor in Middle Georgia," rested solely in the hands of the Anglo-Saxon race. Should whites allow "themselves to be subjugated.... they would prove themselves too degenerate to appreciate liberty." Victory or defeat, men in arms would decide the fate of the South.[28]

Samuel Boykin, meanwhile, set aside concerns about national sins and now seized upon the themes espoused by the "warm-hearted pastor." Ignoring his initial affirmation of a simple and unqualified heavenly providence, as well as later explorations of a passive providence steered by the morals of men, Boykin, seemingly reacting to the moment, called for Southerners to recognize their national duty and seize their own destiny. Battlefield defeats in summer 1863 did not reflect upon the sins of the South, he argued, but rather provided an occasion to rise above misfortune and claim the righteousness and justness of the Southern cause. Sackcloth and ashes forsaken, Gettysburg signaled the need for total commitment to patriotism and unwavering faith in victory. Calling for soldiers to display courage, Boykin pronounced the invincibility of the South and encouraged soldiers to "the shout of defiance.... for as sure of success as the sun shines.... It will not be six months before every one will wonder that he should ever have doubted" victory.[29]

---

[27] "Why Is the War Prolonged?" *Christian Index*, 13 January 1863, 2.

[28] "According to Your Faith Be It unto You," *Christian Index*, 8 June 1863, 2.

[29] "The Crisis of Our National Affairs," *Christian Index*, 24 July 1863, 2; "Despondency," *Christian Index*, 31 July 1863, 2; "Success of Our Cause," *Christian Index*, 31 July 1863, 3.

For Boykin, at this moment, providence remained intact, but now rested in patriotism backed by bullets and artillery. Some fellow Baptists readily agreed with the *Index* editor. One instructed Southerners to retain hope despite the perils at hand, for "let it be remembered that unless we *will it*, we never *can* be conquered." Another portrayed the conflict as no ordinary war and one in which it would do no good to "fold our hands, and wait for the Lord to help us." To the contrary, Southerners "must strain every nerve and make use of every means...guns, powder, men, horses, food, brains and bayonets." Still another argued that the South's hope lay "in the strong right arm of each *man* who can wield a sword or shoulder a gun."[30]

Writing from General Robert E. Lee's camp in November 1863, E. B. Barrett further appropriated the imagery and language of the church in transferring providence from the heavenly realm into an earthly and human context. The battle of Gettysburg, he wrote, was a time and place where "many brave men gave their lives as an offering on the altar of liberty." Sensing the lasting significance of the event, Barrett predicted that "the painful retreat to Virginia, will be theme of many fire-side conversations in days to come." Equating human will, unbending to the point of death, as the hope of the Confederacy, Barrett sanctioned the defense of white freedom as a holy act.[31]

The juxtaposition of human will and God's will merely marked the latest chapter in a decades-long evangelical struggle to frame the two realms. By the time of the Civil War, Northern evangelicals had comfortably embraced human efforts, in the form of social reforms, as a legitimate means of effecting justice in society. Southern evangelicals, however, had remained unconvinced. Systematically voicing the position of Southern evangelicals, Presbyterian James Henley Thornwell of South Carolina, a prominent minister in the

---

[30] "Danger and Duty," *Christian Index*, 4 September 1863, 2; "No Ordinary War," *Christian Index*, 18 September 1863, 2; "The Delusive Phantom of Hope," *Christian Index*, 11 December 1863, 1.

[31] E. B. Barrett, "From Gen. Lee's Army," *Christian Index*, 6 November 1863, 1.

South during the Civil War, coined the phrase "spirituality of the church" in defense of a passive acceptance of God's will for humanity. The church, Thornwell argued, "is not a moral institute of universal good, whose business it is to wage war upon every form of human ill.... It has no commission to construct society afresh.... The problems, which the anomalies of our fallen state are continually forcing on philanthropy, the Church has no right directly to solve. She must leave them to the Providence of God." Human wisdom "sanctified and guided" by God, Thornwell argued, played a complementary role to providence. Specifically, regarding the slavery issue, Thornwell insisted that the church "has no right to interfere directly with the civil relations of society."[32]

While Thornwell appropriated God's will in defense of slavery prior to the war, in 1862 he turned to a providence dependent upon human action. In so doing, he employed themes increasingly familiar to Baptists in Middle Georgia: the necessity of personal and national piety, and faith in soldiers. Of sins personal and national, Thornwell insisted that "dependence upon Providence carries with it the necessity of removing from the midst of us whatever is offensive to a holy God. If the Government is His ordinance, and the people His instruments, they must see to it that they serve Him with no unwashed or defiled hands. We must cultivate a high standard of public virtue. We must renounce all personal and selfish aims, and we must rebuke every custom or institution that tends to deprave the public morals." Thornwell's list of sins was long: "Bribery, corruption, favoritism, electioneering, flattery, and every species of double-dealing; drunkenness, profaneness, debauchery, selfishness, avarice, and extortion" had to be eradicated if the South were to become "the fit instruments of a holy Providence in a holy cause." Yet personal piety remained only half of the equation of human effort needed to achieve "great deeds" in the South's time of peril.

---

[32] Ernest Trice Thompson, *The Spirituality of the Church: A Distinctive Doctrine of the Presbyterian Church in the United States* (Richmond: John Knox Press, 1961) 21–25.

Thornwell also called upon white Southerners to exhibit "the moral power of courage, of resolution, of heroic will" in order to defeat the North. In short, God's providence remained theologically intact, yet the realization of God's will for the South required a priori conditions dependent upon human efforts.[33]

Like Boykin and Thornwell, many Baptists remained both unwilling to dismiss the primacy of God's will and unable to envision Southern defeat. The conversation regarding national and personal sins remained in its infancy, overshadowed by the raw emotions following the devastating defeats at Gettysburg and Vicksburg. The "heroic will" called for by Thornwell the previous year had proven inadequate. A post-Gettysburg world demanded some qualifiers, leading to the further development of a middle ground between the will of God and the determination of Southern warriors. Ebenezer Baptists voiced the belief that God remained on the side of the Confederacy, and although the Almighty presently chastised the South, he would ultimately "help" and "aid" Southerners on the road to victory. Flint River Baptists also remained confident of victory despite recent "severe reverses" that plagued a "bleeding nation." Reaffirming that "above all...the Lord Jehovah is on our side," they nonetheless focused much more on pledging their "fidelity" to and trust in government, President Jefferson Davis, "the skill and efficiency" of Confederate officers, and "the endurance and bravery" of Southern soldiers. Collectively, human effort and the favoritism of God made failure "impossible."[34]

Other Baptists, however, refused to waver from their strict Calvinistic heritage of unqualified providence. Meeting in September

---

[33] James Henry Thornwell, "Our Danger and Our Duty" (Columbia SC: Southern Guardian Steam-Power Press, 1862) 11–13. This document is online at http://docsouth.unc.edu/imls/thornwell/thornwel.html (accessed 14 June 2011), courtesy of the University of North Carolina.

[34] Minutes, Ebenezer Baptist Association, 1863, 4–5, Special Collections, Jack Tarver Library, Mercer University, Macon GA; minutes, Flint River Baptist Association, 1863, 5–6, Special Collections, Jack Tarver Library, Mercer University, Macon GA.

1863 at Mount Zion Baptist Church in Jones County, the Primitive Baptists of the Ocmulgee Association, the previous two years having affirmed God's providential hand upon the just cause of the South, reexamined the big picture. In assessing the will of God, they offered an altogether different statement than that of Southern Baptists. Displeased by the actions of American Christians prior to the formation of the Confederacy, God in his providence determined to punish all Americans North and South, thus bringing about war. The "will of high heaven" remained on the side of the Confederacy in the present conflict, but Southerners were not without guilt. The peculiar American sin borne by Christians, these Primitive Baptists insisted, was "universal love for the whole human race (or at least for those who were at the greatest distance)." Unwavering in the belief that God's providence alone determined the eternal destiny of individuals and nations, the Ocmulgee Baptists labeled as apostate the "religious world" of early- and mid-nineteenth-century America. During that period of growing missionary zeal, "plans and means were invented, unauthorized by the Scriptures" to save the world. Christians falsely believed that "the Gospel must be sent to the heathen, else they would perish" and that God holds believers accountable for their blood. These "deprived carnal inclinations" resulted in "the vengeance of the ever jealous God" upon the American nation. Although the South shared guilt in the attempt to thwart God's will for the world, God would ultimately save his "beloved country." For Ocmulgee Baptists, God's will entailed punishment for human efforts on His behalf, no matter how well intentioned.[35]

Brushing aside questions of providence, evidencing no acknowledgement of the larger Calvinistic paradigm, and ignoring the gloom and doom that overshadowed the Confederacy, Central Baptists in late summer 1863 took another tack, evoking the imagery of mystery in redirecting the conversation. Meeting in Macon County in August, they reached a conclusion that would have been

---

[35] Minutes, Ocmulgee Baptist Association, 1863, 4–5, Special Collections, Jack Tarver Library, Mercer University, Macon GA.

deplorable to their nearby Primitive Baptist brethren. "It is doubtful whether we have ever fully grasped the idea, that under God we are to save the world and the country," they declared. Referring to the spiritual condition of souls, rather than governments or warfare, Central Baptists from this point forward would avoid collective statements concerning the relationship of God's will and the Confederacy, nor would they express support for the Southern cause.[36]

The economic and social foundations of the Confederacy and slavery could not be long neglected when speaking of providence. For some post-Gettysburg and Vicksburg Baptists unwilling to advocate human actions or human will at the risk of creating an impotent God, slavery provided an avenue for affirmation of the Almighty in the face of national crisis. In the midst of struggling with his own questions about providence, Boykin turned to slavery for context. The "mysterious providences" of God would utilize misery and suffering to develop national character and the human resources needed to effect his grand will for the South. Whatever the sins of Southerners, the institution of slavery could not be counted among them. God's ultimate purposes remained unknown, but "must, in some wise be connected with the dark sons of Ham, whose lot has been apparently so providentially cast amongst us, and whose presence, in a servile condition, aroused the North, that insane fanaticism, whose infidel ravings and iniquitous workings brought about this unholy war." No longer certain of battlefield victory, Boykin remained assured that as guardians of the institution of slavery, Southern whites were God's chosen people.[37]

Yet reframing God's will in affirmation of a "just cause"—in reaction to human morality, as appreciation for Southern patriotism, or as reward for steadfastness and battlefield bravery—left less room for spirituality. Some Baptists, in the face of the South's declining

---

[36] Minutes, Central Baptist Association, 1863, 7, Special Collections, Jack Tarver Library, Mercer University, Macon GA.

[37] "He Maketh Wars to Cease," *Christian Index*, 20 November 1863, 1.

fortunes, looked beyond the theocratic, nationalistic God of the Old Testament and sought comfort and meaning in a New Testament concept of providence. Less than two months after Gettysburg, one Baptist suggested that although God remained in charge and on the side of the South, national destiny was not adequate for one's salvation. The more important matter, the writer insisted, was that "each Christian...work out his own salvation with fear and trembling." For this Baptist, "personal religion" stood supreme, and Paul's words in the New Testament book of Philippians addressing the mystery of individual righteousness trumped Old Testament imagery of God directing the fortunes of entire nations.[38]

Other Baptist voices echoed the underlying sentiment of the primacy of personal religion. Rejecting the notion of God's will as a corollary to the Southern cause, one Baptist warned against the "common impression that because ours is a just and right cause, we must infallibly succeed in repelling our foes." A just cause, he noted, did not always translate into triumph. After chronicling the correlation between battlefield reverses and growth in army revivals, the writer concluded that any comfort in the face of adversity should be framed in terms of spiritual blessings, which in turn might lead to "good things" in the end.[39]

Baptists in Middle Georgia by 1864 thus reflected a larger, growing disillusionment and accelerating confusion regarding God's plan for the South. Among evangelicals, discussion of providence, increasingly couched with qualifiers within the context of defeat, replaced once-simple affirmations of God as guardian of the Confederacy. Doubts were not confined to the religious realm, of course. Many small farmers and landless tenants of South Georgia and Alabama, despite volunteering for military service, had silently

---

[38] "Personal Religion," *Christian Index*, 21 August 1863, 2. See Philippians 2:12–13: "Wherefore, my beloved, as ye have always obeyed, not as in my presence only, but now much more in my absence, work out your own salvation with fear and trembling. For it is God which worketh in you both to will and to do of his good pleasure" (King James version).

[39] "Tokens of God's Favor," *Christian Index*, 4 September 1863, 2.

harbored reservations about the Confederacy from the beginning. Initially hoping their wartime service would offer advancement in life, by 1862 their attitudes shifted in the face of hunger, filthy camp living conditions, and the ever-increasing prospect of death. By 1863, these poor sons of the South were deserting in the thousands, and those who remained in the army in the closing months of war had no faith in the Confederacy and no hope for their future.[40]

Although largely a common folk religion, Baptist life in the South, as previously noted, also included a growing class of elites, Samuel Boykin being one of the most prominent. In early 1864, Boykin set out to stem the swelling tide of disillusionment among the lower classes serving in the army. Focusing on human bravery as the hope of the South, Boykin and his editorial staff implored soldiers to remain resolute in the struggle for white freedom. Battlefield losses of the previous years served as "a sacred holocaust to Southern liberty, independence and valor," while the "proud spirit which ever existed in the Southern Cavalier's bosom still burns and blazes." Facing gloomy prospects, hope nonetheless remained. One editorial spoke sadly of the "sea of trouble" characterizing the South, yet declared that the sorrow would pass and victory be achieved. Invoking biblical imagery, the writer likened the Northern invaders to the ancient Egyptian persecution of the Hebrews. Continuing the fight remained the only viable alternative. "Nought remains for us but to fight for freedom until freedom is achieved, as achieved it will be," the writer insisted. More trials and sufferings awaited, while the safety of loved ones rested squarely in the "undaunted valor" of the soldier and the honor of the country could only be preserved by bloody victories won through the bravery of the Southern army.[41]

In the waning days of July 1864, one Baptist pointed to the theme of human effort, rather than providence, as the savior of the South.

---

[40] See for example David Williams, *Rich Man's War: Class, Caste and Confederate Defeat in the Lower Chattahoochee Valley* (Athens: University of Georgia Press, 1998).

[41] "1864!" and "New Year Words for Soldiers," *Christian Index*, 8 January 1864, 2.

Issuing a call to all Southern white men, the writer demanded sacrifice and even death in order to ensure Southern victory. Over three years into the conflict, some men had yet to contribute to the war, he complained. Addressing those men yet remaining at home, the writer issued a call to "gird on their armor and hurry to the front: let those who cannot go make the sick and wounded the special objects of their attention." Acknowledging the wavering of willpower and the collapse of certain victory, he declared, "let the timid be brave, let the hesitating be decided, let croakers take heart, let the doubtful be reassured, let all be bold, confident, cheerful, laborious, self-sacrificing, and success will soon be ours!"[42]

For white Baptists, concurrent with dimming prospects of Southern victory, the final transference of faith and hope from the Almighty to the soldier seemingly reached a pinnacle in late summer. "It is impossible to calculate," one Baptist gushed, "all the happiness, comfort, safety, dignity, honor, glory, wealth and prosperity that hang upon the courage, discipline, constancy and self-sacrificing patriotism of those noble veterans that compose our army. To them we look for all of safety, felicity and national independence that a nation can enjoy; and we look in confidence." Worn, weary, draped with ragged clothing, and witness to despondency and desertions, the heroic Confederate soldier bore the last, desperate hopes of a fading nation. Portraying home-front Southerners as putting their love, trust, and hope in their guardians, men of honor, and battlefield heroism and glory, the writer left little room for the hand of God.[43]

Yet even as some Baptists turned to the solider as savior of a rapidly sinking Confederacy, others remained unwilling to make a total capitulation. A Baptist identified only as "L.T." invoked biblical imagery of struggle as he wrestled with God's apparent inaction, human responsibility, and the prospect of Southern defeat. At best, one could only hope that God might listen to the cries of Southerners. "Look up to God…in the day of trouble…with the wrestling spirit of

---

[42] "Duty of the Hour," *Christian Index*, 29 July 1864, 2.
[43] "Our Army," *Christian Index*, 9 September 1864, 2.

Jacob," he noted, referring to the Old Testament story of the Hebrew patriarch who refused to let an angel of God depart apart from the bestowing of a blessing. Begging God for victory, however, would not alone suffice. Personal sacrifice for the cause of country was necessary, and there was "no time for croaking, for selfishness, for money making.... Every man who can must go to the field, those who cannot, must support the country, feed the poor, make provisions for the army, support the government." Seeking to make sense of what appeared to be a lost cause, L. T. framed spiritual matters as a larger concern. A "fearful crisis" faced the church. While "many of her devout sons" fought valiantly on distant battlefields, home-front Baptists expressed "waning interest" in religious matters. Sanctuaries sat empty, the houses of prayer abandoned. Committed to the Confederacy but unable to mediate the favor of God to the nation, the church stood at the precipice of spiritual devastation.[44]

The Southern situation only grew worse. Four months later, in June, L. T. again voiced concerns. Acknowledging troubling developments on multiple fronts as the fourth year of war unfolded, he called upon soldiers to redouble their efforts, pleaded with home-front Baptists to pray for success and sought to paint a positive portrait of the Confederate army even as General William Tecumseh Sherman bore steadily down upon Atlanta, Georgia. "Sherman is in an unenviable position," L. T. declared. "His troops, having met with several disastrous repulses, must be somewhat intimidated, if not demoralized, his base far in the rear, with thousands of our dashing cavalry hovering around his small Garrisons." The fate of Georgia rested in the hands of General Joseph E. Johnston, whom the writer judged to be competent for the task.

Yet fears were not to be quelled by Johnston alone. L. T. sought to shore up belief in God as well as the army. Turning to the prior theme of the consequences of national sin, he juxtaposed the confession with an assurance that God still remained squarely on the side of the Confederacy. "The Lord Almighty alone can give us

---

[44] L. T., "The Crisis and Our Duties," *Christian Index*, 12 February 1864, 1.

victory, and he alone can make our victories prove blessings to our country. Let us confess and forsake our sins, and turn to the Lord with all our hearts."[45]

Other Baptists expounded upon the theme of the South's fate straddling an intersection of God's desires and man's actions. The human mind permitted only limited insight into the workings of an omnipotent deity, one Baptist argued. The South could find solace that God honored those who honored him, and helped those who helped themselves, a self-help theology that assured a "bright and sublime" future.[46]

Ebenezer Baptists also stood alongside L. T. in affirming God's providence while acknowledging the Almighty had no obligation to grant a Southern victory. Claiming for the South a position of truth and justice, Baptists of the Ebenezer Association admitted the South's "wicked" ways, bowed before God's "Allwise providence," trusted in the justice of his chastising, and expressed hope and belief that success was yet obtainable, dependent "upon the will of God."[47]

Although coupled with the direction of God's will, the specifics of the guilt acknowledged by white Ebenezer Baptists on behalf of the South in late 1864 remained unspecified. Some, by this time, felt uneasy about abuses associated with slavery. A few months prior a Baptist, identifying himself only as "Nicodemus," had suggested that the unjust mistreatment of slaves (not the institution of slavery itself) might be contributing to the South's reversal of fortunes. And a few months afterward, Southern Baptists' leading theologian weighed in on the theme of providence as related to slavery. John L. Dagg, then retired, was a former president of Mercer University and author of Southern Baptists' lone systematic theology volume, *Manual of Theology*, published in 1857. A frequent contributor to Baptist newspapers both in Georgia and throughout the South, the Calvinist

---

[45] L. T., "Notes on the Times," *Christian Index*, 3 June 1864, 3.

[46] "Patience, Unselfishness, Perseverance," *Christian Index*, 9 September 1864, 2.

[47] Minutes, Ebenezer Baptist Association, 1864, Special Collections, Jack Tarver Library, Mercer University, Macon GA, 8.

apologist tackled the issue of slavery and providence at a time when a desperate South contemplated arming slaves to fight the Union. Unlike Ebenezer Baptists, he left little doubt as to the sins of the South. While agreeing with Nicodemus that white failure to evangelize slaves stood as the most damning aspect of slavery, he nonetheless offered a more comprehensive analysis. Arguing that mistreatment of slaves led to Southern chastisement under the hand of God, Dagg admitted that slave owners could be guilty of mistreating their chattel, singling out the sins of not recognizing slave marriages and, most importantly, of not evangelizing slaves. Charging that "multitudes of masters...regard their slaves as mere instruments for making money," the writer scolded guilty slave owners for not making "the distinction between the immortal minds that they control and the brute animals that they protect and use for the sake of gain." Although an institution ordained by God, slavery as executed by Southerners was not yet perfected. "The rod of God is upon us.... Providence will teach us when we have honestly engaged in the work" of slavery done correctly.[48]

Examining the larger landscape, Kenneth Stampp suggests that slavery posed a moral burden upon the mind of the South, while Eugene Genovese argues that some slave owners felt guilt for not living up to the standards of slavery as espoused by the Bible. More pointedly, Richard Beringer concludes that guilt over slavery ultimately contributed to Southern defeat. The guilt thesis, despite various nuances and stiff opposition, nonetheless engages the religion of the South that provided theological rationale for the institution of slavery. Minus historical hindsight and bound by culture, Nicodemus and Dagg merely fretted over abuses of what they viewed as the otherwise proper institution of slavery, most notably as related to the withholding of the Gospel from African Americans. That the inherent

---

[48] Nicodemus, "We Are Not Right in This War," *Christian Index*, 10 June 1864, 1; Cathcart, *The Baptist Encyclopedia*, 1:306. Nicodemus was a Jewish religious leader who approached Jesus under the cover of night for fear of being ridiculed by the other leaders who opposed Jesus. See the Gospel of John, chap. 3.

immorality of the institution itself might imperil the South, they could not, or would not, address. Yet Nicodemus' observation in June 1864 proved prescient: "Well may we fear and tremble for ourselves and our beloved institution," he mourned.[49]

While limited doubts concerning slavery troubled some Baptists, and L. T. and Ebenezer Baptists sought middle ground between God's sovereignty and man's free will, some Baptists, remaining defiant to the end, refused to question God's providential favoritism of the South. Striving to accentuate the positive, Flint River Baptists in September 1864 insisted "we feel grateful to God our bleeding country is not in a worse condition." Noting that the South entered the war "wholly unprepared" militarily, they attributed to "the mercy of God" the South's survival "through three years and a half of fierce conflict with a cruel and relentless foe." Despite setbacks in the form of territory and lives lost, the "goodness of the Lord" guaranteed an "invincible army." While questions of God's providence and human free will paralyzed some Baptists, Flint River Baptists stood unwavering in their belief that God had long determined Southern victory. "We are sure," they declared, "the proper source of our

---

[49] Nicodemus, "We Are Not Right in This War," *Christian Index*, 10 June 1864, 1; A number of historians have examined the theme of Southern guilt over the institution of slavery Kenneth Stampp, in *The Imperiled Union: Essays on the Background of the Civil War* (New York: Oxford University Press, 1981) posits slavery as a moral burden upon the mind of the South, so much so that defeat and the destruction of slavery resulted in a sense of relief. In *A Consuming Fire: The Fall of the Confederacy in the Mind of the White South* (Athens: University of Georgia Press, 1998) Eugene D. Genovese examines guilt over slavery in the context of religion in the South. Mitchell Snay, in "American Thought and Southern Distinctiveness: The Southern Clergy and the Sanctification of Slavery," *Civil War History*, 35/4 (December 1989): 311–28, examines clergy efforts to overcome moral opposition to the practice. Richard Beringer, Herman Hattaway, Archer Jones, and William N. Still, Jr., in *Why the South Lost the Civil War* (Athens: University of Georgia Press, 1987) conclude that guilt over slavery was one identifiable factor that contributed to Confederate defeat. For a comprehensive historical analysis, albeit dated, of the guilt thesis, see Gaines M. Foster, "Guilt over Slavery: A Historiographical Analysis," *The Journal of Southern History* 56/4 (November 1990) 665–94.

ultimate success is the goodness and power of our Heavenly Father." Some Baptists serving in the army mirrored the outsized confidence of home-front Flint River Baptists. T. J. Cumming, ministering among the 12th Georgia camped near Bunker Hill, agreed. "God has blessed us," Cumming insisted. "The troops here seem to have bright hopes in view of future prospects. Let all who profess to love God, both at home and in the army, lift their hearts continually in prayer to God, and trust him for the result." Cumming's positive outlook fits Jason Phillips's description of "diehard rebels," soldiers who were assured of their own invincibility, a perception fostered to a significant degree by the insular nature of Southern religion and culture. Within this faith-sustained crucible, the foundations of the Lost Cause myth took shape, according to Phillips. As such, on the home-front in Middle Georgia, Flint River Baptists joined rebel soldiers in lending their faith to the emerging narrative of a righteous nation that could not be conquered by the weapons of men.[50]

Perhaps T. J. Cummings and Flint River Baptists, while not disagreeing with Samuel Boykin's confidence in military victory, looked with puzzlement upon the editor's ever-evolving formula for Southern hope. Feigning surprise and frustration that some Southerners doubted that the courage of Southern soldiers would ensure victory, Boykin offered another argument in his equation for success. The ungodly characteristics of the enemy—"base, cruel, tyrannical and inhuman"—provided ultimate assurance that the South would prevail, he insisted. "We cannot—we will not—believe that the Almighty will give final success to their arms," he insisted. The "blood-thirsty...coldly selfish...heartlessly cruel" Northerner invaders would be repelled by the will of Southerners willing the hand of God.[51]

---

[50] Minutes, Flint River Baptist Association, 1864, 7, Special Collections, Jack Tarver Library, Mercer University, Macon GA; T. J. Cumming, "From the Valley," *Christian Index*, 23 September 1864, 3; Jason Phillips, *Diehard Rebels: The Confederate Culture of Invincibility* (Athens: University of Georgia, 2007).

[51] "Notes on the Times," *Christian Index*, 23 September 1864, 3.

For Boykin, the low point of his soul-searching possibly arrived in December 1864. Following the devastation in Middle Georgia caused by Sherman's army, as well as the ineffectual response of the Confederate defenders, Boykin in his frustration turned his wrath upon the citizens of Macon. Calling for prayer on behalf of the South in the face of desolation, the editor warned that "danger encompasses us on every side, and yet our people are almost prayerless, almost indifferent." Boykin did not mince words, writing that "in this ungodly city of Macon so lately saved from sack and conflagration, not fifteen persons can be induced to meet together and pray." Echoing the words of a Presbyterian newspaper editor, Boykin wrote, seemingly in desperation, "If there is any religion amongst us, if any faith, if any love for our country, if any trust in God, let it now be seen." Even as Boykin called his fellow Maconites to faithfulness to God and country, at least one Baptist church in Macon had recently held a "special prayer-meeting for the country."[52]

Perhaps the perceived apathy of Maconites served to bring the *Index* editor full circle, for one week after skewering his fellow Baptists he returned to early convictions of unquestioned providence. Summing up 1864 as one of "disaster and distress to the Confederacy.... shrouded in gloom and tinctured all over with blood and agony and disappointment.... filled up with ashes and bones and tears and groans," Boykin could find nothing redeeming in the year's events. Amidst gloom and doom, he fell back upon the Calvinist stream that ran deep in Baptist life, seeking to assuage his own despair and offer words of comfort to his readers. Although God had permitted the North to gain battlefield successes over the Confederacy, the affliction was from God and its rightness could not be questioned. Seeking comfort in theology and scripture, Boykin continued: "Yes, God *ordains*! Blessed be His holy name forever.... God knows what is best for us.... farewell 1864! You have been a trying year to us; but not one tear hast thou brought, not one smile

---

[52] "Prayer for Our Country," *Christian Index*, 22 December 1864, 1; "Personal," *Christian Index*, 22 December 1864, 3.

has though quenched, not one sigh hast though caused, but what our heavenly Father *ordained*. Consoling thought!" God remained in control, and Baptists could rejoice in his unchanging sovereignty.[53]

The theme of Southern salvation through heavenly chastisement, building since the painful battlefield reversals of 1863, became commonplace for home-front Baptists in the closing months of war. A providence clothed in blessing and prosperity was now long abandoned by most Baptists. For some, faith in God's sovereignty necessitated factoring military defeat into God's plan. Explaining the meaning of salvation for the South took on a new sense of urgency. Baptist angst played out against the backdrop of the beginnings of the Lost Cause myth, a narrative that in the wake of Southern defeat, displaced slavery as central to Southern culture and framed the Confederacy's valiant soldiers as unable to overcome impossible odds against an unjust foe. Although defeated on the battlefield, the smoldering South could take comfort in maintaining the high moral ground to the bitter end.[54]

For Baptists, the Lost Cause opened the door for a synthesis of worldly abandonment, spiritual growth, and self-justification. While some Baptists in prior years had sought to turn attention to spiritual things and away from earthly matters, the same message now seemed more pertinent. For one Baptist in January 1865, the ravages of war and impending defeat served to turn the South's attention back to God. Sufferings brought about by war taught a new devotion to and understanding of the Bible, of which one important lesson was that the evil God visited upon His chosen people was for the purpose of their ultimate salvation. Yet another self-justifying lesson learned pointed to the greater sins of Northerners who had "for years imagined they were morally elevated above every other people in Christendom." Yet their "atrocious deeds" including the "robbery

---

[53] "Farewell to 1864," *Christian Index*, 29 December 1864, 2.
[54] See Gary W. Gallagher and Alan T. Nolan, eds., *The Myth of the Lost Cause and Civil War History* (Indianapolis: Indiana University Press, 2000).

and murder of unarmed citizens, women and children" clearly revealed their nature as anything but godly.[55]

At the same time, Samuel Boykin fingered covetousness, the "love of money," as the primary human sin from which God's providence should be interpreted. "We love money or property more than we do our Saviour," he charged. "We give little to the poor, little to the church, little to the heathen; but we give a great deal of time, a great deal of thought, a great deal of labor and a great deal of money to increase our stores." Boykin's warnings took place against the backdrop of public anger over spiraling inflation and food shortages throughout the South. "We too inordinately love our own broad lands, our numerous slaves, our stocks and hoarded cash," he continued, obviously speaking to the elites of Southern society. "Before this fell spirit even patriotism has been made to bow; and men are willing to sacrifice country, liberty, and all the glorious rights and immunities of independence, if by so doing they can save their own property."[56]

Yet while some Baptists on the home-front scrambled to salvage God's sovereignty as the Confederacy sank, other Baptists ministering within the army camps remained unwilling to concede defeat. Army correspondent J. W. J., writing from Virginia in February 1865, offered assurance that Georgians in the Petersburg campaign, albeit tired of the war and ready to return home to family and loved ones, remained defiant. The full extent of the correspondent's unflagging optimism poured forth in his overall assessment of the status of the Confederate army in Virginia. In the face of mounting losses suffered by the Confederacy, he found no reason for discouragement, instead insisting that Union General Ulysses S. Grant's plans had been foiled and Confederate losses "repair[ed]...beyond the expectation of all." Despite questionable commitment on the home-front, the Georgia Baptist minister willed

---

[55] "The Discipline of War," *Christian Index*, 19 January 1865, 4.
[56] "God's Controversy with Us—Its Cause," *Christian Index*, 26 January 1865, 2.

determination upon the troops and victory within the trenches of Petersburg. A second correspondent in Virginia, Semei, refuted any cause for despondency. "The army is cheerful," he declared, "and our prospects of success as bright as ever before."[57]

Meanwhile, as *Index* associate editor Sylvanus Landrum determined to remain in Savannah despite Union occupation, a Georgia Baptist pastor in Milledgeville sought to instill into home-front Baptists in Middle Georgia the determination credited to the state's Baptist soldiers. His message magnified human effort and left little to the providence of God. "*Endure* and *persist*," the Rev. Palmer insisted. The two words summarized "the whole secret of honorable and glorious success" in the Southern cause. Doubts and fears held no place in the Southern mind. Southern independence deserved "every sacrifice" citizens were asked to make. "Upon its altars let us lay ourselves, our property, our comfort, our *all*—a holocaust to freedom and honor!" A Baptist identified only as Pheneas echoed Palmer's call for persistence, but subjugated human effort beneath simple faith in the will of God. The travails of the South he identified as originating from "want of faith." Steadfast belief in the kingdom of God would lead to a rescue from the "fiery furnace," a reference to the Old Testament story of God coming to the rescue of four faithful men who were cast into a furnace. Like Daniel and his companions in the Bible, God would rescue the South before he would allow it to suffer ultimate defeat. All that was required of God's people was simple faith in God's omnipotence.[58]

Ultimately, Baptist convictions about the theological mysteries of God's sovereignty and human free will grew increasingly fractured as the military fortunes of the Confederacy grew ever dimmer. Confident assurances of God's providential blessings upon the South faltered in summer 1863, never to fully recover. Once questioned,

---

[57] J. W. J., "Our Army Correspondent," *Christian Index*, 2 February 1865, 1; Semei, "Our Richmond Correspondent," *Christian Index*, 2 February 1865, 2.

[58] "Bro. S. Landrum," *Christian Index*, 23 February 1865, 2; "Endure! Endure! Endure!" *Christian Index*, 2 February 1865, 2; Pheneas, "Have Faith in God," *Christian Index*, 23 February 1865, 1.

God's presence in the life of the Confederacy competed with actions of human bravery and persistence to rescue the sinking nation. In the end, God's sovereignty, when acknowledged, smoldered in the ashes of national defeat, speaking to both past sins and future spiritual hopes.

Perhaps Samuel Boykin, two weeks prior to Appomattox, best expressed the path that providence trod in the four years of the Civil War. Acknowledging the mysteries of God and limits of human emotion, the editor declared, "in our bereavements we have seen a frowning providence hiding a smiling face; and in our victories we have read the favor God extends to a righteous cause." Yet the attributing of battlefield defeats and victories to God undergirded a truth far greater than the war: "triumph and joy, suffering and sorrow, hardships and peril, have all brought us near to our Maker." Defeated, Southerners nonetheless could claim a spiritual victory that recast providence as the extension of a just God, rather than a reflection of human certainty. "The great lesson for us, as a people, to learn is to bow in submission to God's chastisements, and seek, by turning from our sins and working righteousness, to gain his favor and procure for our sorely tried land the benefits of his blessing and forgiveness."[59]

---

[59] Samuel Boykin, "Lessons of War—No. 1," *Christian Index*, 30 March 1865, 2.

CHAPTER 2

CHURCH AND STATE REVISITED

Marching northward toward Washington, D.C., Pierce Young of Forsyth, Georgia, paused in Staunton, Virginia, on 14 June 1861 to purchase a "Butiful Diary" for his bride-to-be, Julia Stanford. Far from home and family, Young felt both excitement and loneliness. Packaging the diary with a book titled *A Guide to Virginia Springs*, the soldier express-mailed the items to Stanford. Upon receiving them 19 June 1861, the young lady claimed to prize the diary and guide "more than gold of Ophir."[1]

Both Baptists, Young and Stanford experienced the war at several levels. While Young fought for the Confederacy, Stanford prayed for the South's soldiers and eagerly read and listened for news from the battlefront. Realizing that the future of their South lay on the battlefield, the two young Southerners also understood that their own future depended upon the whims of war. Supporting the Confederacy entailed the prospect of great personal loss.

For Baptists at large, the war posed risks beyond those of national defeat, theological anguish or loved ones lost. One Baptist gave succinct voice to what he perceived as the greatest theological danger posed by the Civil War: the temptation for Baptists to abandon their foundational belief in the separation of church and state. Identified only as "Brother Wilson," in June 1861 he offered a dissenting voice to pro-Confederacy resolutions passed by the Southern Baptist Convention the preceding May. The Convention according to Wilson had "transcended their constitutional powers" when addressing the war and Confederacy. Messengers should have

---

[1] Julia A. Stanford, diary, Spencer King Papers, Special Collections, Jack Tarver Library, Mercer University, Macon GA, 14–20 June 1861.

addressed such a secular subject as "citizens...after the adjournment of the Convention," he declared. Samuel Boykin, *Christian Index* editor, took exception to Wilson, defending the resolutions and insisting that the Baptist principles of separation of church and state had not been breached because the resolution was voted upon by individuals and expressed the opinions of individuals. Both striving to claim the mantle of separation of church and state, Wilson and Boykin's arguments reflected a conundrum confronting Baptists of the South during the Civil War.[2]

Established in the earliest days of Baptists in early-seventeenth-century England, and transported to the New World in 1638, Baptist insistence upon the separation of church and state did not waver in the ensuing centuries. Persecuted by colonial theocracies, Baptists in the New World, beginning with Roger Williams and the first Baptist church established on American soil, fought long and hard for the right of all persons to worship, unhindered, one god, many gods, or no god. Unity on this principle, while putting Baptists at odds with other religious groups, superseded theological, polity, and regional differences among the various Baptist groups in America. Instrumental in the establishment of the First Amendment to the United States Constitution, Baptists in the nineteenth century settled into the role of guardian of separation of church and state.[3]

Nonetheless, religious principle confronted conditions unique in the post-Revolutionary War South. John Leland, the recognized leader of Virginia Baptists in the 1780s and 1790s, reflected the road traveled by white Baptists in the South. A consistent champion of separation of church and state, Leland galvanized Baptist efforts to secure religious liberty and churchstate separation both in Virginia

---

[2] *Christian Index*, 19 June 1861.

[3] For more on seventeenth- and eighteenth-century Baptist commitment to the separation of church and state, see Edwin S. Gaustad, *Liberty of Conscience: Roger Williams in America* (Grand Rapids: Eerdmans, 1991); Edwin S. Gaustad, *Faith of Our Fathers: Religion and the New Nation* (San Francisco: Harper & Row, 1987); Timothy L. Hall, *Separating Church and State: Roger Williams and Religious Liberty* (Urbana: University of Illinois Press, 1998).

and the newly formed American nation during the last two decades of the eighteenth century. On the overlapping issue of slavery, however, Leland and his fellow Baptists expressed changing viewpoints. As the Virginia (and Southern) economy increasingly depended upon slave labor in the early nineteenth century, Leland the abolitionist gradually altered his views, as did other one-time-antislavery Baptists in the South. Whereas Leland once longed to see the day when blacks were free from their oppression, an older Leland, then relocated to New England, scolded abolitionists and defended slave owners. Whereas the early Leland called upon government to free slaves, he later argued that slavery was a moral issue, beyond the realm of government interference. By 1839, against the backdrop of increasing national hostilities over the issue of slavery, the now-proslavery Leland reframed slavery as a civil issue only, apart from the realm of religion and morality. Reflecting the larger consensus of Baptists in the South, Leland's conclusion represented an effort to accommodate the proslavery position within a church-state separation framework. Ultimately, the compromise would prove problematic.[4]

As Leland's transformation unfolded, Baptist leaders in the South, despite positing slavery as a political rather than religious issue, increasingly addressed slavery from a religious perspective, bringing a literal interpretation of the Bible to bear in an apologist fashion. Providing a moral basis, grounded in religion, for the

---

[4] See Bruce Gourley, "John Leland: Evolving Views of Slavery, 1789–1839," *Baptist History & Heritage Journal* 40/1 (Winter 2005): 104–16. Few Virginia congregations and associations followed the lead of John Leland and Baptist General Convention of Virginia in opposing slavery. In response, the BGCV in 1793 backed away from abolitionist sentiment, declaring slavery to be a "civil" issue. In nearby Kentucky, the Elkhorn Baptist Association in 1805 declared slavery a "political subject" with no religious dimensions. See Rueben E. Alley, *A History of Baptists in Virginia* (Richmond VA: Virginia Baptist General Board, 1973) 124–27; James David Essig, "A Very Wintry Season: Virginia Baptists and Slavery, 1785–1797," *Virginia Magazine of History and Biography*, 88/2 (April 1980): 181; William W. Sweet, *Religion on the American Frontier: The Baptists, 1783–1830* (Chicago: University of Chicago Press, 1931) 508.

political and social realities of the South, Baptists thrust themselves into civic affairs. In 1823, a contemporary of Leland, Baptist pastor and statesman Richard Furman of South Carolina, summed up the manner in which religion buttressed the civil institution of slavery. "The influence of a right acquaintance with that Holy Book," Furman declared in speaking on the subject of slavery, "tends directly and powerfully, by promoting the fear and love of God, together with just and peaceful sentiments toward men, to produce one of the best securities to the public, for the internal and domestic peace of the State."[5]

Meanwhile, in the Northern states, many Baptist leaders, reflecting a broader reading of the Bible that framed slavery as a moral issue, brought the Bible to bear against slavery. John R. McKivigan and Mitchell Snay argue that Baptists in the North to varying degrees had staked out antislavery positions by 1840. McKivigan and Snay place Freewill Baptists alongside Quakers and Scottish Presbyterians as the most ardently abolitionist religious groups, as all three refused to accept slaveholders into membership. New School Presbyterians, Congregationalists and Unitarians, in contrast, refused to formally adopt an abolitionist stance, yet harbored many members holding abolitionist views. By the mid-1840s, Northern Methodists and Baptists reflected a similar pattern. Arguing the incompatibility of slavery in a democratic society, some Baptists joined the broader abolitionist movement that marked a new chapter in church-state relations. Whereas Baptists in the South transferred slavery from the religious sphere to the political realm in an effort to negate questions of morality and preserve the semblance of church-state separation, Baptists in the North joined other

---

[5] Richard Furman, *Exposition of the Views of the Baptists, Relative to the Coloured Population in the United States* (Charleston: A. E. Miller, 1838). Furman's letter was penned in 1823 and later published. It is reproduced online at http://facweb.furman.edu/~benson/docs/rcd-fmn1.htm (accessed 14 June 2011).

Northern evangelicals in an effort to interject religious morality into government legislation regarding the issue of slavery.[6]

Examining the denominational schisms preceding the Civil War, Goen concludes that despite the separation of church and state in America, "Protestant evangelicalism, with its millennial visions and its immense energies in seeking to establish the kingdom of God on earth, mightily reinforced nationalism." He argues that Protestant bonds in early nineteenth-century America represented national unity, and the denominational breakups prior to the Civil War represented the ripping apart of the national fabric. The thesis of denominational harmony shattered with the ascendancy of Southern slavery, however, overshadows ideological and theological fissures within Protestantism at large and individual denominations in particular. Admitting the difficulty of arguing for a bond among Baptists in antebellum America, Goen tenuously concludes that the development of mission organizations in the early nineteenth century served to encapsulate the unity of the denomination. Such a conclusion necessarily downplays the growing denominational differences over missionary activity. Inexplicably, Goen does not adequately address a significant doctrine shared throughout Baptist life from the colonial era through the antebellum era: the separation of church and state.[7]

Six years after John Leland's death, Baptists in the South in 1845 chartered their own course in the formation of the Southern Baptist Convention. From its inception, Southern Baptist leaders publicly voiced their commitment to slavery, a regional, civil institution by

---

[6] John R. McKivigan and Mitchell Snay, *Religion and the Antebellum Debate over Slavery* (Athens: University of Georgia Press, 1998) 355; see also C. C. Goen, *Broken Churches, Broken Nation* (Macon GA: Mercer University Press, 1985).

[7] In *Broken Nation*, Goen's examination of Baptists only briefly and partially addresses the issue of separation of church and state, noting that some Baptists by the turn of the nineteenth century considered slavery a civil issue and emancipation a political matter to be avoided in religious circles (*Broken Churches, Broken Nation*, 166–67). His treatment of Baptist unity is found on pp. 59–61. For a treatment of the larger dynamic of slavery in public and political life, see Orville Vernon Burton, *The Age of Lincoln* (New York: Hill and Wang), 2007.

then endowed with a moral, religious foundation. William B. Johnson, elected as the first president of the newly formed Southern Baptist Convention, declared slavery a civil issue only. Borrowing a scriptural phrase long used by Baptists in support of the separation of church and state, Johnson pledged that Southern Baptists would "never interfere with what is Caesar's" and were now free "to promote slavery" since it was not a religious issue. The fracturing of Baptists North and South over the issue of slavery thus nuanced the long-held unity among Baptists at large in regards to the issue of separation of church and state. By confining slavery exclusively to the civil realm, a once-divisive issue was neatly resolved. Religious arguments for emancipation and the resulting disruption of the political status quo would clearly cross the line of separation of church and state, while support of slavery merely reflected acknowledgement and support of civil law.[8]

Southern Baptists' hearty endorsement of the civic institution of slavery altered church-state demarcations. Baptists leading up to and during the Revolutionary War had insisted the American democratic cause was consistent with their own long-held convictions concerning individual freedom for all people, transcendent of the biblical mandates claimed by colonial theocracies and state churches at large. Southern Baptists from 1845 to 1860, in contrast, turned to the Bible to defend the white Southern enslavement of African Americans and denounce Northern abolitionists. In so doing, Baptists joined other Southern denominations in utilizing religious dogma to expressly support proslavery laws and legislation. Ebenezer Warren's proslavery January 1861 sermon in Macon, in addition to positing the providential hand of God upon the South, summed up the Southern Baptist position of the South as an amalgamation of civic and religious spheres. "Both Christianity and Slavery are from Heaven," Warren argued. Secession was necessary in order to ensure a

---

[8] Proceedings of the Southern Baptist Convention (Richmond, Va: Southern Baptist Convention, 1845), 19.

government that protected godly institutions such as slavery from the grasp of Satan.[9]

Warren's words served notice that the Baptist heritage of separation of church and state faced an old foe in new clothing: nationalism. Having resisted the colonial theocracies of an earlier era, Baptist leaders in the South now called upon congregations to support a new nation established by the will of God for the preservation of a Christian faith dependent upon the civic institution of African slavery. The pastor's rallying cry for a Southern defense of slavery did not go unheeded among his congregants. Throughout February and March 1861, prayer meetings for the Confederacy were held first daily and then thrice weekly at Macon's First Baptist Church. When the Confederate Congress adopted the "Stars and Bars" as the flag of the Confederacy on March 4, Mrs. Thomas Hardeman of Macon First worked all night making the first Confederate flag that would fly on Georgia soil the following day.[10]

Warren was also at center stage when the Georgia Baptist Convention met in late April in Athens. Opening the meeting with a sermon, the Macon minister declared Baptists in the South "the light of the world." A highlight of the gathering, the report on the "condition of the Country" spelled out a series of resolutions that were embraced by delegates. Collectively, the resolutions provided a church-state framework that could accommodate nationalism.

First, the report enthusiastically endorsed the new Confederate government, declaring "we consider it to be at once a pleasure and a duty to avow that, both in feeling and in principle, we approve, endorse and support the Government of the Confederate States of America." The delegates, speaking as "citizens," then resolved for the "union of all the people of the South in defence of the common cause." They also expressed "the confident belief that…the Baptists of

---

[9] *Christian Index*, 13 February 1861, 3; *Macon Telegraph*, 7 February 1861.

[10] H. Lewis Batts, *History of First Baptist Church of Christ at Macon* (Macon GA: Southern Press, 1969) 48. Minutes, Macon First Baptist Church, 1:112, Special Collections, Jack Tarver Library, Mercer University, Macon GA, box CH 4.

Georgia will not be behind any class of our fellow citizens in maintaining the independence of the South by any sacrifice of treasure or of blood." Whereas the second resolution made some effort to distinguish between church and state, the third resolution thoroughly blurred the lines between the two entities. "Almighty God," the report stated, had thus far "blessed our arms and our policy." Furthermore, "the Baptist Churches of this State, be requested to observe the first and second days of June next, as days of fasting and prayer, that God will deliver us from all the power of our enemies and restore peace to our country."[11] The message was clear: God was a Confederate, and thus Georgia Baptists owed their allegiance to the Confederacy.

Inviting the government to influence congregations, the fourth resolution simply stated that "the Confederate Government be requested to invite the churches of all denominations within the Confederacy, to unite in observing said days of fasting and prayer." At the time, virtually all Georgia "churches" were Protestant churches led by white men. In the face of denominational barriers prior to the sectional conflict, the war provided opportunity to unite white-led churches of all denominations under the umbrella of Confederate Christians. Delegates sought to make certain that Confederate leadership at both the national and state level were assured of the wholehearted support of Baptists in Georgia, in turn welcoming political directives in the religious sphere.[12]

Two weeks following the annual GBC meeting, the Southern Baptist Convention returned to Georgia for the first time since its formation in 1845. As at that time, Baptists in Middle Georgia were well represented when the SBC convened in Savannah in 1861. Two of the four vice-presidents during the annual meeting were Georgians, and both had attended the 1845 Augusta meeting: Thomas Stocks from Greensboro and Patrick Mell of Mercer University.

---

[11] Minutes, Georgia Baptist Convention, 1861, 5–6, Special Collections, Jack Tarver Library, Mercer University, Macon GA.

[12] Ibid., 6.

Whereas the 1845 Augusta meeting took place for the express purpose of spiritual disunion with the North, the 1861 Savannah meeting celebrated and sanctified political disunion. Convened one month after the formation of the Confederate States of America, SBC delegates promptly appointed a Committee "on the state of the country." The Baptists assembled in Savannah issued a statement "distinctly, decidedly, emphatically" applauding the formation of the new Southern nation and pledging "hearty cooperation" with the Confederate administration. The pledge of unreserved Baptist support for the new nation contrasted with the meeting sixteen years earlier in which Baptists of the South announced a spiritual break from the North in order, they claimed, to avoid the taint of abolitionist politics and preserve the sanctity of church-state separation.[13]

"The Special Committee on the State of the Country" served as a highlight of the meeting. Mell sat on the committee as the representative of Baptists in Georgia. Nationalistic rhetoric resounded in the report. The "fanatical" North had deprived the South of her rights, and Southern withdrawal from the Union was done in accordance with "sacred rights and honor, in self-defence." Southern peace efforts were dismissed by the North, which intended to "loose hordes of armed soldiers to pillage and desolate the entire South."[14]

As in the recent convening of the Georgia Baptist Convention, separation of church and state took a backseat in resolutions concerning the Confederate nation. Although vowing not to forget the "spirit of Jesus," SBC messengers declared that "every principle of religion, of patriotism, and of humanity" compelled Baptists to defend the South. Messengers voiced approval of the formation of the Confederate States, and pledged to "assiduously invoke the Divine direction and favor in behalf of those who bear rule among us...that their enterprise may be attended with success; and that they may attain a great reward...in contributing to the progress of the

---

[13] SBC, *Proceedings* (1845); Proceedings of the Southern Baptist Convention (Richmond, VA: Southern Baptist Convention, 1861), 19.

[14] SBC, *Proceedings* (1861) 62.

transcendent Kingdom of our Lord Jesus Christ." Pledging their "hearts" and "hearty cooperation" to Jefferson Davis, his cabinet and Congress, those present called upon their fellow Baptists to be fervent for the cause of both country and God, so that the "labor is not in vain." Reinforcing these sentiments, the four-day meeting ended with a resolution invoking "the special protection of heaven" upon the border cities of the South.[15]

In the space of two weeks, in two separate gatherings in the state of Georgia, Baptists circumvented centuries-old religious convictions by rhetorically joining God and government. While Samuel Boykin and Brother Wilson argued over whether or not Baptists had breached the wall between church and state at the convention level in the weeks following, others did not bother to discuss at all the fine points of Baptist theology.

Unbridled nationalistic enthusiasm said to be sanctioned by God, occasionally couched with seemingly obligatory calls for humility in the face of God's blessings, flowed more freely from the penned words of some Baptists than did calls for caution or careful attempts to build a theological framework in which the sacred and the secular could exist alongside one another without breaching the Baptist heritage of separation of church and state. The anonymous writer of the *Christian Index* editorial, "The Present War: How Do We Know that We Are Right," argued that the South was justified because the people had a right to change the structure of government and the South simply acted in self-defense against a hostile invader. Another unsigned editorial addressed the "The Uses of the War," declaring the North as "the most arrogant, self-reliant and presumptuous people on the face of the earth" who had the presumption to enslave "Government, Constitutions and even Christianity" under the banner of "Yankee power." The wrath of God evidenced in the Old Testament would be visited upon those who sought to subjugate Christianity. Yankee power would be no match for the wrath of God. "The American Union," the anonymous writer

---

[15] Ibid., 17, 63–64.

charged, "had become as irresponsible to God as Nebuchadnezzar was, when he stood self-deified amidst the magnificence of Babylon. God saw that it needed humiliation and purgation, and disruption and war became his ministers—let us hope of mercy as well as retribution." Yet Southerners were not free of the stain of guilt. "We too, not as we trust chargeable with the same guilt, may be made through war, the subjects of a salutary discipline. We have not given God the glory or our peculiar and distinguishing institutions; we have not ascribed due honor to him for our conservatism, our abounding wealth and our pure religion." Guilt notwithstanding, "triumph we must, for God is with us," declared the writer. In short, the South alone held legitimate claim to God's favor. Nation and deity could not be understood apart from one another.[16]

Yet by July, the church-state issue had provoked public disagreements among Baptists. Arguing for the necessity and justification of war, B. L. Ross summarized the unabashed mingling of the secular and sacred: "the gospel, salvation, the Bible, the character and honor of Christ, are the unparalleled and all absorbing interests committed to our [Southern] hands for preservation and perpetuation," he wrote. An unsigned editorial in the *Christian Index* championed the SBC resolutions on the state of the country against an anonymous editorial in the *Tennessee Baptist* that criticized the statements as out of bounds on the grounds that a body of Baptists did not have the authority to make non-religious statements. Yet another editorial, proposing "A Few Earnest Words to Pastors and Church Members," lamented that some pastors were preaching nationalism from the pulpits and discussing the war on pastoral visits. The writer warned pastors to confine their sermons to spiritual themes and to avoid burdening already troubled families with news and rumors from battlefields. "Brethren of the ministry, we earnestly exhort you not to let your minds be diverted from your legitimate business by the excitements of the day. The care of souls is your business: we beseech you to give a more earnest attention to it

---

[16] *Christian Index*, 10 July 1861.

according as war and the rumors of war distract the hearts of your people and tend to diminish their spirituality." Baptists, in short, were not unified in equating the Confederacy with the Kingdom of God.[17]

Dissident voices aside, the rhetorical mingling of church and state extended throughout the war and beyond individual voices, in the process tapping into Calvinistic underpinnings in Baptist life. In fall 1861, Baptists of the Flint River Association weighed in on the issue, setting a tone that others would follow. Expressing little concern about the separation of church and state, Flint River Baptists boasted, "with pride, that there is no class of citizens in the Southern States who have proven themselves more patriotic and loyal than the Missionary Baptists." The "Report on the State of the Country" further noted that "Although this is an assembly of Christians, we are desirous to express our feelings on the state of the Country, because, as christians and citizens, its affairs are near and dear to our hearts." The four resolutions of the report were heartily adopted: approval of the South's separation from the North and the formation of the Southern Confederacy; the pledging of Baptists as citizens to the defense and support of the new nation; unwavering confidence in the ability, integrity, and patriotism of Confederate president Jefferson Davis and vice-president Alexander Stephens; and thankfulness to God for Southern battlefield victories in the opening months of war. After stating their convictions, Flint River Baptists invoked the future blessings of God, offering prayers that he would guide and sustain the Confederacy in its righteous purposes, thus ensuring victory over the North. Tightly joined were the bonds of Southern citizenship and heavenly fellowship.[18]

Subsequent events did not deter Flint River's nationalism. Following demoralizing military losses in summer 1863, they met again and reaffirmed their unbending optimism in the Confederacy.

---

[17] *Christian Index*, 10, 17, 24 July 1861.

[18] Minutes, Flint River Baptist Association, 1861, 7, 11–12, Special Collections, Jack Tarver Library, Mercer University, Macon GA.

Acknowledging "severe reverses" and large losses of men and weapons, Flint River Baptists nonetheless insisted that the enemy's losses were much greater and "we have achieved several of the most brilliant and signal victories which history has ever recorded." How should victory and loss be interpreted by God's faithful? Flint River Baptists, professing to examine both the past and present, saw "no good reason for despondency or discouragement." Confidence in the justness of the Southern cause remained, and victory seemed inevitable. Pledging themselves and their possessions "to our Government," the Baptists of the Flint River Association made no distinction between the mission of the church and the role of the state. Earth and heaven both were on the side of the Confederacy, assuring the impossibility of failure. Confederate President Davis, army officers, and soldiers all invoked the fullest confidence of these Baptists of Middle Georgia: "We here unanimously record our deliberate and solemn conviction that, with such a President, such officers, and such privates, and such a cause to maintain and vindicate as we now have, and above all, with Lord Jehovah on our side, as He evidently is, to fail is impossible." While Central Association Baptists had lost confidence in the prospects of the Confederacy and Ebenezer Association Baptists believed that salvation of the South rested upon the salvation of Southern men from the debauchery of the army camps, Flint River Baptists insisted all the harder that the Confederacy was immune to failure because the South's noble leaders and soldiers were graced by the very power and presence of God.[19]

Traditionally less prone to muddy the waters between church and state, some Primitive Baptists nonetheless enjoined God and country. While Flint River Baptists equated God's righteousness with that of the Confederacy, Ocmulgee Primitive Baptists portrayed the

---

[19] Minutes, Flint River Baptist Association, 1863, Special Collections, Jack Tarver Library, Mercer University, Macon GA; minutes, Central Baptist Association, 1863, Special Collections, Jack Tarver Library, Mercer University, Macon GA; minutes, Ebenezer Baptist Association, 1863, Special Collections, Jack Tarver Library, Mercer University, Macon GA.

war in eschatological terms. Quoting Luke 21:10–25, in which Jesus warned of coming wars, persecution, death, and destruction, Ocmulgee Baptists declared that "the Scriptures are now fulfilled, we are now involved in a bloody war." Appropriating the "God of love and peace" as the commander of the South who demanded that his people discharge all their duties "as citizens and christians," they framed the Confederacy as God's own nation. Noting that "we as a Southern Confederacy have duly appreciated the blessings and privileges we have enjoyed under a Government better calculated to promote human happiness than any hitherto devised by the wisdom of man," Ocmulgee Baptists called upon the faithful to defend the "country highly favored of the Lord." The call to arms and ideology was unequivocal: "let us evince to the nations of the earth that the Government of our Southern Confederacy has our confidence and esteem, and that with united hearts and hands we shall sustain it." In short, Ocmulgee Baptists stamped God's blessings upon the Confederacy and declared war as the duty of Baptists, all the while voicing little to no concern regarding the separation of church and state.[20]

Exuberance over early battlefield victories long subsided, Baptists struggled more with the dual themes of temporal defeat and spiritual salvation in the latter years of the war. In 1864, Baptists of the Ebenezer Association passed three resolutions concerning the war. Rhetorically, they accepted the South's bleak outlook as the providence of God, taking upon themselves, on the behalf of the Confederacy at large, blame for battlefield losses. Nonetheless, Ebenezer Baptists insisted that truth yet resided on the side of the Confederacy. "We believe that in successes as well as in reverses, in

---

[20] Minutes, Ocmulgee Baptist Association, 1861, Special Collections, Jack Tarver Library, Mercer University, Macon GA. By way of contrast, the remaining three Primitive Baptist associations in Middle Georgia, also meeting in fall 1861, offered no commentary regarding the war. See Minutes, Echoconnee Primitive Baptist Association, 1861; minutes, Ebenezer Primitive Baptist Association, 1861; minutes, Towaliga Primitive Baptist Association, 1861. All located in Special Collections, Jack Tarver Library, Mercer University, Macon, GA.

adversity as well as in prosperity, the footprints of a just God are ever visible to a christian people." God's justice could not to be questioned, even in the face of the reverses of the past year. Being punished by God merely reinforced the righteousness of the cause of the South. Acknowledging the wickedness of the South without going into details, Ebenezer Baptists bowed to the chastising rod of God, professed humility, and expressed confidence that the Southern cause would yet prevail. Ever aware of their denomination's heritage of separation of church and state, yet bathed in Calvinist theology that subjected all human effort to the sovereign designs of God, delegates publicly insisted "while we would make no effort to blend Church and State, we believe that our final success depends upon the will of God."[21]

Ebenezer Baptists' public affirmation of the principle of separation of church and state, a disclaimer deemed necessary when positioning the Confederacy as God's chosen nation, openly revealed the dueling theological positions Baptists struggled to hold together in tension. While some Baptists individually and corporately did not allow their faith heritage of church and state relations to prevent the rhetorical joining of heavenly and earthly kingdoms, Baptists with few exceptions stood together upon one church-state issue: government sponsorship of army chaplains. Unlike Methodists and Presbyterians, Baptists largely rejected government salaries for chaplains, citing firm adherence to the separation of church and state. Against the backdrop of state-funded Methodist and Presbyterian army chaplains and a shortage of chaplains among Baptists, J. G. Johnson in 1863 expressed concerns and uncertainty as to remedying the problem. Despite considering the option of petitioning the Confederate government for assistance, his Baptist heritage did not permit him to follow the example of other denominations, for he perceived state-supported ministers as "without example in the Word of God" and effecting a "union of Church and State." The solution to

---

[21] Minutes, Ebenezer Baptist Association, 1864, Special Collections, Jack Tarver Library, Mercer University, Macon GA.

the lack of Baptist work among the soldiers, according to Johnson, was for the home-front to provide generous financial support to salary chaplains. He requested that pastors appeal to their congregations to support army missions.[22]

Yet within army camps, separation of church and state sometimes took a backseat to the harsh realities of war. The few Baptist chaplains in Stonewall Jackson's army offered their own assessment of the "great spiritual destitution" within the ranks as a result of a shortage of ministers among the soldiers in late spring 1863. Supporting, with reservations, government-funded chaplains, Jackson's Baptist chaplains nonetheless took a different tack in appealing to Baptists in Georgia. "That sincere Christian, Lieutenant General T. J. Jackson," the chaplains reported, "has given special encouragement to the work of supplying the corps with chaplains—not one-half of the regiments of infantry are supplied. Some entire brigades have no chaplains at all. In the artillery attached to the corps, the destitution is still greater." Declaring that no more than 200 chaplains worked throughout the entire Confederate army, the chaplains noted that 5,000 to 6,000 ministers could be counted throughout the Confederate States. Jackson's chaplains agreed with Johnson that pastors and churches should take steps to alleviate the severe shortage of chaplains. With summer approaching, Jackson's chaplains encouraged home-front pastors to leave their comforts and "labor among the soldiers." Their prescription for solving the chaplaincy crisis consisted of asking churches to grant their pastors

---

[22] J. G. Johnson, "Chaplains," *Christian Index*, 18 May 1863, 1. Whereas the Methodists and Episcopalians petitioned the Confederate Congress for government support of army chaplains, Baptists did not (see *Journal of Confederate Congress*). In addition, from the 22 July 1862 edition of the *Christian Index* onward, articles addressing the subject of army chaplains routinely appeared in print. Some local church and associational records from 1862 forward also discuss army chaplains. For a broader analysis of denominational army chaplains, see John W. Brinsfield, William C. Davis, Benedict Maryniak, and James I. Robertson, Jr., eds., *Faith in the Fight: Civil War Chaplains* (Mechanicsburg PA: Stackpole Books, 2003).

"furlough for a few weeks to labor in the army" while paying expenses associated with the mission work.[23]

Baptist leaders' refusal to embrace government-salaried chaplains thus ironically ensured shortages of Baptist chaplains, leading to scenes like that which took place in July 1863 when James O. Cumbie left the comforts of home to preach to Georgia soldiers. Visiting the 32nd Georgia Infantry near Savannah for two weeks, Cumbie preached among the soldiers, speaking to "large and seriously attentive" gatherings of men who expressed interest in his words, with as many as 100 "coming forward for prayer." During the last three days of revival services, military drills were halted and "the whole time devoted to religious services." Cumbie's short-term mission trip among the soldiers came at his personal expense. To show their appreciation, the soldiers took up a collection for the evangelist.[24]

Yet Cumbie's two-week preaching tour of army camps proved only an exception to the norm. One of few Baptist chaplains within the army in 1863, A. M. Marshall of the 12th Georgia Infantry lamented the lack of ministry among the soldiers. Struggling for a solution to the chaplaincy shortage that would not infringe upon separation of church and state, he disclosed: "I am the only chaplain in the brigade, and have tried to the best of my ability to supply the whole brigade with preaching, and have preached so much that my voice has begun to fail me." The minister explained to Baptists in the association that "there are in this brigade [Doles's] six companies that are made up within the bounds of the Central Association; three of these companies belong to the 44th regiment, which has no chaplain. Besides, the 4th and 21st regiments are also without chaplains." Marshall pleaded with Central Association Baptists to support their soldiers, men who were making great sacrifices, who lived in constant danger of death, and who were "begging for the gospel."

---

[23] W. M. Huff, "Letter," *Christian Index*, 1 June 1863, 1.

[24] James O. Cumbie, "Thirty-Second Ga. Regiment," *Christian Index*, 13 July 1863, 1.

Methodists and Presbyterians, benefiting from government funding, were "sending their best ministers to the army," thus shaming Baptists for their lack of action. Unwilling to speak only in generalities, Marshall offered a solution to the problem of inadequate work among the soldiers, declaring that the association should assist ministers in stepping down from their pulpits to work among the soldiers. He closed, "I hope, dear brethren, that you will do something towards preaching for the brigade, composed of so many companies within the bounds of the Central Association."[25]

The Central Association reacted to Marshall's request by encouraging support of army missions, and the pages of the *Index* recorded the responses in the ensuing months. In October, George W. White, a licensed minister from Crawford County currently serving in the 27th Georgia Infantry, wrote the *Index* offering his service as an army missionary. On December 16, when White's offer apparently went unanswered, Marshall again wrote a letter to the *Index*, pleading with Samuel Boykin to use his influence to encourage the churches of Central Association to raise funds for the appointment of Rev. Van Hoose as chaplain to George P. Doles's Brigade, in which there were "8 companies from the bounds of the Central Association." Having previously written Ebenezer Warren, pastor of First Baptist Macon, Marshall had not yet received a reply. "There are about three regiments in this brig. without chaplains," he noted, and "in Rodes' division there are about 15 or 20 Methodist chaplains and only 2 or three Baptist chaplains." A Baptist soldier in the 3rd Georgia Regiment similarly noted that all the chaplains in his entire brigade were Methodist. Marshall hoped Baptists in Middle Georgia would rise to the challenge of ministry among the soldiers.

Yet one month later, *Index* editors lamented the continuing inaction of churches of the Central Association. Despite the

---

[25] A. M. Marshall, "To the Central Association," *Christian Index*, 18 September 1863, 1; Clyde G. Wiggins III, ed., *My Dear Friend: The Civil War Letters of Alva Benjamin Spencer, 3rd Georgia Regiment, Company C* (Macon GA: Mercer University Press, 2007) 110.

association authorizing the appointment of Van Hoose, the churches failed to provide enough financial support. Boykin voiced irritation, demanding, "Come, brethren, wake up! The Central must do its share in army missions; and *each church* must do *its* share." The association finally came through, and Hoose began his army mission service in January along the coast of Savannah. Preaching among the encamped Georgia regiments, he found few chaplains but eager soldiers, reporting that "the congregations are very large, and a more attentive, interested one I never saw."[26]

The uneasy intersection of theological principle and the spiritual needs of soldiers remained a point of contention throughout the remainder of the war, comprising an ongoing theme within the pages of the *Christian Index*. Gardiner Shattuck argues that despite military defeat, religious enthusiasm in army ranks helped advance the cause of religion in the South. Yet despite appreciation of army revivals, Baptists placed church-state separation above the evangelization of soldiers. Although their churches failed to provide enough army ministers, Georgia Baptists ultimately refused to step across the wall of separation between church and state in order to fulfill army chaplaincy needs. John W. Brinsfield's extensive research of chaplaincy records reveals the extent of the problem. He identifies 3,694 commissioned chaplains in the Confederate and Union armies. Methodists, Baptists, and Presbyterians represented the three largest denominations in the Confederacy, with the three groups claiming memberships of roughly 750,000, 650,000, and 220,000 respectively. Yet of 938 identifiable Confederate chaplains, 47 percent were Methodist, 18 percent Presbyterian, and only 16 percent were Baptist. Brinsfield notes that both Methodists and Baptists acted slowly in responding to the need for army chaplains, but the former eventually met the challenge. Although he offers no conclusive explanation for

---

[26] Minutes, Central Baptist Association, 1863, Special Collections, Jack Tarver Library, Mercer University, Macon GA; "Brief Mention," *Christian Index*, 9 October 1863, 1; A. M. Marshall, "From a Chaplain," *Christian Index*, 8 January 1864, 1; "Brief Mention," *Christian Index*, 15 January 1864, 1; A. Van Hoose, "To the Baptists of the Central Association," *Christian Index*, 26 February 1864, 2.

the variance in overall percentages, Baptists' refusal to accept government funding clearly impacted the numbers of Baptist chaplains.[27]

While unwilling to receive government funding, at least some Baptists eventually expressed a willingness to work with the Confederate government in identifying potential chaplains from among army ranks. With no end in sight to the chaplaincy shortage, Georgia Baptists in late 1864 requested permission from the Confederate government to appoint certain current soldiers as chaplains. The services of these individuals would in turn be paid for by Baptist churches. Confederate President Jefferson Davis politely refused the request, however, in the process drawing criticism from the Baptists of Georgia.[28]

Ultimately, Georgia Baptists chose adherence to the principle of separation of church and state in the face of chaplaincy needs during the Civil War, and Baptist ministers in Middle Georgia (and elsewhere) did little to voluntarily alleviate the problem. Yet while declining state help in evangelizing Confederate soldiers, Baptists of the Civil War era, unlike their forebears, were decidedly of the opinion that civil authorities give preferential treatment to the weekly Christian holy day. Championing church and state separation in the early nineteenth century, John Leland and other Baptist leaders had

---

[27] Gardiner H. Shattuck, Jr., *A Shield and a Hiding Place: The Religious Life of the Civil War Armies* (Mercer University Press, 1987); Brinsfield, Davis, Maryniak, and Robertson, Jr., eds., *Faith in the Fight*, 61–62. The author notes that some denominations appointed missionaries in addition to chaplains. In the case of Southern Baptists, seventy-six "domestic missionaries" were appointed to work among the soldiers.

[28] "Correspondence with the President," *Christian Index*, 14 October 1864, 1. The letter to Davis and Davis's reply were reprinted in the *Index*. Georgia Baptists sought to alleviate their own chaplaincy shortage by requesting permission to appoint certain current soldiers as chaplains, whose services would be paid for by Baptist churches. Davis refused the request.

argued that the government should not afford Sunday—or any other religious holy day—special treatment.[29]

"A man cannot give greater evidence that he is destitute of the spirit of Christianity," John Leland wrote in 1830, "and ignorant of its genius, than when he makes, or urges others to make, laws to coerce his neighbor in matters of religion." Yet Baptists in the South during the Civil War were convinced otherwise. Displaying views inconsistent with their forbears but currently popular, Baptists in Middle Georgia stood ready to do their part in making certain that the Confederate government enforced homage to the weekly Christian holy day. The Jewish holy day, the actual biblical Sabbath, was of no concern to Baptists. The government had a duty to honor Sunday only, the one day of the week set aside for spiritual worship and contemplation for Christians. Government infringement upon the weekly day of worship, Baptists insisted, amounted to a violation of Christian rights, a breaching of the wall of separation of church and state.[30]

---

[29] Brad Creed, "John Leland and Sunday Mail Delivery: Religious Liberty, Evangelical Piety, and the Problem of a 'Christian Nation'" (*Fides Et Historia*, 33–2 (Summer/Fall 2001) 1–12. In 1810, Congress passed legislation formalizing the common practice of sorting and delivering mail seven days a week. Over the next two decades, mainline Christian denominations other than Baptists opposed the 1810 act, and in 1828 formed the General Union for the Promotion of the Christian Sabbath, enacting boycotts and petitioning Congress. The following year two Baptists, General Richard M. Johnson (1812 war hero and chair of the Senate Committee on the Post Office and Post Roads) and Obadiah Brown (pastor of First Baptist Church in Washington, D.C.) authored a senate report on the "Subject of Mails on the Sabbath" that denied efforts to repeal the 1810 law and reiterated America's founding as a secular nation. On 8 January 1830, John Leland scolded Christians who insisted that the government halt Sunday mail delivery. "Whenever a legislature legalizes holy days, creeds of faith, forms of worship, or pecuniary reward for religious services, they intrude into the kingdom of Christ," Leland charged. The Baptist evangelist also insisted, "the only way to prevent religion from being an engine of cruelty, is to exclude religious opinions from the civil code." See L. F. Greene, ed., *The Writings of the Late Elder John Leland* (New York: G. W. Wood, 1845) 561–66.

[30] Greene, ed., *Writings of John Leland*, 568; minutes, Washington Baptist Association, 1861, 13, Special Collections, Jack Tarver Library, Mercer University,

Defending the sanctity of the Sabbath, Civil War Baptists in Georgia echoed some well-known figures North and South. On 6 September 1861, Union General George McClellan had issued an order demanding "a more perfect respect for the Sabbath." The general prohibited "all work" on the Sabbath and declared that "no unnecessary movements shall be made on that day" in order that the soldiers "shall attend Divine service." On 16 November 1862, President Abraham Lincoln issued a general order for "Sabbath Observance" among the United States armies, "a becoming deference to the best sentiments of a Christian people, and a due regard for the Divine will." Within the Confederacy, General Thomas "Stonewall" Jackson, a Presbyterian, insisted that his troops observe the Sabbath unless battle loomed. But Jackson did not merely ensure that worship took place on the Sabbath. "Jackson's observance of the Sabbath was fastidious. He neither read a letter nor posted a letter on the Sabbath day, and he believed that the government was violating God's law in carrying the mail (i.e. working) on that day. It was one of the most important duties of the legislature, he maintained, to stop such work." According to Stephen L. Longenecker, Jackson considered the "Old United States" too extreme on the separation of church and state. Furthermore, the general "was not a typical Presbyterian" and his fellow church members considered him "unusually disciplined and eccentric."[31]

Macon GA, microfilm reel 1246; minutes, Antioch Baptist Church, Washington County, 1862, Special Collections, Jack Tarver Library, Mercer University, Macon GA, microfilm reels 375, 503. For a broad overview of the history of the Sabbath, see Craig Harline, *A History of the First Day from Babylonia to the Super Bowl* (New York: Doubleday, 2007).

[31] "General McClellan on the Sabbath," *Harpers Weekly* (21 September 1861): 595; "Sabbath Observance," *Harpers Weekly* (29 November 1862): 755; Russ Campbell, "The Battle Rainbow: Jackson and His Chaplains," *Military History Online*, 2003 (published online at http://www.militaryhistoryonline.com/civilwar/articles/battlerainbow.aspx (accessed 14 June 2011); Stephen L. Longenecker, *Shenandoah Religion: Outsiders and the Mainstream, 1716–1865* (Waco: Baylor University Press, 2002) 89.

Meanwhile, the Confederate government never took a firm stance on Sabbath observance. A. C. Dayton of Cartersville, Georgia, joined the members of Antioch Baptist in Washington County in chiding Confederate officers for drilling, parading, and building entrenchments on Sundays. Liable to be shot as mutinous soldiers if refusing orders, soldiers were unable to obey God without rebelling against officers and, by extension, the Confederate government, Dayton reasoned. "Let Christians in every corner of our land cry out...petition and remonstrate" the government until God comes to "our side," Dayton implored. Ebenezer W. Warren echoed Dayton. "Drills and reviews on the holy Sabbath," Warren insisted, placed the Confederacy "in defiance of the authority of heaven."[32]

Baptist indignation concerning Sabbath violations sanctioned by the Confederate government was widespread and deep. Meeting in 1862, the Georgia Baptist Convention passed a resolution to petition the Confederate government to avoid violations of the Sabbath in the form of military drills and related activities. A second resolution requested the preparation and distribution of a tract on the subject of violating the Sabbath. The bromide was to be printed and circulated among the soldiers. Local churches also joined in the protest against Sabbath-breaking. On 19 August 1862, the *Index* reprinted a resolution passed by Shiloh Baptist Church of Marion County in which the congregation "unanimously resolved to petition our Government to cease as much as possible, under the present circumstances, the violation of the Holy Sabbath day."[33]

Among the various evils of camp life, Baptists considered Sabbath-breaking the worst of sins. Yet despite Baptist assurances that God was on the side of the South, soldiers and officers regularly violated the day of the week recognized as holy. Baptist complaints about soldiers' failure to honor Sunday as a day of worship thus

---

[32] A. C. Dayton, "Is God on Our Side?" *Christian Index*, 17 June 1862, 3; E. W. Warren, "Drunkenness and Sabbath-Breaking," *Christian Index*, 1 April 1862, 2.

[33] Minutes, Georgia Baptist Convention 1862, 7, Special Collections, Jack Tarver Library, Mercer University, Macon GA; "Resolution," *Christian Index*, 19 August 1862, 3.

represented the primary complaint lodged against the Confederacy by Baptists in Middle Georgia. One writer charged the South prior to the war of being a nation of Sabbath-breakers, and faulted the dishonoring of God's day as the cause of the war. The "wretched condition" of the armies in spring 1862 was blamed partially on "drunkenness, vulgarity, gaming, and profanity," yet such vices were secondary to "the great sin of all, Sabbath-breaking." Another writer, although positioning the Confederate government on "God's side" for prohibiting profanity in the nation's articles of war, scolded the government for forcing soldiers to violate the Sabbath.[34]

At least one officer responded to the complaints of Sabbath violations. Following proclamations by General Robert E. Lee to end the practice of Sunday drills, Central Association Baptists quickly offered words of praise: "this body, with gratitude to God, have seen the act of Gen. Lee, commander-in-chief of our armies in Virginia, in ordaining that all drills, parades and reviews, except for the purpose of inspection, shall be dispensed with in the Army on the holy Sabbath, so that our soldiers may attend divine worship."[35]

Lee's assurances offered, the issue gradually moved to the periphery in Baptist life in Georgia as confidence in the Confederacy soared following battlefield victories. But in the wake of battlefield reverses in 1863, A. C. Dayton, now residing in Perry, revisited the issue of the Sabbath in a letter to the *Index*, scolding Baptists and others for neglecting the subject. God had "accepted" the 1862 Sabbath protests against the sin of the government and granted the South success in battles, according to Dayton. In the meantime, Congress ignored the Sabbath protests and persisted in its "wicked rebellion against the King of kings," the preacher charged. In response, God removed his favor from the South, resulting in battlefield losses. Yet "even the people of God themselves seem to

---

[34] S. D. E., "Inklings of Camp Life," *Christian Index*, 25 March 1862, 3; "Camp Life" was composed at Camp Brown, near Savannah.

[35] Minutes, Central Baptist Association, 1862, 10, Special Collections, Jack Tarver Library, Mercer University, Macon GA.

have forgotten their own protest of the former year," Dayton warned. The Georgia Baptist Convention in 1863 "met...and never so much as asked what had become of their memorial" on the subject, and no Baptist organizations were now "taking any action in regard to the great sin of our nation."[36]

Despite concern regarding Sabbath violations, the following week an unsigned editorial voiced disagreement with Dayton over the severity of Sabbath-breaking. Although "Sabbath-desecration is a fearful evil in the sight of the Lord, and one that invokes the outpourings of his anger," the writer refused to classify it as a national sin, instead arguing that the Confederacy, with the possible exception of England, held the Sabbath in higher honor than any other nation. Sabbath drills and maneuvers by the army, practices Baptists loudly protested the previous year, were noticeably absent from the list of Sabbath violations deemed largely irrelevant by Dayton's opponent.[37]

At least one Baptist cautioned his fellow believers against seeking state mandates to force public compliance with Christian Sabbath beliefs. Anonymously expressing disapproval of Dayton's efforts to secure Confederate legislation regarding the observance of the Sabbath, he voiced support for a stricter understanding of the separation of church and state that represented traditional Baptist views prior to the Civil War era. "We are opposed to all attempts to sustain the institutions of religion, by secular power," the dissenting Baptist noted. "All we ask of Caesar is to let us alone. This is the ground occupied by Baptists from time immemorial."[38]

---

[36] A. C. D. of Houston Female College in Perry, Georgia, "Is It True," *Christian Index*, 11 September 1863, 1. A. C. Dayton, a prominent minister in central Georgia in the latter half of the war, often utilized his initials in letters to the *Index*.

[37] "A Great National Sin," *Christian Index*, 18 September 1863, 2.

[38] "Sabbath Desecration: A Misunderstanding," *Christian Index*, 18 September 1863, 2. The theme of separating "Caesar" from religion hearkens to Roger Williams, the founder of Baptists in America, who in 1644, published a pamphlet titled "The Bloudy Tenent of Persecution," in which he called for religious freedom for all—"Paganish, Jewish, Turkish, or Antichristian." He wrote

That anonymous voice of caution aside, other Baptists, in the wake of government inaction, heightened their rhetoric against the Confederacy. In addition to government-mandated military activity on the Sabbath, Baptists expressed frustration that the Confederacy allowed soldiers to engage in vices on the weekly day of worship. Boykin considered inappropriate Sunday camp activities—including profanity, gambling, and drunkenness—as "national sins" reflective upon the Confederacy's failure to honor the Sabbath. The editor's arguments represented an increasingly contorted view of the separation of church and state, erasing any clear-cut lines of demarcation. God's insistence on personal purity, Boykin insisted, encompassed all the citizens of his chosen nation, not just the churched.[39]

While railing against vice-laden Sundays in the camps, Baptists recognized a larger, and perhaps more disturbing Sabbath reality within the Confederacy: a disinterest in religion. One sign of individual purity on the part of Southerners was to be found in Sabbath attendance. Yet merely one year after the beginning of the war, one unnamed writer lamented the decline of interest in the worship of God, observing that the South seemed no more religious at the present than it had at the beginning of the war. To the contrary, the opposite seemed "true in many parts of our land. The God who delivered our forefathers from bondage, and gave to them the goodly land which we have inherited, has been ignored by many, and the homage which is His due has been rendered to Caesar!" Perhaps the irony of depending upon the state to enforce the Sabbath, while at the same time condemning non-churched citizens for worshipping the state, did not occur to the anonymous writer.[40]

"that no civil magistrate, no King, nor Caesar, have any power over the souls or consciences of their subjects in the matters of God and the crown of Jesus."

[39] "A Skeleton of a Fast Day Address," *Christian Index*, 18 March 1862, 1; "Why God Afflicts Nations and the Remedy," *Christian Index*, 29 April 1862, 2; "National Sins—What Are They?" *Christian Index*, 29 October 1862, 2.

[40] "Read and Ponder," *Christian Index*, 8 April 1862, 1.

One pseudonymous writer tied several themes together, calling upon Baptist pastors to resist sin in the land and reconcile church and state under the banner of Christian morality and respect for the Christian Sabbath. "Ministers of the gospel are watchmen," he declared. The watchmen were to be at their appointed posts, seeking the good of souls, and warning of impending dangers. They should also preach against both personal and national sins, calling all offenders to repentance. The pastor lived in two worlds, and "as a patriot, and a citizen, he must feel deeply for the interests of his invaded country; and as a Christian minister, he cannot feel less than at other times for the spiritual and eternal wants of people." The writer encouraged ministers to publish their views of both worlds in the form of tracts, sermons, and essays, as well as in letters to soldiers in the army. Pastors were also to set the example in supporting the Confederate leaders and nation through prayers, and interceding before God on the behalf of "our guilty people, who have departed from God, and incurred His just displeasure by the indulgence of avarice, pride, uncleanliness, and many other evil works."[41]

The hand-wringing came not only from the home-front. Baptist missionary Jesse Campbell, declaring himself the only Baptist missionary among the Georgia soldiers for the previous eighteen months, observed in 1863 that "Profane swearing, Sabbath-breaking, and drunkenness prevail in the army to a lamentable extent." Campbell's firsthand experience spoke to both of the problems arising from Baptist refusals to allow government-sponsored chaplains and Baptist beliefs that the Confederacy should support the Christian day of worship. Yet not all news was bad. During the harsh winter of 1864, an anonymous army chaplain reported to *Index* readers that General Robert E. Lee "received with the utmost cordiality" a contingent of chaplains who advocated for "better observances of the Sabbath."

---

[41] Paulous, "A Word to Pastors and Churches," *Christian Index*, 1 April 1862, 1.

The general expressed interest in the request and issued an order that the request of the chaplains be met.[42]

Compared to some other evangelicals, in short, Baptists in Middle Georgia expressed a heightened interest in ensuring Sabbath purity, perhaps an interest afforded by their distance from the battlefront. Methodists and Presbyterians of Virginia's Shenandoah Valley, according to Longenecker, exhibited, in contrast, a lack of interest in public Sabbath morality. In addition, whereas Middle Georgia Baptist churches routinely expelled members who failed to attend Sunday services, Presbyterians of the Shenandoah Valley "seldom disciplined for Sabbath-breaking." Longenecker attributes the lack of interest in Sabbath morality to Methodists and Presbyterians having moved into the mainstream of religion by the middle of the nineteenth century. Although Baptists' numerical strength in Georgia, as well as the fact that many Baptist leaders in Georgia were large slaveholders, indicated the denomination had achieved mainstream status by the war era, Baptists did not allow their apparent mainstream status to prevent them from challenging perceived godlessness in the public sphere.[43]

Late in the war, an unexpected turn of events offered a new perspective on the Sabbath issue. When a period of revival swept the Confederate armies in late 1863 and early 1864, offering spiritual hope in the face of long battlefield odds, Samuel Boykin re-assessed his view of the Sabbath and the Confederacy. No longer a nation living in rebellion against God, the Confederacy, through the difficult

---

[42] J. H. Campbell, "From Our Army Evangelist," *Christian Index*, 16 March 1863, 1; W., "Army Correspondence of the Index," *Christian Index*, 26 February 1864, 1.

[43] Longenecker, *Shenandoah Religion*, 89. For an analysis of the wealth and stature of Georgia Baptist leaders in the mid-nineteenth century, see Robert G. Gardner, *A Decade of Debate and Division: Georgia Baptists and the Formation of the Southern Baptist Convention* (Macon GA: Mercer University Press, 1995). Failure to attend church was one of the most common reasons for being expelled from Middle Georgia Baptist churches. As noted previously, in Georgia, Baptists approximated Methodists numerically, with Southern Baptists alone approaching the Methodist population, 650,000 to 750,000.

war years, had been used by God to bring religion to the forefront of Southern consciousness. Boykin voiced his belief that profanity in the camps was in decline and noted that Confederate officials now required Sabbath observances. Yet God's displeasure continued to evidence itself in battlefield defeats, indicating that Southerners were not yet "devout, humble-minded, sin-hating, God-loving people." In the face of such unrighteousness, the editor called upon Southern ministers to be faithful to God, country, self, and soul, mindful of "the millions who are to come after us."[44]

Boykin's concern with matters heavenly and earthly, personal and national, echoes Reid Mitchell's observation that revival carried different meanings among soldiers. But while Boykin hoped the spiritual wave would result in dramatic personal commitments to God and victory for the Confederacy, Mitchell argues that "Confederate religion did not sink deeply into the souls" of soldiers. Rather, "death, suffering and hardship" preoccupied the minds of the South's defenders more than "southern independence or Confederate defeat." No longer concerned about whether their cause was holy, they simply sought "blessed assurance" of a victory beyond earth's battlefields.[45]

Yet another dimension of the Sabbath issues involved instances of the state legislating the content of Christian worship. While some Baptists took offense at the Confederate government allowing military drills and sinful activities on the Christian Sabbath, others showed no hesitation in obeying government proclamations to celebrate and support the state on the day of Christian worship. Such government proclamations took place both on the eve of the formation of the Confederacy and during the war years. Prior to the

---

[44] "Religion—and the War," *Christian Index*, 7 October 1864, 2.

[45] Reid Mitchell, "Christian Soldiers?: Perfecting the Confederacy," in Randall M. Miller, Harry S. Stout, Charles Reagan Wilson, *Religion and the American Civil War* (New York: Oxford University Press, 1998) 308. For further analysis of revivalism among the Confederate armies during the second half of the war, see Drew Gilpin Faust, "Christian Soldiers: The Meaning of Revivalism in the Confederate Army," *Journal of Southern History* 53/1 (February 1987): 63–90.

outbreak of war, Madison Baptist Church of Morgan County stood out among Baptist congregations in Georgia for addressing the growing sectional crisis. On 3 November 1860, as the much-contested United States presidential election approached, a layman brought a seemingly impromptu motion to the Madison Baptist congregation, requesting the pastor "make the condition of our country as an object of special prayer on sabbath." Accordingly, the church's next Sunday gathering "was observed by the church as directed by" Governor Joseph Brown. The motion for special prayer, in reality, had been prompted by a political request. And despite his Baptist faith, the governor had not been dissuaded from calling upon Christian churches to focus on the State on the day of worship.[46]

The Confederate government also issued directives concerning the Christian Sabbath. Following the First Battle of Manassas, New Bethel Baptist Church in Washington County proclaimed, "in [compliance] with a proclamation of Congress that we the Baptist church of New Bethel observe tomorrow the 4th Sabbath in July as a day of thanksgiving & prayer for the grand victory achieved by the confederate arms at Manasses Junction. Sunday morning church met according to appointment & observed the day in solemn service Bro. A Ivey by request preached a good & appropriate sermon for the occasion." Julia Stanford, attending Forsyth Baptist Church in Monroe County the same day, recorded her feelings about the nationalistic celebration in her congregation that Sunday, reflecting common perceptions of the Confederacy as God's chosen nation. "This has truly been a day of thanksgiving to God for the Kindness bestowed upon our soldiers and for the victory at Manassas and for the bounteous harvest that make[s] glad our land. Truly the Lord is our God and our God is the Lord."[47]

---

[46] Minutes, Madison Baptist Church, Morgan County, 1860–1865, Special Collections, Jack Tarver Library, Mercer University, Macon GA. Governor Joseph Brown's church membership during the war was with the Milledgeville Baptist Church.

[47] Minutes, New Bethel Baptist Church, Washington County, Special Collections, Jack Tarver Library, Mercer University, Macon GA, microfilm reel

From secession to Appomattox, Baptists in Middle Georgia and the state at large struggled with the ambiguity that lay between the patriotism they felt as Confederate citizens and their long-held separationist traditions. Throughout the war they remained conflicted over church-state issues. Rhetorically, many Baptists disregarded a heritage of church-state separation in equating the Confederacy with the Kingdom of God.

At the same time, Baptists evidenced a complex relationship with the state. They expressed unity regarding government funding of military chaplains. Unlike Methodists and Presbyterians, Baptists voiced steadfast opposition to state-supported chaplains, remaining firm in their position even in the face of failure to recruit enough volunteers to minister among soldiers. Although a few Baptists dared to ponder the benefits of permitting government-appointed chaplains, Baptists viewed such a move as a clear violation of the separation of church and state. When in desperation they petitioned the government to allow churches to appoint and fund certain Baptist soldiers as chaplains, Confederate President Jefferson Davis rebuffed them.

Sunday, the Christian day of worship, revealed a departure from historical norm in church-state dynamics, and again illustrated the unevenness of Baptist thought in time of war. Whereas their faith forebears taught that government should be neutral toward religious days and neither advocate nor hinder religious worship, Baptists in Middle Georgia evidenced a strong insistence that the Confederate government show favoritism to the Christian Sabbath, to the point of suspending military drills and mandating soldiers' social activities on Sundays. In the larger context, Baptists turned to the state to enforce public respect for the Sabbath at a time when other Southern evangelicals expressed little interest in the matter. And although the Confederate government did not legislate Sabbath morality as

---

504; Stanford, diary, Spencer King Papers, Special Collections, Jack Tarver Library, Mercer University, Macon GA, 28 July 1861.

Baptists wished, some Baptists nonetheless eagerly acquiesced to government calls for nationalistic-themed worship services.

In short, the Civil War served to confuse the Baptist heritage of church-state separation, and derailing it in some instances discarding tradition altogether. The tearing of the separatist fabric took place against the larger confluence of evangelicalism, republicanism, and slavery that Drew Gilpin Faust argues both formed and ripped apart a Confederate national consciousness a process that Anne Sarah Rubin posits began only when the South realized the war would not end quickly. For Baptists, the theological church-state turnabout began prior to the war, as evident in John Leland, his contemporaries in the South, and the generation following who shifted the issue of slavery from the religious sphere to that of a civic matter. Freeing their religious consciousnesses, white Baptists in the South enabled a moral defense of African slavery based on biblical obedience to civil rulers and suitable to prevailing white racial views. Defending the peculiar institution that undergirded Southern culture and economy proved but a step from equating the South with the Kingdom of God, a marriage consummated with the formation of the Confederate States of America and tested in the fires of war. Unfortunately, the envisioned church-state union, although never truly realized, created internal friction among Baptists of Middle Georgia and jeopardized long-standing faith commitments.[48]

---

[48] Drew Gilpin Faust, *Creation of Confederate Nationalism: Ideology and Identity in the Civil War South* (Baton Rogue: Louisiana State University Press, 1988); Anne Sarah Rubin, *A Shattered Nation: The Rise and Fall of the Confederacy, 1861–1868* (Chapel Hill: University of North Carolina Press, 2005).

CHAPTER 3

A FLEETING HOPE:
SOUTHERN BAPTIST ARMY MISSIONS

Yoked together in the antebellum South, missions and slavery served as the midwife of the Southern Baptist Convention, a union long under-recognized by denominational historians. Not until the latter half of the twentieth century did some denominational historians recognize slavery as a primary causation of the 1845 separation between Northern and Southern Baptists. Instead they pointed to mission philosophies, geographical dynamics, and national politics as the rationale for the formation of the Southern Baptist Convention. That is to say, they generally echoed the arguments of Richmond journalist Edward A. Pollard. In his 1866 history of the Confederacy, entitled *The Lost Cause: A New Southern History of the War of the Confederates*, Pollard reimaged the South and reinterpreted Southern defeat, insisting that slavery had served as a secondary issue to politics and other regional differences.[1]

Post-Civil War historians notwithstanding, Southern Baptists of the antebellum and wartime South openly recognized slavery as crucial to their missionary enterprises. Against the backdrop of growing national tensions over slavery, the peculiar institution formally intersected national Baptist mission efforts in 1840, when Elon Galusha, a New York pastor serving as a vice-president of the Triennial Convention, the foreign missions organization of Baptists in

---

[1] Edward A. Pollard, *The Lost Cause: A New Southern History of the War of the Confederates*, (New York: E. B. Treat & Co., 1866); Walter B. Shurden and Lori Redwine Varnadoe, "The Origins of the Southern Baptist Convention: A Historiographical Study," *Baptist History & Heritage* 37/1 (Winter 2002): 71–96. While Southern Baptists focused on mission efforts, Primitive Baptists eschewed denominational mission efforts as unsanctioned by scripture.

America, became the first president of the American Baptist Antislavery Convention. The ABAC promptly issued a statement condemning slavery as a perversion of God's will, castigating slaveholders as unchristian, and demanding emancipation for slaves. Galusha signed the statement and mailed copies to Baptist pastors throughout the South. Baptists in Georgia reacted quickly and angrily. Georgia Baptist Convention leadership protested in writing to the missions board, receiving assurances of the board's neutrality in regard to slavery.[2]

Eight of the forty-six associations in Georgia Baptist life additionally issued statements critical of Northern Baptists' abolitionist stance. The Ebenezer Association decried the Antislavery Convention's "threats against us as holders of slaves" and representation of Baptists in the South as "tyrants and bloody murderers," and responded by proclaiming "utter detestation of the principles, accusations and threats contained in the address to Southern Baptists, believing them to be unfaithful, untrue, unchristian, unscriptural." Likewise, the Flint River Association expressed "disapprobation of Northern fanatics, who are disposed to uproot our Southern institutions." The neighboring Georgia Association voted to withhold funding from mission efforts until "more fully advised upon this subject." The Washington Association reprinted a letter from the Sparta Baptist Church, which stated, "That portion of our brethren at the North, who are misguided, either by ignorance or ill counsel, called Abolitionists, we, as Baptists, would entirely disclaim. We cannot hold as brethren those who entertain their sentiments." In response, that Association voted to take no action on the church letter, other than to continue to withhold funds until the matter was resolved.[3]

---

[2] Robert G. Gardner, *A Decade of Debate and Division: Georgia Baptists and the Formation of the Southern Baptist Convention* (Macon GA: Mercer University Press, 1995) 4–7. Minutes, Georgia Baptist Convention, 1840, Special Collections, Jack Tarver Library, Mercer University, Macon GA.

[3] James Adams Lester, *A History of the Georgia Baptist Convention, 1822–1972* (Atlanta: Baptist State Convention of Georgia, 1972) 821; minutes, Ebenezer

At the local church level, at least 3 of Georgia's 971 Baptist churches issued public statements as well in 1840 and 1841. In addition to the letter from the Sparta Baptist congregation, the Bethesda Baptist Church in Greene County immediately issued a call for investigating "the propriety of a Southern board of Foreign mission. Resolved that we as a church are in favour of a Southern Board of Foreign Missions." On the other hand, Palmyra Baptist Church in Lee County declared that the potential "dissolution of the fellowship betwixt the North and South would be an event which we would deeply deplore...an evil highly injurious to the cause of religion in general...calculated to bring other evils of great magnitude in its train." The Palmyra Church requested that Triennial Convention delegates from the South "do their utmost to avert so great a calamity...without conceding any thing to the...Abolitionists."[4]

Tensions between Baptists North and South temporarily eased in 1841 following a dialogue between leaders of the two groups, but during the course of the next three years the growing influence of the American Baptist Antislavery Society among Northern Baptists again led to increasing uneasiness among Baptists in the South. That tension came to a head in 1844 when the American Baptist Home Mission Society, reversing a prior stance of neutrality toward the issue of slavery, refused to "entertain the application" of James Reeve, a prominent Georgia pastor and slaveholder. In late December of that same year, the Triennial Convention rejected the missionary appointment of an Alabama slaveholder.[5]

Baptist Association, 1840, 4–5, Special Collections, Jack Tarver Library, Mercer University, Macon GA; minutes, Flint River Association, 1840, 3. Minutes, Georgia Association, 1840, 3–9; minutes, Washington Baptist Association, 1840, 3–9, Special Collections, Jack Tarver Library, Mercer University, Macon GA.

[4] V. T. Cates, ed., *Conference Minutes of the Bethesda Baptist Church, Union Point, Greene County, Georgia* (Alto TX: East Texas Genealogical Society, 1991) 19 September 1840. Minutes, Palmyra Baptist Church, Lee County, 27 March 1841, Special Collections, Jack Tarver Library, Mercer University, Macon GA.

[5] Gardner, *A Decade of Debate*, 8–17. The Georgia and Alabama missionary nominations were viewed by Baptists in the South as test cases for discerning how

Thus, as 1845 dawned, the growing rhetoric over slavery made a parting of ways between Baptists in the North and South inevitable. Virginia Baptists took the initiative in calling for a South-wide convention. On 20 March, the Georgia Baptist Executive Committee concurred and extended an official invitation for Baptist leaders throughout the South to meet for a consultation in Augusta "before the 2nd Lord's Day in May" for the purpose of ascertaining "the best means of promoting the Foreign Mission cause and other interests of the Baptist Denomination in the South." The executive committee of Georgia's Central Baptist Association adopted a supportive resolution leaving little doubt as what "other interests" meant. "The crisis some of us have so long looked for has come," the resolution declared. "Let us meet it as becomes the Disciples of our blessed Lord and Master; but also as Southern men, conscious of our rights both civil and religious." Virginia Baptists perhaps most clearly stated the position of Baptists in the South: "We wish not to have a merely sectional Convention. From the Boston Board we separate, not because we reside at the South, but because they have adopted an unconstitutional and unscriptural principle to govern their future course. The principle is this—That holding slaves is, under all circumstances, incompatible with the office of the Christian ministry."[6]

In the weeks leading up to the Augusta meeting, Georgia Baptists' *Christian Index* made certain that readers understood the relationship between missions and slavery. The success of Southern Baptist mission efforts depended upon the peculiar Southern institution. "The most influential [Baptist] ministers in S. Carolina, Georgia, Alabama and Mississippi are slaveholders; and, wielding more influence than others, are the best qualified to act as agents in the South—they would be the most *successful* agents," insisted the

---

the Triennial Convention would deal with the issue of slaveholders serving as missionaries.

[6] Minutes, Georgia Baptist Convention Executive Committee, 20 March 1845, Special Collections, Jack Tarver Library, Mercer University, Macon GA; *Christian Index*, 4 April 1845; *Religious Herald*, 10 April 1845, 2.

Index. The rights of slaveholders were uppermost in the mind of the editor as he commented on the friction between Baptists North and South: "While we continue united in the same organization, our rights will be continually liable to invasion, and their invasion will ever excite strife." In short, slavery was necessary for the "purity" of Christianity, a correct understanding of scripture, and the success of mission efforts.[7]

Southern Baptists in Georgia participated in the reconfiguration of missions and slavery. As individuals and in community, Middle Georgia Baptists struggled to uphold their loyalty to the missionary enterprise. On the heels of denominational schism, Southern Baptists as a whole remained officially impervious to the growing slavery-driven sectional crisis of the 1850s as convention meetings focused on missions, education, and other spiritual matters, seemingly ignoring the outside world other than as a mission field. Associations in Georgia followed the same pattern. The *Christian Index*, however, regularly reprinted secular news near the back of the paper, including accounts of some of the more notable events of the decade, such as the Kansas Nebraska Act and the ensuing skirmishes over slavery on the western frontier.[8]

In the midst of the growing political storm over the issue of slavery, many Baptists in Middle Georgia on the eve of war remained focused on missions—foreign, domestic, and Native American. Delegates to the Central Baptist Association in late summer 1860, for example, listened to a missionary sermon and received a report that lamented a lack of attention to missions. The report noted the failure of the association to provide for an associational missionary the previous year and charged that churches in the association evidenced "no special interest" in terms of missions, indicating "we are fast

---

[7] "The Southern Convention Again," *Christian Index*, 4 April 1845, 3; "The Press and the Mission Board" and "The North and the South," *Christian Index*, 11 April 1845, 3.

[8] See annual minutes of the Southern Baptist Convention and Georgia Baptist Convention, 1845–1859, Special Collections, Jack Tarver Library, Mercer University, Macon GA.

becoming Anti-Missionary in all but name." The stern words evoked a response from the delegates, who resolved to hold "four Missionary Mass meetings during the ensuing year." They further requested that pastors discuss missions "more frequently to the Churches," and "send out a Missionary to either the Indians or some foreign field." The outside world made no intrusion upon the huddled Baptist delegates, in other words, other than concerns related to the salvation of lost souls. In a similar fashion, the available minutes of local churches in the Central Association in 1860 are void of references to the growing sectional crisis or the outside world in general.[9]

Yet despite years of rhetoric and resolutions concerning missions, this primary directive of Southern Baptists took a hit immediately following the firing upon Fort Sumter. Meeting in late April, the Georgia Baptist Convention learned that national Southern Baptist leaders had decided "domestic" mission efforts would be confined to the Confederate states. In addition to limiting the geographical scope of missions, financial hardship caused by secession and war forced the firing of "about 50" of the board's missionaries, leaving a total of 69 employed. Ebenezer W. Warren, pastor of First Baptist Church in Macon, addressed the financial crisis, seeking to cast the situation in a positive light. "Our political troubles have rendered the future uncertain," he stated, "and our people have been disposed to hold their money, that they might be prepared for any emergency. Very large amounts of money have been given to our volunteer companies, who have gone to defend our country. These

---

[9] Minutes, Georgia Baptist Association, 1859, 45, Special Collections, Jack Tarver Library, Mercer University, Macon GA; minutes, Central Baptist Association, 1860, Special Collections, Jack Tarver Library, Mercer University, Macon GA; minutes, Georgia Baptist Convention, 1860, 46, Special Collections, Jack Tarver Library, Mercer University, Macon GA; minutes, Flint River Baptist Association, 1860, Special Collections, Jack Tarver Library, Mercer University, Macon GA. The minutes of the Central and Flint River associations focus on missions, evangelism, polity, and theological issues. The general conclusion about local churches is drawn from examining all available 1860 minutes of churches within the Central Baptist Association, as well as a sampling of central Georgia Baptist churches not affiliated with the Central Baptist Association.

amounts were well deserved by our patriotic soldiery, and therefore were nobly contributed by our citizens." Warren continued, apologetically, "We were not surprised, with these facts before us, that our boards should be embarrassed and compelled to retrench." Yet Warren quickly issued a challenge. "What is to be done in the future? Shall the cause of Christ and of souls suffer further?... Let us meet the crisis, prove equal to it, and by the help of God bear the tottering ark through its present severe trial."[10]

The drastic curtailment of mission efforts did not go unnoticed among the Baptist public in Georgia. Following the state convention, the editor of the *Christian Index*, while praising Georgia Baptist leaders for voicing unanimous and wholehearted support of the Confederacy, expressed criticism of the decreased attention given to missions. "Nothing was done to encourage State missions, Colportage, or a systematic collection of funds, all thinking, no doubt, that troublous times was a fair excuse," Samuel Boykin concluded. "But to our mind, troublous times is an urgent reason why Christians should work harder than ever for Jesus and give more liberally than before to spread the Gospel. Zeal for our heavenly country should at least equal zeal for our earthly country." Two months later Boykin warned his readers against neglecting financial support of mission causes against the backdrop of excitement regarding the war. Despite wholehearted support for the Confederacy among Georgia Baptist leaders, unease among the ranks of Georgia Baptists, including those of Middle Georgia, developed as the war immediately drained financial support from mission causes.[11]

Immediate and widespread, the threat to missions also existed at the associational level of Baptist life, an arena in which elites and common folk worked side by side. Meeting in August 1861 at Bethel Baptist Church in Jasper County, the Central Association counted

---

[10] Minutes, Georgia Baptist Association, 1861, 8–11, Special Collections, Jack Tarver Library, Mercer University, Macon GA.

[11] *Christian Index*, 8 May 1861, 2; "A Few Earnest Words to Pastors and Church Members," *Christian Index*, 17 July 1862. Colportage referred to the distribution of Bibles and other religious reading material among soldiers.

among its members some of the most influential Baptists in the state. Forty delegates strong, the meeting featured a number of Georgia Baptist leaders, including Samuel Boykin, Ebenezer W. Warren, and Adiel Sherwood. Of the 22 churches represented in person or by letter, Macon First Baptist was the largest (760 members) and most influential, represented by Boykin and Warren. Both held prominent places on the program and were two of nine elected delegates to the upcoming Georgia Baptist Convention. Of the nine men elected as delegates to the GBC, eight were present at the associational meeting. Of the eight, seven were from the five largest churches.

Most of the Baptists present nonetheless represented small, rural Baptist churches and were not among the ranks of Georgia Baptist leaders. Only 7 of the 22 churches claimed more than 100 members. In five of these seven churches, African-American slaves outnumbered whites, reflecting the prominence of planter members. Of the remaining 15 churches with memberships of less than 100, only 3 had majority African-American membership, reflecting the prominence of small farmers and yeoman. In short, the gathering of the Central Association contained a minority presence of Baptist elites, representing city and planter, and a majority presence of Baptists representing poorer white Baptists living in the countryside and small communities.[12]

---

[12] Minutes, Central Baptist Association, 1861, 3–9, 14, Special Collections, Jack Tarver Library, Mercer University, Macon GA. Although local church records are incomplete partially due to a lack of diligence in preserving them, smaller congregations throughout Middle Georgia tend to have less complete records than larger congregations. Pulpit resources certainly factored into the equation; large churches such as Macon First Baptist had a full-time preacher, while many smaller congregations met only once a month and depended upon a circuit-riding preacher who was charged with two to four congregations. Even with the decline of slavery as the war progressed, this author found no evidence that larger congregations in Middle Georgia with large slave constituencies shuttered their doors. Such congregations continued to pay their pastors, albeit at sometimes lower wages, even as support of mission work waned. Geography contributed to the ability of large churches to remain functional; unlike North Georgia, Middle Georgia remained on the periphery of the war even in the later months. When forced to flee Atlanta in fall 1864, for example, some Baptists temporarily settled

Penning the Report on Missions of the Central Association, Sherwood acknowledged that "the times are hard." Focusing on the need to fund a missionary among Native Amercians residing within Georgia, the long-time pastor declared that "if we contribute when money is hard to obtain, it becomes a sacrifice, and shows our love for his cause." Although seemingly well received at that time by delegates, one year later Sherwood expressed disappointment that Central Baptists had not rallied around the cause of missions. "In the midst of the horrors of the war which is now desolating our borders," Sherwood's Report on Missions lamented, "little has been done in the way of missionary labor." From this point, matters would only grow worse.[13]

Despite financial problems in 1861, Native American missions continued to capture the popular imagination of Southern Baptists throughout Middle Georgia, and at least one association responded with financial support. During the same month that Central Baptists lamented the need for Native American missions, a Native American missionary headlined a camp meeting just north of Macon in Forsyth. Julia Stanford expressed great excitement about the revival services. "Camp Meeting begins next Thursday," wrote Stanford on Sunday, 18 August. In the agrarian South of the nineteenth century, camp meetings were an integral part of the region's identity. Mark Wetherington, in his study of South Georgia during the war and Reconstruction, estimates that no more than one-third of Georgians actually attended church. Yet the popularity of protracted revivals, featuring visiting preachers from distant states, extended beyond the regularly churched in a rural nineteenth-century Georgia that afforded few opportunities for plain folk to gather for socializing and

---

in Macon and attended First Baptist Macon. In some instances, such as the First Baptist Church of Milledgeville, no war-time records remain for large congregations. Nonetheless, secondary and anecdotal sources do not suggest widespread, or even sporadic, closures occurred in the larger Baptist churches of Middle Georgia.

[13] Minutes, Central Baptist Association, 1861, 6; 1862, 9, Special Collections, Jack Tarver Library, Mercer University, Macon GA.

entertainment beyond kinfolk connections. Indeed, camp meeting afforded the best opportunity of the year for the hosting church or churches to recruit new members.[14]

Stanford had never attended such an event, but "should like to go.... I do hope the Lord will bless...with a glorious revival." Her interest in the revival services centered on her desire to hear Reverend Benjamin Murrow, a missionary to Creek peoples of the Western frontier. She noted his arrival on the train and found "truly interesting" a pre-revival lecture he delivered on the subject of Native American history and early missionary activity. God, in Stanford's mind, remained concerned that the Native Americans hear of his love. "From the Red men comes the cry, come over and help us. Oh that men would go. God has done so much for us and so little for him. Oh, that I could love him more & more." Murrow's story enamored the young Stanford. "I love so much to hear of his work among the Red men & of his successes & misfortunes. The cause is near my heart or rather my heart is in the matter."[15]

The emphasis on Native American missions spilled over into the associational meeting of the following month. On 22 September, Stanford attended the annual Flint River Baptist meeting held at Shiloah Baptist Church in Monroe County. Featured speakers included three missionaries to Native Americans, two of whom were Natives, D. M. Foreman and J. T. Foster. The three speakers so impressed the Baptists in attendance that the association collected a mission offering and voted to financially support one of the three for

---

[14] Julia A. Stanford, diary, Spencer King Papers, Special Collections, Jack Tarver Library, Mercer University, Macon GA, 18 August. For an analysis of common folk in rural South Georgia, see Mark V. Wetherington, *Plain Folk's Fight: The Civil War and Reconstruction in Piney Woods Georgia* (Chapel Hill: University of North Carolina Press, 2006).

[15] Stanford, diary, Spencer King Papers, Special Collections, Jack Tarver Library, Mercer University, Macon GA, 16 August.

the coming year. "It did my soul good to hear these red men preach," Stanford noted.[16]

Stanford's excitement about missions could not counteract widespread concerns among Baptists of Middle Georgia. Nor did the enthusiasm generated by Murrow's tour of Middle Georgia prevent the Native American missionary from voicing his own concerns. Attending the annual meeting of Rehoboth Baptists at Traveler's Rest Baptist Church in Macon County, he spoke of "a dark and gloomy cloud...hanging over us as a nation and as a Christian people...the advancement of God's cause, the salvation of souls, we fear will be interrupted for a season, and crippled." Delegates at the Rehoboth meeting echoed Murrow's apprehension, worried that war would harm the cause of missions. Expressing fear that religious education, a corollary of missions, would suffer as well in war, Rehoboth Baptists voiced concern that the "mental culture" of Southern children was being neglected. Prophetically, delegates solemnly declared, "we fear that we may, at a future not very distant, be dependent upon a foreign, and at present hostile country for teachers." Afraid not only of the present disruption of Southern mission efforts, Rehoboth Baptists lamented the future possibility of Northern missionaries in the South.[17]

Baptists of the Ebenezer Association in late 1861 joined those of the Central, Flint River, and Rehoboth bodies in expressing anxiety about mission activity. Avoiding overt expressions of patriotic sentiments, Ebenezer delegates agreed to set aside a day of fasting and prayer and expressed concerns regarding the adverse affect of

---

[16] Stanford, diary, Spencer King Papers, Special Collections, Jack Tarver Library, Mercer University, Macon GA, 18 August, 22 September; minutes, Flint River Baptist Association, 1861, 4, Special Collections, Jack Tarver Library, Mercer University, Macon GA. D. M. Foremon and J. T. Foster were Cherokee. The "Report of Committee on Missions" noted that Foremon, Foster, and Murrow "have delighted us by their sermons, addresses, and conversation." The association agreed to financially support Foster for the next year. The Native American nations' loyalty to the Confederacy is prominently noted.

[17] Minutes, Rehoboth Baptist Association, 1861, 2–6, Special Collections, Jack Tarver Library, Mercer University, Macon GA.

the war upon mission efforts. Noting the growing emphasis on missions prior to the war, the mission committee's report fretted over the war-caused reduction in the number of domestic missionaries and expressed concern that Baptists would no longer be able to sustain those remaining on the field. Ebenezer Baptists also worried about the bleak prospects for foreign missions. In the face of declining opportunities for traditional mission activity, the association cast about for new fields of service. Ebenezer Baptists appropriated Baptist soldiers serving in the Confederacy as missionaries "battling against the host of darkness." Soldier missionaries, the committee declared, deserved the sympathy and gratitude of Baptists of the South, who should ensure that the soldiers' wants were adequately supplied. Yet the association sounded a note of caution, observing that "the citizens of the States are so absorbed with our National affairs, as to be disqualified for spiritual service." Within mere months of the war's beginnings, the Ebenezer Association recognized both the spiritual danger and opportunity the conflict afforded.[18]

While Central and Flint River Baptists focused on preaching the Gospel to Native Americans (and collected money to assist in the matter), mission efforts among Africans seemed of little importance. Central Baptists offered no support—verbally or financially—for such efforts. Flint River Baptists acknowledged the need to preach among "the ancestors and kindred of those who till our fields," yet took no action on the matter. Julia Stanford offered her own insight into the disparity. While enamored with the Native American race in the distant West, she expressed disdain for the African race in her own hometown: "Runaway Negroes caught I anticipate trouble with the race ere long—They are getting too high."[19]

---

[18] Minutes, Ebenezer Baptist Association, 1861, Special Collections, Jack Tarver Library, Mercer University, Macon GA.

[19] Minutes, Central Baptist Association, 1861, 5, 6, 10, Special Collections, Jack Tarver Library, Mercer University, Macon GA; minutes, Flint River Baptist Association, 1861, 3, 8, Special Collections, Jack Tarver Library, Mercer University, Macon GA; Stanford, diary, Spencer King Papers, Special Collections, Jack Tarver Library, Mercer University, Macon GA, 25 June.

As the war moved into its second year, traditional Baptist mission efforts fared even worse as verbal and financial commitment to work among Native Americans and Africans plummeted. By spring 1862, with initial Southern hopes of a quick victory dashed and amidst the formative stages of a Confederate identity, Southern Baptist leaders increasingly turned their attention to mission opportunities among the men in the field. Expressing "gloomy forebodings" regarding the war, a March editorial in the *Christian Index* noted "sunshine on the dark clouds" in the enterprise of army missions, framing such efforts as a "nobler struggle" than the war because the spiritual conversion of soldiers served the purpose of subjecting the world to God. In short, the imperative of missions, serving as the focal point of Southern Baptist evangelistic efforts outside the local church since the inception of the Southern Baptist Convention, demanded an actionable response. With all prior mission opportunities hindered by the war, unsaved Confederate soldiers represented the only remaining avenue of preserving the missionary identity of Southern Baptists.[20]

Redirected mission efforts now underway, Baptists sought the best means to achieve soldier conversions. In July 1862, Chaplain D. G. Daniell observed the influence of Christian newspapers among the soldiers. Noting the "avidity" with which such papers were received, Daniell purposed to double to sixty the subscriptions he had secured for his regiment. Believers were fed spiritually, and non-believers were inspired at the sight of the "interest" among the soldiers. The chaplain reported the case of a non-churched lieutenant who financially supported Christian newspapers. Noting the presence of four weekly services and "three preachers in camp," he rejoiced that "a few conversions have occurred in the regiment" and "the religious

---

[20] A.E.D., "An Encouraging Aspect of the War," *Christian Index*, 11 March 1862, 1. For a discussion of the forming of Confederate identity, see Anne Sarah Rubin, *A Shattered Nation: The Rise and Fall of the Confederacy, 1861–1868* (Chapel Hill: University of North Carolina Press, 2005).

element of the regiment is being drawn out." Avoiding the word revival, Daniell nonetheless declared, "I am not discouraged."[21]

Daniell's focus on spiritual conversion reflected one aspect of the religious military press. Kurt Berends examined the religious life of Confederate soldiers through the pages of the Southern religious military press, concluding that by the second half of the Civil War, Southern ministers at large were convinced that the key to sectional victory was a converted army. Utilizing religious newspapers, Baptists, Methodists, and Presbyterians in the South portrayed soldiers as God's warriors and proclaimed manliness and commitment to the Confederacy as Christian virtues. Maintaining faith in the primacy of personal salvation, Southern churches, through the religious military press, rallied for sectional victory, while at the same time providing rationale for the possibility of defeat. Berends observes that this message conveyed social implications far beyond the war itself, shaping the religion of the Lost Cause as a civil religion, but also perpetuating a manly Christianity.[22]

The members of Sandy Creek Baptist Church in rural Morgan County would likely have read Daniell's report from the camps printed in the pages of the *Christian Index* rather than the latest war news from a New York or Virginia daily paper, unless the latter were reprinted in the *Index*. Shortly after the chaplain's commentary on army missions, the congregation voted to give two dollars for "colportage among the Soldiers." By the following summer, as other local churches in Middle Georgia addressed mission work among

---

[21] D. G. Daniell, "Letter from a Chaplain," *Christian Index*, 22 July 1862, 3. Daniell previously pastored in Dublin, and also established the first Baptist church in the Atlanta area. See B. D. Ragsdale, *Story of Georgia Baptists* (Atlanta: Executive Committee of the Georgia Baptist Convention, 1938) 314, 335, 348, 357.

[22] Kurt O. Berends, "'Wholesome Reading Purifies and Elevates the Man': The Religious Military Press in the Confederacy," in *Religion and the American Civil War*, ed. Randall M. Miller (New York and Oxford: Oxford University Press, 1998) 131–66. See also Peter S. Carmichael, *Lee's Young Artillerist: William R. J. Pegram* (Charlottesville: University Press of Virginia, 1995). Carmichael examines the young Confederate soldier William Pegram in portraying how Confederate soldiers were certain they were fighting for a holy cause.

Confederate soldiers, the Sandy Creek church again provided funding for army missions, collecting $8.50 "for Colportage among the Soldiers" and $6.50 "for sending the *Christian Index* to the Soldiers."[23]

In August and September 1862, Baptist associations across Middle Georgia increasingly turned their attention to army missions. The Ebenezer Association reflected the missions shift then taking place in Baptist life. Noting that some former Native American missionaries had transferred to the army camps due to the dire spiritual condition of Southern soldiers, Ebenezer Baptists refocused their mission vision. "Deprived in a great degree of religious instructions and religious influences, and surrounded with circumstances tending to develop their feelings of revenge, rather than their Christian graces, a responsible duty devolves upon us, to send among them ministers of the Word." The situation among the soldiers demanded the immediate attention of faithful Baptists. The South's defenders, far from home and cut off from most religious influences, faced overwhelming temptations of vice. Heroic mission efforts were necessary in order to save the heroes of the South from moral dangers, even as the destiny of the new nation seemed doubtful. "The glory and hope of our country is fast passing away," one report lamented. Another report offered words of contrition, bewailing the anger of God upon the South, yet obediently submitting to the chastisement. In the face of diminished national prospects, delegates urged churches to keep their doors open, pay their local ministers, and contribute to army missions.[24]

For their part, Rehoboth Baptists began a transition from traditional mission efforts to a focus upon the needs of soldiers and young women. Former Native American missionary Benjamin Murrow, by now working unofficially among Southern soldiers,

---

[23] Minutes, Sandy Creek Baptist Church, Morgan County, 1862–1864 (GBCR, Mercer, microfilm reel 124).

[24] Minutes, Ebenezer Baptist Association, 1862, Special Collections, Jack Tarver Library, Mercer University, Macon GA.

influenced Rehoboth Baptists' perceptions of mission needs. His pleas of support for army missions led delegates to redirect mission funds at large to evangelism among the soldiers, distributing Bibles, tracts, and other religious reading material. Rehoboth Baptists also lamented the ramifications of the loss of soldiers' lives, concluding that the education of Baptist young people was in jeopardy. In addition to army mission efforts, delegates thus turned their attention to young women in particular, declaring that in the face of immense losses of the lives of young men in the war, "the education of the young for some time to come will devolve more than ever upon females."[25]

---

[25] Minutes, Rehoboth Baptist Association, 1862, 6–8, Special Collections, Jack Tarver Library, Mercer University, Macon GA. The Flint River and Rehoboth associations, both of which supported Native American missionary Benjamin Murrow, provide a snapshot of the gradual demise of Native American mission support. Within the Flint River Baptist Association, Native American missions garnered more funding than other mission activities from 1860 to 1862. In the 1860 church year, associational churches contributed $78.57 to Native American missions, $74.90 to domestic missions, $54.70 to foreign missions, $9.80 to African missions, and $8.92 to the Colporteur Society. In 1861, the total amount designated to specific mission causes decreased in the wake of financial hardships in the South, yet the gap between categories increased as $31 went to Native American missions; $20 to foreign missions; $18 to domestic missions; $5 to African missions; and none to the Colporteur Society. In the face of growing inflation, the trending gap dramatically increased in 1862 as Native American missions received $253.70 in funding while foreign missions garnered only $39.40 and neither domestic missions, foreign missions (including African missions) nor the Colporteur Society received any support. In addition, two new categories emerged: a "Colored Agent" received $14 for work among slaves, while $45 was collected for Georgia soldiers. Giving statistics for 1863 indicate the ascendancy of army missions ($375.28) against a peaking interest in Native American missions ($379.68) while domestic missions ($33.83) received support from only one congregation and foreign missions was not funded. The trend to army missions and away from Native American missions continued in 1864 as army missions garnered $238.50 of support against $139.90 given for Native American missions, $35 for foreign missions, and none for domestic missions. During 1865, against the backdrop of the South's defeat, the churches of the Flint River Association contributed a mere $32.50 for all mission purposes. A total of three churches contributed the sum total, and no specific breakdowns of the contributions were recorded. Although wartime minutes for the Rehoboth Baptist Association exist for only 1861 and 1862, the predominance of Native American missions is much

Flint River Baptists also turned their focus to army missions in 1862, albeit in a more cheerful manner. Declaring army missions an "interesting and important field," Flint River Baptists omitted any reference to negative aspects of army life. Declaring the Domestic Mission Board adequately engaged in providing Bibles and religious literature to "fathers, husbands, sons and brothers" fighting for the Southern cause, the association expressed satisfaction with army mission efforts. During the remainder of the war, army missions garnered increasing attention from Flint River Baptists, while the sins of camp life never merited a single comment. Although soldiers needed spiritual help, apparently the peopling of the army by fathers, husbands, sons, and brothers of the South's Baptists precluded any appearance, or at least acknowledgement, of immorality in the camps.[26]

At this point, Baptists' mission vision reflected the realities of a nation increasingly isolated from the outside world by a prolonged war. *Index* editors interpreted that isolation as the will of God. God's

---

more pronounced than in the Flint River Association. In 1861, Rehoboth Association churches gave a total of $1233.30 to Native American missions, with twenty of twenty-two reporting churches providing funding. By way of contrast, foreign missions received a total of $17 funding (by way of one church designating the $17 total to African missions) while neither domestic missions nor the Colporteur Society received any support. The following year, Rehoboth churches supported Native American missions to the total of $592.20 in contributions, compared to $94 given for tracts for soldiers, and no funding of home or foreign missions. While these two associations represent general trends found in many associations in Georgia during the war era, the overwhelming support of the Rehoboth Associations of Native American missions in 1861 and 1862 is not typical, and can be explained by the influence of Native American missionary Benjamin Murrow who was adopted, in effect, by the association. In short, Native American missions captured the imagination of Baptist churches in Middle Georgia in such a way as to elicit much financial support on the eve of war and during the early years of the war, only to cede ground to army missions by the middle of the war. See minutes of the Flint River Baptist Association, 1860–1865, and Rehoboth Baptist Association, 1861–1862, Special Collections, Jack Tarver Library, Mercer University, Macon GA.

[26] Minutes, Flint River Baptist Association, 1862, 9; 1863, 4–5, 8; 1864, 3–4, 6, Special Collections, Jack Tarver Library, Mercer University, Macon GA.

providence had opened the army mission field following the closing of other mission opportunities. One editorial called upon home-front Baptists to embrace the new "golden opportunity" with "christian liberality, effort and sacrifice." Resorting to hyperbole in magnifying the importance of the Confederacy, the editorial declared, "'never before, in the history of nations or of wars, was there such an opportunity for the display of christian zeal, for benefiting one's own country, or for softening the rigors of war and the cruelties of man." By saving the soldier, the nation would be blessed of God.[27]

Reports from the camps in late 1862 evidenced some successes. Stationed in Virginia, missionary Abner B. Campbell of the 9th Georgia Infantry reported the successes of small tent meetings held with previously unchurched soldiers. Meanwhile, *Christian Index* associate editor Sylvanus Landrum and Jesse Campbell, father of Abner, preached to and prayed over soldiers stationed in Savannah. The army evangelist also preached in a hospital located near Savannah, finding the scene much more somber. Armed with tracts and hymn books, Campbell ministered to "poor invalids" with "pale faces and emancipated forms...trembling voices and...tearful eyes gazing wistfully upwards, as they sung the sweet songs of Zion."[28]

Demand for religious literature in the winter 1862/63 proved great. Yet while the *Index* urged Georgia Baptists to contribute funds needed to send tracts, Bibles, and newspapers to the soldiers via missionaries, funds collected did not meet all demands. Chaplain R. K. Porter of Cobb's Legion, headquartered near Fredericksburg, Virginia, reported a lack of sufficient reading material for soldiers. Unable to count upon outside help, Chaplain Porter reported that the men had taken up a collection to purchase fifty copies of the *Index*. The *Index* sent the requested fifty copies to Cobb's Legion, urging

---

[27] "Soldier's Colportage," *Christian Index*, 16 December 1862, 2.
[28] A. B. Campbell, "Experience of an Army Chaplain," *Christian Index*, 2 December 1862, 2; "From Our Army Evangelist," Jesse H. Campbell, *Christian Index*, 23 December 1862, 3.

Georgia Baptists to fund an additional 1,000 copies for distribution among regiments in Virginia and the western theatre.[29]

Growing as the war progressed, army missions took the form of placing evangelical tracts in the hands of soldiers, distributing Bibles among soldiers, financing denominationally paid chaplains, and sending copies of religious newspapers such as the *Christian Index* to enlisted men. The primary concern addressed by literature and chaplains was that of souls, whether in the form of eliciting conversion or offering encouragement in living out one's faith. Coinciding with revivals among army ranks, by 1863, Baptist mission efforts focused almost solely on army missions. Rather than seeking to save the souls of Native Americans, Chinese, or Africans, Southern Baptists trained their attention on the souls of Southern white men. In January 1863, army missionary G. F. Williams, corresponding from Chattanooga, described evangelistic successes and failures among Confederate soldiery, while noting some evidence of revival. Williams visited and preached in the camps, sometimes finding it difficult to assemble an audience, but in other cases preaching to crowds. At one meeting, "some fifteen indicated a desire to obtain religion," signifying "good indications of a revival."[30]

In a similar fashion, Jesse Campbell offered mixed reviews of religious affairs in army life in Georgia during winter 1863. Campbell distributed over 1,000 New Testaments as well as thousands of tracts, in turn witnessing hundreds coming forth for prayer and manifesting "serious concern for their souls." Yet he questioned the effectiveness of mission efforts. Uncertain that he had accomplished any good, he wrote that only "God knoweth." Army mission work he considered "the most exciting, absorbing, and, in some respects, the most promising work I have ever performed," even in the face of inconclusive results. Twenty-two months into the war, Campbell

---

[29] "Index for Soldiers," *Christian Index*, 23 December 1862, 2. Kurt O. Berends, in "Wholesome Reading Purifies," 131–66, argues that religious reading material, popular among Confederate ranks, stressed personal religious experience while also reinforcing patriotism.

[30] M. T. Sumner, "Army Missions," *Christian Index*, 13 January 1863, 1.

offered a sobering assessment of mission work among the soldiers. Declaring himself the only Baptist missionary among soldiers in Georgia for a period of eighteen months—and now one of five total—the minister from Middle Georgia expressed some satisfaction that his perseverance eventually resulted in the recruitment of chaplains for "several regiments" and the placement of reading material among the soldiers.[31]

Campbell's observations notwithstanding, the focus on army missions gathered momentum during the spring and summer months of 1863 as the *Christian Index* published extensive correspondence from missionaries in the camps. Ivy W. Duggan of the 49th Georgia, camped "on the banks of the Rappahannock in Virginia," reported that "religious feeling," already present for "some months," was on the rise. The weather played a role in public religious expressions, as warmer weather allowed for twice daily religious services. Duggan reported "large numbers" of soldiers embracing religion. The spiritual results found manifestation in that which Baptists most understood: baptism. Hymn singing accompanied the baptism of new converts. Religious tunes reminded participants of church life back home, part of the larger evangelical revival atmosphere that conveyed comforting memories of home and hearth. J. J. Hyman held night services among the 49th Georgia, noting that "the sweet strains of music from the voices of the war-torn soldiers were heard to echo and re-echo up and down the valleys and hills where so many Georgians had fallen in defense of their country." The interest in religious matters finally led to a construction of a baptismal pool near the camp, with many conversions resulting.[32]

---

[31] J. H. Campbell, "From Our Army Evangelist," *Christian Index*, 16 March 1863, 1.

[32] Ivy W. Duggan, "From the Wilderness," *Christian Index*, 8 June 1863, 1; J. J. Hyman, "A Chaplain's Report," *Christian Index*, 6 July 1863, 1. From Duggan: "Yesterday morning we repaired to a stream near our camps, and our chaplain baptized four young men of our regiment. This morning we started to the same place to baptize another. As we approached the water, we saw a large crowd assembled there, and on arriving we found brother Barrett, Chaplain of the 45th

J. S. Dodd, pastor of Bethsaida Baptist Church in Fayette County, reported on revivals among the 6th Georgia, 19th Georgia, 23rd Georgia, 27th Georgia, and 28th Georgia regiments. Eager soldiers prepared an arbor for revival services, and hundreds arrived prior to the designated preaching time. After the first service, "a very large number came forward and requested special prayer." Services continued for eight days, and Dodd recounted the experience as the most "gracious work of divine grace" in his memory, with hundreds of rejoicing soldiers crowding the altar, "some shouting aloud the praises of God." The impact was such that the chaplain reported that swearing and card playing ceased during the duration of his stay.[33]

Not everyone accepted reports of warm-weather revivals at face value, however. Although he readily published missionary accounts, *Index* editor Boykin expressed some skepticism over reports of mass conversions. He worried that ministers were largely being deceived by soldiers who merely acted the part expected of them in the presence of men of the cloth. Calvinistic influences in Baptist life historically led to questions about emotionally oriented revivals, a point reflected in Boykin's criticisms of army revivals. "All wicked men are not fools," the editor charged. "Many of them know how they ought to feel and talk and act, and while they loudly denounce hypocrisy in professors of religion, play the hypocrite themselves most successfully in the presence of ministers of the gospel." Ministers in turn were "often deceived," he noted, and in turn

---

Ga. Reg., preparing to baptize a young man of his regiment. The two were baptized, and we returned to our camps.... When we assemble here in the groves of Virginia, we seat ourselves upon the leaves that cover the ground, and sing the same old songs that we sang with you long ago. No sweet voice of mother, sister, or wife, softens our music here, but we trust that your voices mingle with ours in harmony at the mercy seat." For a broader discussion of why soldiers embraced religion, see Steven E. Woodworth, *While God Is Marching On: The Religious World of the Civil War Soldiers* (Lawrence: University Press of Kansas, 2001). Reasons included echoes of familiar rituals from home, a desire to find a moral anchor in the midst of war, and in preparation for the inevitably of death.

[33] J. S. Dodd, "Gen. Colquitt's Brigade," *Christian Index*, 6 July 1863, 1; J. S. Dodd, "Bethsaida and Ebenezer Baptist Churches," *Christian Index*, 6 July 1863, 3.

unintentionally deceived others in reporting the successes of the revivals. Fears of religious pluralism may have contributed to Boykin's negative assessment, implied by his odd charge that some soldiers were converting instead to the "principles of Mormonism."[34]

Boykin's questions about the effectiveness of Southern army revivals reflect an ongoing debate among historians. In the decades following the Civil War, military chaplains William W. Bennett and J. William Jones recounted their experiences serving among the Confederate armies and related the widespread conversions they witnessed. That thousands of soldiers experienced spiritual conversions as a result of army revivals remains uncontested among historians, although actual numbers are difficult to pinpoint. Gardiner H. Shattuck, Jr., examining both Confederate and Union revivals, estimates that while some 100,000 conversions probably took place among Southern armies, Union conversions may have been twice as many. These figures represent up to 10 percent of all soldiers, and do not include all soldiers who attended revival services. Among individual soldiers who had conversion experiences, statistical long-term measurements of the impacts of the moment of spiritual decision are simply unknown for lack of data. Reflecting broader themes, some historians have sought to examine the motives underlying the moment of conversion. Stephen Woodworth, for

---

[34] Samuel Boykin, "The Moral Effects of the War," *Christian Index*, 21 August 1863, 2. The nineteenth-century Calvinist, in order to embrace revivalism, had to "concede that God was benevolent and not wrathful, merciful not stern, reasonable not mysterious...that man was active not passive in his salvation, that grace was not arbitrarily or capriciously dispensed like the royal prerogative of a sovereign but offered freely to all men as the gift of a loving Father to his children." William H. McLoughlin, *The American Evangelicals, 1800–1900* (Gloucester MA: Peter Smith, 1985) 4. In addition to challenging Calvinistic theology, the Civil War era paralleled growth in religious pluralism. "Southern clergy did grow ever more weary of Northern Christians who seemed to be straying into a godless wilderness to chase after 'Mormonism, Millerism, Comeoutism, Universalism, or with an Americanized edition of German rationalism." Bertram Wyatt-Brown, "Church, Honor, and Secession," *Religion and the American Civil War*, ed. Randall Miller (New York: Oxford University Press, 1998) 100.

example, demonstrates that some soldiers embraced the revivals in an attempt to find a moral center in the midst of war, while for others religion provided comfort while daily facing the prospect of death and attendant eternity. Drew Gilpin Faust argues that Confederate revivals, while sometimes effecting change in personal piety, served on a larger scale as a vehicle for corporate understanding of God's plan in the midst of death, destruction, and defeat. Faust also echoes Woodworth in the observation that for many individual soldiers, revivalist religion provided a mechanism for coping with the ever-present specters of mortality and death.[35]

Long-term effects on soldiers and later analysis aside, Georgia Baptists in late 1863 gradually decided that the triumph of religion in the ranks they accepted as fact ultimately rested upon the faithfulness of home-front Christians. Portraying the plight of Southern soldiers as "half clad, barefoot and blanketless—exhausted by long marches, panting beneath a scorching sun, or shivering upon the wintery blast," the Ebenezer Association insisted that the unselfish sacrifices of the sons, husbands, and brothers of the South demanded a response. Physical death was lamentable; spiritual death even worse. With the help of an ever-present God and the duty demanded by Christian patriotism, spiritual victory at least seemed evident. The numbers told the story of salvation emerging from the battlefield: thanks to the faithfulness of home-front believers, Baptist missionaries had distributed 379,995 pages of tracts; 2,601 New

---

[35] William W. Bennett, *A Narrative of the Great Revival which Prevailed in the Southern Armies* (Philadelphia: Claxton, Remsen & Haffelfinger, 1877); J. William Jones, *Christ in the Camps: Or Religion in Lee's Army* (Richmond: B. F. Johnson, 1887); Gardiner H. Shattuck, Jr., *A Shield and a Hiding Place: The Religious Life of the Civil War Armies* (Mercer University Press, 1987); Drew Gilpin Faust, "Christian Soldiers: The Meaning of Revivalism in the Confederate Army," *Journal of Southern History* 53/1 (February 1987): 63–90; Woodworth, *While God Is Marching On*; Drew Gilpin Faust, *This Republic of Suffering: Death and the American Civil War* (New York: Alfred A. Knopf, 2008). Woodworth combs the diaries and letters of soldiers for reasons why soldiers embraced religion, while Faust addresses the subject of religion and death in chap. 6, "Believing and Doubting: What Means the Carnage?"

Testaments; 4,787 religious newspapers; and 3,479 other religious books. Despite the fact that much of the army stood in disarray and the nation suffered immensely, the effects of an abundance of religious material among the soldiers represented an encouraging development on a bleak landscape. On the same fields where Southern soldiers butchered the enemy, Southern souls were readied for heaven. In short, Baptists of the Ebenezer Association in 1863 sought to transform the South's battlefield losses into a painful yet triumphant and joyful salvation.[36]

While Ebenezer Baptists remained hopeful of the spiritual state of Southern soldiers, Central Baptists evidenced a bleaker outlook. Ebenezer Baptists' previous assertion of Confederate soldiers as missionaries fighting the forces of evil proved chillingly wrong in the minds of Central Baptists. Declaring Confederate soldiers evildoers, Central Baptists asked, "What must be done to stay this tide of spiritual desolation?" The war had revealed the depths of sinfulness in the hearts of the Anglo-Saxon race. Yet the wholesale slaughtering of hundreds of thousands was not the issue. Fear of personal immorality, not the mass killings, imperiled the souls of men. "The gospel is the only remedy for all moral evils; it is the only star of hope that now appears to guide us on safely amid the threatening aspects which surround our beloved Zion," Central Baptists pronounced.[37]

The fear of spiritual shallowness embedded within the fabric of Southern life, bubbling up so quickly in the face of temporal warfare, placed Baptists of the Central Association in an awkward situation. Rather than strengthening the Confederacy with the sure imprint of God's blessing through holy rhetoric from the pulpit, they suddenly viewed themselves in an epic struggle for the spiritual welfare of their denomination and nation. As the attention of Baptists turned from temporal to spiritual struggles, the battlefield and camps

---

[36] Minutes, Ebenezer Baptist Association, 1863, Special Collections, Jack Tarver Library, Mercer University, Macon GA.

[37] Minutes, Central Baptist Association, 1863, 6, Special Collections, Jack Tarver Library, Mercer University, Macon GA.

reflected their new emphasis. In 1863, the association redirected mission efforts, positioning army missions over and above foreign missions and viewing the army as a great missionary field. Mirroring Boykin's concern for genuine spiritual conversions within army ranks, and perhaps reflecting the personal influence of the Macon-based editor, the association asked local churches to fund army missionaries and purchase religious reading material for soldiers. Confessing that Baptists had not been faithful in financial support of missionary endeavors, Central Association Baptists agreed to fund a full-time army missionary equipped with "religious reading" and supported by pledges solicited from congregations. In addition, messengers recommended additional contributions for the distribution of thousands of copies of the *Christian Index* among Confederate soldiers. Against the backdrop of new and disturbing realities, messengers spent an hour in solemn prayer for the country on the last day of the meeting.[38]

With Southern Baptist associations in Middle Georgia increasingly focused on army missions in late summer and early fall 1863, Boykin set aside his earlier concerns about soldier conversions. The lack of missionaries on the field warranted a stern word to the Baptists of Georgia. The Domestic Mission Board of the Southern Baptist Convention, funded by churches throughout the South, had only fifty missionaries afield. Boykin commended the men for leaving home and families to minister to soldiers, but scolded the churches of Georgia for not doing their full part to support the mission effort. He asked in frustration, "Shall we appeal to you in vain for funds to be raised for this cause? Shall we call *in vain* upon the churches to take up immediate and liberal collections for army colportage?" In the appeal for "Domestic Missions," no other mission efforts were mentioned. The greatest concern of all Southern Baptist mission

---

[38] Minutes, Central Baptist Association, 1863, Special Collections, Jack Tarver Library, Mercer University, Macon GA. Despite the growing rhetoric concerning army missions, the Central Association, as previously noted, struggled to generate interest in army missions among member congregations in the latter half of 1863 and early 1864.

efforts by this time, army missions nonetheless lacked the support that some Baptist leaders envisioned.[39]

While home-front believers thus exhibited mixed signals concerning support for army missions, soldiers serving in Robert E. Lee's army rejoiced in the revivals that took place in the months following the terrible loss at Gettysburg. "After our return to camps" following Gettysburg, wrote E. B. Barrett of the 45th Georgia Regiment, "the work of Grace commenced afresh with greater power than was enjoyed in the Spring." The revival fires yet burned brightly in the fall months, and "hundreds of wayward transgressors are now rejoicing in the pardoning love of Jesus." Daily services took place at noon and prayer meetings at night, with many conversions among the various Protestant denominations.[40]

Lee's army notwithstanding, the winds of revival did not blow evenly in late 1863. Visiting Georgia troops on a tour of army camps throughout Florida, associate *Index* editor Joseph S. Baker was dismayed to learn that Baptist soldiers were reticent to identify themselves. Only at Camp Cooper, near Fernandina, did "two or

---

[39] "Domestic Missions," *Christian Index*, 11 September 1863, 2. An editorial titled "Foreign Missions" appeared on the same page of the *Index* and suggested that neglect of offerings for foreign missions might be cause for Southern sufferings. In addition, it noted the use of promissory notes to sustain the remaining foreign mission work of the Southern Baptist Convention.

[40] E. B. Barrett, "From Gen. Lee's Army," *Christian Index*, 6 November 1863, 1. Fall 1863 witnessed a notable increase in army revivals, ushering in a period that became known as the Great Revival among the Army of Northern Virginia. In *A Shield and a Hiding Place*, Shattuck argues that by late 1863, revivals in Southern armies, anchored in personal conversion experiences, were more intense than those among Northern ranks. Reid Mitchell, "Christian Soldiers?: Perfecting the Confederacy," in Randall M. Miller, Harry S. Stout, Charles Reagan Wilson, *Religion and the American Civil War* (New York: Oxford University Press, 1998) 297–309, questions whether Southern soldiers were more religious than their Northern counterparts. Berends, "Wholesome Reading Purifies," argues that by the second half of the war, Southern ministers largely embraced the revivals, convinced that the key to sectional victory was a converted army. Sidney J. Romero, in *Religion in the Rebel Ranks* (Lanham MD: University Press of America, 1983) 129, concludes that "there seems little doubt that the church was the single greatest institution in the maintenance of moral in the Confederate army."

three Baptist brethren" make themselves "known to me as such. In other camps Baptist brethren have failed to do this." Nonetheless, Baker was impressed by the signs of revival he witnessed. At Camp Cooper, he found a crude tabernacle constructed for use in worship services. The simple structure was "a large shed with an angular roof covered with clapboards...fenced around with poles to keep cattle from seeking shelter under it. The seats were made of flattened logs."[41]

Though far away, Virginia retained the attention of Baptists of Middle Georgia as the winter months arrived. From the Army of Northern Virginia, missionary A. E. Dickinson reported numerous soldier conversions and declared that more Baptist ministers were entering the chaplaincy. An anonymous correspondent noted a Virginia regiment in which eighty of ninety men were "evangelical" believers, with all eighty attending "Bible classes." Yet some army camps in Virginia still awaited Baptist chaplains. "We are greatly in need of a good Chaplain," wrote an anonymous soldier from "Camp Cutt's Batt. Art." at the Rapidan River as the new year dawned.[42]

The revivals persisted despite lack of leadership and in face of nature's fury. Braving the harshness of winter, some soldiers walked barefooted through the snow to attend nightly prayer meetings held outdoors for lack of a chapel, at least according to the report of a pseudonymous army correspondent writing from the camps of Virginia. Lamenting the lack of Baptist chaplains compared to other denominations, the writer appealed to ministers to work among the soldiers. On a positive note, he rejoiced over "a great many marriages within our lines this winter."[43]

Officers from Middle Georgia serving in Virginia played a notable role in promoting religion among the troops. Captain John T.

---

[41] J. S. Baker, "Dr. Baker's Report," *Christian Index*, 4 December 1863, 1.

[42] A. E. Dickinson, "Revival among the Soldiers," *Christian Index*, 8 January 1864, 1; SEMEI, "Richmond Correspondence of the Index," 8 January 1864, 1; A Soldier, "From the Army," 22 January 1864, 1.

[43] W., "Army Correspondence of the Index," *Christian Index*, 26 February 1864, 1.

Wingfield of Wilkes County served in the 9th Georgia, commanding the Irvin Militia. "He is a sample of the polite, high-toned, and christian gentlemen," wrote a traveling army missionary. Despite spending ten days with the company, day and night, the writer had heard "but *one* single profane expression." Evidences of soldier piety notwithstanding, the writer commented, as had many observers beforehand in other camps, that the soldiers were in great need of a chaplain.[44]

The 88th Georgia, in winter 1864 stationed near Summerville Ford, Virginia, was fortunate enough to have a Baptist chaplain, James M. Brittain. He reported that the soldiers had built a chapel capable of seating 200 persons. Although grateful for the crowd that "always" assembled at the services, no "outward show of a revival" manifested itself. He wistfully remembered "the rich revival of last summer" during which "many of the sons of Georgia found God" in the forests of Virginia. Yet the revivals of 1863 paled compared to Brittain's grand vision of a new "*sweeping revival*—one that will gather into its balmy wings every soldier of the Confederate army!" Such a revival would unite the spiritual and temporal, and no enemy would then be able to withstand "the children of Zion in battle array."[45]

Sometimes the work of chaplains included matters far from spiritual. In February 1864 an *Index* army correspondent reported on chaplain activity in William Mahone's brigade. In addition to leading chapel services, Bible classes, and prayer meetings, the two chaplains serving in the five regiments of the brigade also taught "classes in

---

[44] ZADOC, "Notes of a Short Trip to the Army of Northern Virginia," *Christian Index*, 11 March 1864, 1. In addition, the writer noted he met "with my old friend Capt. George M. Patterson; a 'Mercer boy' of days gone by, now commander of a battery in Cutts' Battalion. It was gratifying to learn, that Capt. Patterson not only stands high as a military officer, but that he also maintains his christian integrity."

[45] James M. Brittain, "From the Camp," *Christian Index*, 11 March 1864, 2. Brittain's visions of lasting revival proved unfounded. Shattuck, *A Shield and a Hiding Place*, notes that the Great Revival in the Northern Army of Virginia came to an end in the face of Grant's movements in May 1864 (99).

spelling, reading, writing, English grammar, Geography, Astronomy, Mathematics, Latin, Greek, &c." The practical instruction was much needed, the army correspondent reported, as many men previously did not know their alphabet, but now were "reading very well." Nonetheless, spiritual matters lay at the heart of army revivals as John B. Gordon's Georgia Brigade in late March and early April 1864 experienced the blessing of "a most precious revival of religion." An observer noted the three chapels were "crowded every night with deeply interested listeners" while "a number have professed conversion, and a much larger number are still enquiring the way of life."[46]

Another correspondent later commented on the unintended effects of camp life upon certain soldiers, in the process providing a glimpse into socio-economic frictions. Camp life resulted in the educated and illiterate being thrown together, the result being that the latter achieved a degree of education. At the same time, the more wealthy men, previously unaccustomed to manual labor, developed a better work ethic and improved their physical condition. Such results would benefit future generations of Southerners, the writer determined.[47]

Yet the conversion of souls remained the ultimate measure of success, as Chaplain J. L. Pettigrew reminded *Index* readers. Revivals in the 31st Georgia Regiment continued unabated, Pettigrew insisted. Soldiers attested to souls saved daily. Over 100 conversions took place in a two-month span. Preaching took place nightly, and prayer meetings daily. Even the "most wicked and profane men...have been converted, and are now exerting all their influence for the salvation of those whom they once sought to ruin." An army missionary in

---

[46] W., "Army Correspondence of the Index," *Christian Index*, 18 March 1864, 2; W., "Army Correspondence of the Index," *Christian Index*, 15 April 1864, 2.

[47] Star, "Correspondence from the Army of Tennessee," *Christian Index*, 6 May 1864, 1.

Virginia reported a "very general revival throughout the army" and rejoiced at having baptized sixty-seven soldiers in the past month.[48]

Despite apparent successes of army revivals, army ministers from Baptist ranks remained in short supply as winter gradually gave way to spring. The *Index's* army correspondent in Virginia noted that Lee's army contained only four Baptist chaplains and no missionaries. Offering pointed criticism of home-front ministers, "who, beneath the quite shade of their own vine and fig tree are enjoying that ease which becomes not laborers in the Lord's vineyards," the correspondent berated preachers for their cold souls and listless faith that permitted thousands of soldiers to walk down the path to hell. In order to stimulate home-front preachers, remove the shame of Georgia Baptist ministers and meet the needs of the soldiers, the writer suggested that preachers visit the army camps of Virginia, where soldier revivals might reinvigorate the ministers' faith.[49]

The intense interest in army missions on the part of some thus contrasted with a shortage of Baptist ministers among the soldiers, as noted in the previous chapter. Three years into the war and in the face of mounting battlefield defeats, spiritual leadership among the soldiers as a result lagged to such an extent that *Index* writers felt compelled to openly and harshly scold Baptist preachers in Middle Georgia serving solely on the home-front. The scarcity of evangelistic work among Georgia regiments led Boykin to propose looking beyond any help from the home-front. Flatly dismissing "home ministers" as men of "indifference and backwardness," the editor proposed that soldiers look within their own ranks for men who could serve as chaplains. Fellow soldiers could then petition their officers to commission select soldiers as chaplains. Boykin observed that three soldiers from John B. Gordon's Brigade, all ordained

---

[48] Chaplain J. L. Pettigrew, "Religion in the Army: Camp Gordon's Brigade," *Christian Index*, 13 May 1864, 2; W., "Army Correspondence of the Index," *Christian Index*, 13 May 1864, 2.

[49] W., "Four Chaplains and Not a Single Missionary," *Christian Index*, 22 April 1864, 1.

Baptist ministers, had expressed interest in serving as chaplains. Months later, Boykin noted with appreciation two state army missionaries—one from Tennessee and one from Virginia—who were "laboring in our midst in Macon." The city's preachers apparently remained focused on their own pulpits.[50]

Army revivals, taking place despite the scarcity of missionaries and chaplains, led Boykin to question the reasons for camp successes while "the churches at home, so strangely, remained cold and lifeless." The editor concluded that worship services conducted in the "open air" must allow a more robust and complete religious experience. "Nature and Revelation are two coordinate systems of divine truth: the two systems are media of access to God. Nature is a great Teacher, and, if studied in the light of Revelation, leads us unerringly towards the Creator."[51]

One anonymous Baptist portrayed army missions as nothing less than the primary hope of the South. Against the backdrop of numerous reports of prolonged revivals, the writer positioned army missions as the most important matter requiring the attention of the Confederacy. Glorifying Southern soldiers as heroes, and placing missions in the context of patriotism, the writer pointed to religion as the saving grace of the Confederate nation. In light of such successes, and in order to ensure further advances, Baptists of the South "should pour out" their "money like water" in support of army missionaries.[52]

Meanwhile, and echoing the personal accounts that chaplains Bennett and Jones would later chronicle, hundreds of soldiers from the "heart of Georgia," weary and muddy from yet another day of digging fortifications, solemnly gathered under a clear, starry night outside Petersburg, Virginia, in late summer 1864. Sitting upon the ramparts and perching on the edges of the trenches laboriously dug, facing another day of hard work when the sun arose, the battle-

---

[50] "How to Get Chaplains," *Christian Index*, 22 April 1864, 1; "Personal," *Christian Index*, 29 July 1864, 2.

[51] W., "An Interesting Inquiry" *Christian Index*, 13 May 1864, 2.

[52] "To the Baptists," *Christian Index*, 22 July 1864, 2. As noted previously, Berends's "Wholesome Reading Purifies" echoes this point.

hardened men with calloused hands and lonely hearts enjoyed a respite from the volley of bullets and drudgery of shoveling. While some soldiers spent the evening gambling and others found solace at the bottom of a cheap bottle of alcohol, the assembled men searched their souls for a peace that transcended war. Moonlight glistened off of earnest faces leaning forward, ears straining to hear every word the preacher offered. After a simple Gospel message, an invitation was offered and "an old familiar hymn" pierced the still night, wafting across field and fortification. A hundred men with solemn faces, some with glistening eyes, slowly arose and stepped to the front of the crowd, bowing in prayer. The sound of hundreds of men praying displaced the musical notes as the heroes of the Confederacy poured out their fears and hopes under the Virginia moonlight.[53]

Night after night in Virginia during the waning days of summer 1864, Baptist soldiers from Middle Georgia and elsewhere gathered faithfully to hear preaching, sing hymns, and pray. Nonetheless, illustrating the ambivalence among home-front Georgia Baptist ministers that repeatedly evoked sharp criticism and exasperation in the pages of the *Christian Index*, their brigade, now well over three years into the war, remained without a Baptist chaplain or permanent missionary.[54]

While their brethren near Petersburg dug fortifications by day and listened to revival messages at night, Ebenezer Baptists, meeting at Evergreen Baptist Church in Pulaski County, took partial exception to the bleak outlook previously voiced by Central Baptists, as well as laments concerning a lack of Christian workers among soldiers.

---

[53] W., "Army Correspondence of the Index," *Christian Index*, 2 September 1864, 3.

[54] Ibid. The absence of Baptist chaplains among Georgia regiments is a theme repeated throughout the war years, as voiced in the pages of the *Christian Index*. Denominational histories do not reflect this theme, although John W. Brinsfield et al. notes that Baptists contributed a lower percentage of chaplains than other denominations in the South (John W. Brinsfield, William C. Davis, Benedict Maryniak, and James I. Robertson, Jr., eds., *Faith in the Fight: Civil War Chaplains* [Mechanicsburg PA: Stackpole Books, 2003] 61–62).

Wishful hopes and acknowledgment of God's sovereignty over the battlefield a fading memory, to Ebenezer Baptists the Confederacy's ultimate defeat appeared inevitable by late 1864. Instead of dwelling on temporal setbacks, delegates enlarged their vision of spiritual victory, as associational committees focused their attention on salvation *within* the armies and among the children of soldiers. Chastising fellow Baptists who could not see beyond the wickedness of the soldiery, and acknowledging that "even many ministers of the Gospel had abandoned their high and holy calling, and by their profanity and profligacy had scandalized the religion of Jesus," Ebenezer Baptists pointed to mission work among the armies whose fruit included at least 142,000 soldier conversions. Yet many more souls needed rescuing. Horrendous though the suffering of the heroic soldiery, true victory was at hand, and the faithfulness of Christians on the home-front would seal the mighty triumph. Baptists on the home-front would do well to remember the sacrifices made on battlefields and in the camps. Describing the beleaguered Confederate soldiers as cheerful, hopeful, and fully devoted to the Southern cause, Ebenezer Baptists castigated home-front efforts to secure the salvation of soldiers' souls as poor, pitiful, and contemptible in comparison. In light of such great and inspiring sacrifices by the nation's defenders amidst the death and destruction of war, Baptists on the home-front had a solemn responsibility. Churches were to assure that religious reading material permeated the camps. To ministers fell the task of preaching spiritual salvation to the soldiers whose bodies stemmed the tide of Northern invasion.[55]

The Baptists of the Ebenezer Association glossed over one irony—the fact that the males of God's chosen nation had proven en masse to be sinners in need of salvation—while creating another. In the course of theologizing the war, the need for battlefield victory had evaporated, replaced by the certainty of spiritual victory achieved by the faithfulness of Christians on the home-front. "Flesh and blood"

---

[55] Minutes, Ebenezer Baptist Association, 1864, Special Collections, Jack Tarver Library, Mercer University, Macon GA, 11–12.

were doomed to fail, but thanks to missionary work among the soldiers the "sword of the spirit" turned sacrifice into salvation and assured true victory that would in turn be entrusted to the younger generations, who through Sabbath School training were the future hope of the Confederacy. A relatively new development in Baptist life, Sunday school for children suddenly took on a new urgency. Ebenezer Baptists thus found consolation in the face of the growing ranks of orphaned children of soldiers, a mission field that could be served by Sunday schools.[56]

Other mission fields were now largely forgotten. Ebenezer Baptists noted of foreign missionaries, "we seldom hear from them" in our "isolated condition." Flint River Baptists echoed the disconnection: "We have been cut off from our missionaries in heathen lands, and hence have heard but little of their labors." Some remained in the field, subsisting on borrowed credit and receiving little support from churches. In a similar fashion, Flint River Baptists reported no correspondence with the one missionary to the Native Americans still supported. Yet while Ebenezer and Central Baptists viewed army missions as their primary ministry focus, Flint River Baptists, despite considering as important the "spiritual interest of our dear soldiers," understood the army mission field as a temporary training ground for teaching "the importance of mission work" in order that "we be better prepared to send the gospel to the heathen." Isolated and under siege, the state of the Confederacy focused attention on army missions and hindered virtually any connection between Southern Baptists in Middle Georgia and missionaries on foreign or domestic fields. Flint River Baptists, however, refused to dwell upon the sins of Southern soldiers, clinging to a pre-war mission framework even while engaging army missions.[57]

---

[56] Ibid. In the post-war years, Boykin became a leading writer of Southern Baptist children's Sunday school material. See William Cathcart, *The Baptist Encyclopedia*, 2 vols (Philadelphia: Louis H. Everts, 1881) 2:124.

[57] Minutes, Ebenezer Baptist Association, 1864, 11–12, Special Collections, Jack Tarver Library, Mercer University, Macon GA; minutes, Flint River Baptist

Meanwhile, some local Southern Baptist congregations in 1863 and 1864 mirrored the shift to army missions as reflected at the associational level and in correspondence to the *Christian Index*. Sandy Creek Church's embracing of army missions in 1862 proved to be an indicator for other congregations, as the following year witnessed numerous Baptist congregations providing support for ministry among Confederate soldiers. In addition to periodical prayer meetings on behalf of the Confederacy and war effort, New Bethel Church of Washington County and the Washington Association, unlike most Baptist churches in Middle Georgia, often referred to Confederate soldiers in church records. Although all Baptist churches in Middle Georgia likely had members, or relatives of members, serving in the Confederate army, New Bethel distinguished itself by frequent discussions of its soldiers in church minutes during the latter half of the war. On 21 March 1863, for example, "Bro. Thomas Wood presented a letter from his Son John A. Wood who was in Virginia requesting his letter of membership be deposited with this church the letter was [received]." The following month, the church received "as correspondent letter from Joseph M. Smith & John A. Wood members of this church from Virginia." In September of the same year, New Bethel received "a letter from & a certificate from C. S. Meadows from the 49th Ga Regmint in [Virginia] wishing to become a member of this church after reading the letter and the recommendation from Rev. John Hyman on motion he was [received] into the fellowship of the church."[58]

Association, 1864, 5–6, Special Collections, Jack Tarver Library, Mercer University, Macon GA.

[58] Minutes, New Bethel Baptist Church, 1863, Special Collections, Jack Tarver Library, Mercer University, Macon GA; Caney S. Meadows, rosters, Georgia 49th Infantry Regiment, http://www.researchonline.net/gacw/rosters/49thcomh.htm (accessed 14 June 2011). With eighty-six members, it was a mid-sized church within the association. A corporal in Company H at the time of the letter, Caney Meadows was promoted to sergeant in August 1863, later captured at the Battle of Petersburg, and released at Point Lookout in June 1865.

Army missions impacted the New Bethel congregation through the person of John J. Hyman. Ordained as an army chaplain on 12 April 1863, Hyman served for the remainder of the war as a chaplain in the 49th Georgia in the Army of Northern Virginia. Organized on 22 March 1862, the 49th Georgia remained intact through the war and was present at Appomattox when Lee surrendered. Hyman's charges heralded from throughout Middle Georgia, and included the Wilkinson County Invincibles, Telfair County Volunteers, Washington County Guards, Taliaferro County Volunteers, Wilcox County States' Rights Guards, Irwin County Volunteers, Laurens County Volunteers, Washington County Cold Steel Guards, Hancock County Pierce Guards and Pulaski County Greys. Spiritual conversions, considered by Baptists as the measuring stick of success on the mission field, were numerous in Hyman's ministry. Nineteenth-century Baptist historian William Cathcart described Hyman as "one of the best chaplains in the army," because of the 260 soldiers the chaplain baptized. The records of New Bethel indicate that his ministry to Georgia Baptist soldiers extended beyond the 49th Georgia. In November 1863, a letter from Hyman arrived at New Bethel, stating that "he had Baptised W. T. Price of the 48th Ga. Reg. who was recommended by Rev. J. Hyman as this church being his choice upon the recommendation of Bro. Hyman he was received into the church."[59]

---

[59] Cathcart, *The Baptist Encyclopedia*, 1:566; minutes, New Bethel, Special Collections, Jack Tarver Library, Mercer University, Macon GA; John J. Hyman, http://www.researchonline.net/gacw/rosters/49thfiel.htm (accessed 14 June 2011); Caney S. Meadows, http://www.researchonline.net/gacw/rosters/49thcomh.htm (accessed 14 June 2011); William T. Price http://www.researchonline.net/gacw/index/index401.htm (accessed 14 June 2011). Soldier Alva Spencer of the 3rd Georgia Regiment wrote of Hyman in April 1864: "I have seen Mr. Hyman, a Baptist minister of Thomas Ga. Brig., baptize and receive into the baptist church, nine of our best soldiers. One of the number was from my company." See Clyde G. Wiggins III, ed., *My Dear Friend: The Civil War Letters of Alva Benjamin Spencer, 3rd Georgia Regiment, Company C* (Macon GA: Mercer University Press, 2007) 110. After the war, Hyman served as a pastor and

The New Bethel church maintained a concern for soldier members and a steady interest in army missions. In April 1864, church members listened to the reading of a "corresponding letter" from soldiers Joseph Smith and John Wood, although the contents of the letter were not recorded in church minutes. The following month, "Reced a letter & supplication from John Howard, army missionary from friendship Association Recommending A. H. Page of the 32nd Ga. Reg. who hand [had?] been Reced. upon Experience & Baptism To New Bethel church Bro. Page was Reced into the church fellowship." In September, "Reced a letter & a cirtificate from Bro. J. J. Heyman chaplain of the 49th Ga. reg Stating that he had Baptised D. J. Adkins on a profession of faith & recommended him to the fellowship of the church & at his request he was received."[60]

Bethel Baptist in Jasper County, a rural congregation holding membership in the Central Association, also addressed army missions in September 1863. The congregation "received bro Lucian B Thigpen in the fellowship of the church on a certificate from the 14th Georgia Reg who hered his experience & baptized him." Two months later church members demonstrated their appreciation of army missions and their concern for the souls of the brave defenders of the Confederacy. A visiting army missionary, "bro O Whittle," led the worship service on 14 November, after which the "church met in conference and the church gave bro Whittle all money that was on hand intended for mission...to be appropriated to the use of the soldiers buying religious reading the amount of money on hand was $13.00." Following this outpouring of support for the evangelization of soldiers, church members were doubtlessly pleased when during the December conference meeting, "an application for membership was made by W D Vaughan by certificate from the chaplain of the 14th Georgia Reg which was received." Following the reception of

---

moderator of the Mount Vernon Association, which included some churches located in Middle Georgia counties.

[60] Minutes, New Bethel Baptist Church, Special Collections, Jack Tarver Library, Mercer University, Macon GA; Asa H. Page, http://www.research online.net/gacw/index/index377.htm (accessed 14 June 2011).

Vaughan into membership, Bethel church records fell silent regarding the war and Confederacy.[61]

Madison Baptist Church in Morgan County, a city church and the third largest congregation in the Central Association, expressed support for army missions. After nearly three years of silence concerning the war, in January 1864 the congregation discussed the subject of army missions and decided "to take up a collection from the congregation for that object at some suitable time."[62]

Middle Georgia churches holding membership in other associations also redirected mission efforts as a result of the war. On 4 July 1863, the Siloam Baptist Church in Greene County voted to support army missions when they "agreed to take up a collection for sending the [*Christian*] *Index* to the soldiers." On 5 September of the same year, the congregation voted "to collect money to send to the Association for the support of the gospel among the Soldiers." As the war drew to a close, the church on 1 October 1864 accepted into membership "brother J. D. Andrews upon the certificate of the Chapplain W. L. Curry" of the 50th Georgia Infantry. Siloam's evangelistic efforts among Southern soldiers had borne fruit.[63]

The same day Siloam voted to support army missions, Bethlehem Baptist in Morgan County "received W L A Whitten, upon a certificate of his profession of repentance & faith in Jesus and also of his having been duly baptized by a Rev. Mr. Marshall, a baptist minister at camp near Massaponax Va said certificate by J M Stokes,

---

[61] Minutes, Bethel Baptist Church, Jasper County, 1861–1865, Special Collections, Jack Tarver Library, Mercer University, Macon GA, microfilm reel 247.

[62] Minutes, Madison Baptist Church, Morgan County, 1861–1864, Special Collections, Jack Tarver Library, Mercer University, Macon GA. The 14 May 1861 church records contain a verbatim copy of that year's Georgia Baptist Convention resolutions concerning the war and Confederacy. No further mention of the war took place until the January 1864 army missions discussion.

[63] Minutes, Siloam Baptist Church, Greene County, 1861–1864, Special Collections, Jack Tarver Library, Mercer University, Macon GA, microfilm reel 523; National Park Service Civil War Soldiers and Sailors System, http://www.itd.nps.gov/cwss/ (accessed 14 June 2011).

chaplain of 3rd Regiment Volunteers." Whitten, himself a member of the 3rd Georgia, found salvation and a spiritual home even as his fellow Confederates retreated from Gettysburg. The beneficiary of army missions, Bethlehem on 20 August 1864 voted to take up a collection for "army mission," although no amount was noted and other details were omitted.[64]

On 5 September 1863, Lebanon Baptist Church in Crawford County took up an offering of $18.50 for "Indian Missions & to send the Gospel to the soldiers." Concerned about the spiritual welfare of soldiers to the bitter end of the war, on 4 April 1865, the church "made a collection for Bro. J. B. Taylor Jr. who is laboring for our soldiers in the tented fields." The chaplain supported by Lebanon Baptist was James B. Taylor of Virginia, serving under William Henry Fitzgerald Lee, the second son of Robert E. Lee. After the war, Taylor would pastor in Virginia, retaining the gratitude of Baptists far from his home.[65]

Meanwhile, Henry County's Indian Creek Baptist Church on 29 August 1863 took up an offering of $50.60 for "Soldier funds." And in Bibb County, the twenty white members of Midway Baptist Church voted to lend support to army missions in the form of sending "the *Confederate Baptist Banner* to 34th Ga Regiment." As in other congregations, slave members—totaling fifteen in the Midway church—had no voice in the matter.[66]

---

[64] Minutes, Bethlehem Baptist Church, Morgan County, 1861–1864, Special Collections, Jack Tarver Library, Mercer University, Macon GA, microfilm reel 377.
[65] Minutes, Lebanon Baptist Church, Crawford County, 1862, Special Collections, Jack Tarver Library, Mercer University, Macon GA, microfilm reel 638; Cathcart, *The Baptist Encyclopedia*, 2:1135; *Antietam on the Web*, http://aotw.org/officers.php?officer_id=86 (accessed 11 November 2006).
[66] Minutes, Indian Creek Baptist Church, Henry County, 1863–1865, Special Collections, Jack Tarver Library, Mercer University, Macon GA, microfilm reel 41; minutes, Midway Baptist Church, Bibb County, 1864, Special Collections, Jack Tarver Library, Mercer University, Macon GA, microfilm reel 69; minutes, Rehoboth Baptist Association, 1861, 12, Special Collections, Jack Tarver Library,

Diverging Loyalties

One congregation's journey into the spiritual quandary posed by the war led to emotional moments, hesitation, and unforeseen irony. Located in Greene County and a member of the Georgia Association, the Bethesda Baptist Church, a large congregation of 170 members, had long been a significant congregation within the state. The seventh-oldest Baptist church in the state, Bethesda's previous pastors included Georgia Baptist giants such as Silas Mercer, Jesse Mercer, and Adiel Sherwood. As the war commenced, yet another prominent pastor, Henry H. Tucker, filled the pulpit. A former attorney from Forsyth, Tucker afterwards entered the ministry and in 1856 moved to Greene County upon his appointment to Mercer University as professor of Belles-Lettres and Metaphysics. In addition to his scholarly responsibilities, Tucker accepted the pastorate of Bethesda Baptist in 1857. When war enveloped the South, the Bethesda congregation did not formally address the conflict until 12 December 1861. Even then, Dr. Tucker's notice to the congregation that he might be compelled to forsake his flock to serve in the Confederate Army proved to be premature. Following Tucker's unnecessary warning, another year-and-a-half passed until the subject of war again surfaced in church minutes. This time the occasion brought joy: a young man brought up in the congregation and now serving in the Confederate Army had given his life to Christ.[67]

Mercer University, Macon GA. The *Confederate Baptist* was a publication of South Carolina Baptists. Membership statistics are from 1861.

[67] Minutes, Bethesda Baptist Church, Greene County, 1861–1864, Special Collections, Jack Tarver Library, Mercer University, Macon GA, microfilm reel 11; R. L. Robinson, *History of the Georgia Baptist Association* (Union Point GA: R.L. Robinson, 1928) 47–52, 258; Cathcart, *The Baptist Encyclopedia*, 2:1171–1172; B. D. Ragsdale, *Story of Georgia Baptists* (Executive Committee of the Georgia Baptist Convention, 1938) 300, 385. Bethesda Baptist Church membership stood at 170 in 1864. Silas and Jesse Mercer, father and son, played instrumental roles in the founding of the Georgia Baptist Convention and Mercer University. Following the war, Henry H. Tucker was elected president of Mercer University in 1866, and in the 1880s served as editor of the *Christian Index*.

Long established in the Bethesda church, the Tuggle family personally experienced the Civil War. Serving in the 3rd Georgia Infantry, Edward B. Tuggle wrote his father on 12 May 1863 to tell him the wonderful news of his Christian conversion. The imagery employed by Corporal Tuggle wove temporal and spiritual conflict into a very personal narrative that nonetheless conveyed the joys and hopes of white Southern churchgoers in a troubled age. Tuggle, "quietly encamped" and enjoying "the sweets of another glorious and remarkable victory," gave credit to "the Almighty hand of a kind and just God." The young soldier hoped temporal triumph would convey the love of Jesus to the Northern aggressors. "Oh! that this victory would instill Jesus into the breast of our enemies and cause them to retreat to the land from whence they came and leave us alone to enjoy a peaceful and tranquil country." Acknowledging that not all was going well for the Confederates, Tuggle nonetheless quoted Romans 8:28 in declaring that "all things work together for the good of those that love God. If God is with us, and I believe he is, [he] knows what is best for us, hence we should [illegible] ourselves by submitting to his will." The young soldier then turned his pen to discussing "a subject...concerning which I have not spoken as boldly as I should have done to you and to the world." Professing his belief in "the merits of Jesus Christ, and feeling what would be my lost and ruined condition, was it not for Christ, I am through faith enable to utter the prayer of our Savior, 'Thy will be done not mine.' In obedience to my profession, I yesterday evening put on Christ by baptism."[68]

Edward Tuggle described first hand the revivalist atmosphere among Confederate soldiers in 1863. "There is a great manifestation of the influence of the Holy Spirit in our regiment," the young soldier continued. "Five joined the Church last night, four baptist.... We have religion services every day and God grant that much more good may

---

[68] Minutes, Bethesda Baptist Church, Greene County, 1863, Special Collections, Jack Tarver Library, Mercer University, Macon GA, microfilm reel 11; National Park Service Civil War Soldiers and Sailors System, http://www.itd.nps.gov/cwss/ (accessed 14 June 2011).

result therefrom is my prayer." In closing, Tuggle included a note to the "Dear Brethren of Bethesda Church," in which he confessed "having been convicted of sins" and "converted to God." The soldier continued, "I humbly beseech you to receive me as a member of your church and pray the Lord that I may never bring reproach upon the Cause of Christ" and that "God may...preserve me through this evil world, give me a life of usefulness, and a home at last in heaven." Along with a certificate of baptism and letter of recommendation from John Hyman, chaplain in the 49th Georgia Infantry, Tuggle's letter was read to the Bethesda congregation on 20 June 1863. Afterwards, Tuggle "was received into the church."[69]

Clearly portraying the primacy of the spiritual over battlefield conflict, Tuggle's letter is unique in the annals of Baptist churches in Middle Georgia. Rarely formally read in church, much less copied into church records, the few soldier letters included in church records are much less detailed in nature. Moreover, Bethesda, in common with most other Baptist churches in Middle Georgia, did not maintain a formal listing of members who served in the Confederate Army. The war appears on the surface to have touched the church lightly, with no soldier deaths recorded and only two total deaths reported in the 1864 church year. Tuggle's story, however, perhaps eventually helped persuade the congregation to designate money for the evangelization of soldiers. Long after Tuggle's conversion and acceptance as a church member, Bethesda decided to collect an offering for army missions. The $340 contributed by the church took place on 15 April 1865, six days after Lee's surrender at Appomattox.[70]

Tuggle's profession, baptism, and spiritual concerns came in the midst of the camp revivals that were embraced, and later glorified, by

---

[69] Minutes, Bethesda Baptist Church, Greene County, 1863, Special Collections, Jack Tarver Library, Mercer University, Macon GA, microfilm reel 11. For an analysis of revivals in Civil War armies, see Shattuck, *Shield and a Hiding Place*, 73–110.

[70] Minutes, Bethesda Baptist Church, Greene County, 1861–1865, Special Collections, Jack Tarver Library, Mercer University, Macon GA.

Southern evangelicals. Among Georgia Baptists, Bethesda's tardiness in regards to tangible support of army missions took place against the backdrop of widespread frustrations during the closing months of war. Ministers in the army camps chafed in the face of home-front inaction as summer gave way to fall in 1864. One army correspondent voiced his concerns as he toured Georgia regiments embedded in the trenches near Petersburg. He declared bitterly, "I know of but *two* missionaries now present in this whole army." Reserving harsh criticism for Georgia Baptists, including no shortage of sarcasm, he noted that "those good brethren who resolved at the Georgia Baptist Convention that governmental Chaplaincies were wrong, and they would do the work of army evangelization as voluntary missionaries, must all have gone to General Hood's army. I have seen none of them here, though I constantly hear as I go amongst Georgia troops, 'you are the only Baptist preacher I have seen in a long time.'" Challenging Georgia Baptist ministers directly, the correspondent described a brigade from Middle Georgia that was "largely Baptist" yet had "never had a Baptist chaplain or permanent missionary." He urged part-time preachers in small congregations to do mission work among and help convert spiritually receptive soldiers. Incredulous that Baptists in Middle Georgia refused to support the troops, the writer further scolded ministers on the home-front who spent their time criticizing the theological faults of army missionaries and chaplains. The correspondent pleaded, "is there no earnest working brother among the large Baptist ministry of Georgia who is willing to come and labor among these brave men?" Another Baptist army correspondent at Petersburg, writing at the same time, bemoaned, "I am alone in my brigade. The question, 'Where is our preacher?' is asked until it has become a bore." In the eyes of the few Baptist chaplains and missionaries on the field, home-front ministers were more concerned about comfort and proper theology than meeting the spiritual needs of Southern soldiers.[71]

---

[71] W., "Army Correspondence," *Christian Index*, 2 September 1864, 3; J., "Army Correspondence," *Christian Index*, 3 September 1864, 3.

Accused of ignoring mission needs among distant army camps, Baptist ministers and laypersons in Middle Georgia also expressed little interest in the needs of transient soldiers within their own hometowns. Macon hospitals, increasingly treating Confederate soldiers in the final months of war, received a visit by a Florida minister. Rev. Lewis Price stayed in the city for at least two months, ministering not only to the wounded, but also soldiers stationed in the vicinity of Macon. While praising Lewis, Samuel Boykin scolded the Baptists of Macon for their comparative inaction. Some wounded soldiers lying in the city's hospitals had no clothing or shoes, one observer noted, relating the story of one unclothed soldier who, when dismissed from the hospital for furlough, "left for home in his drawers." Accusing the Soldiers' Relief Societies of being "asleep," the writer chided local Baptists for their lack of charitable concern for the needs of Southern soldiers stationed in their midst.[72]

Soon thereafter, by late October 1864, the Baptists of Macon faced a new opportunity for mission work of an altogether different type. Having fled to Macon, an unspecified number of members of the First and Second Baptist churches of Atlanta, including the pastor of the First Baptist Church, called an organizational meeting and proposed to take steps to reassemble their congregations in Macon while in exile. Agreeing to worship with the First Baptist Church of Macon, the members also decided to meet weekly for prayer and to continue to conduct church business. More receptive to Baptists who walked through the doors of their church buildings than to Baptists from distant towns lying wounded and dying in the city's hospitals, Baptists of Macon welcomed their fellow believers from Atlanta.[73]

Meanwhile, Azor Van Hoose, the army missionary recently employed by the Central Baptist Association, returned home, unable to reach the armies of Tennessee and Virginia because of the presence of Union soldiers in his path. Apologetic to the Central Association

---

[72] "Editorial Items," *Christian Index*, 7 October 1864, 2; "Personal," *Christian Index*, 4 November 1864, 2.

[73] "Baptist Refugee Meeting," *Christian Index*, 4 November 1864, 1.

churches that had supported his mission efforts, yet resigned to his fate, the former missionary resumed preaching duties in Middle Georgia. Following Van Hoose's return, A. E. Dickinson, the superintendent of army colportage in Virginia, noting a lack of preaching and religious literature among soldiers, pleaded with fellow Georgia Baptists to provide financial resources to send Christian literature to Confederate soldiers. Requesting financial support in the face of spiraling inflation, Dickinson maintained that "hundreds of regiments" remained devoid of Baptist chaplains, while "thousands of our brave men are asking earnestly for the Word of God."[74]

One Georgia Baptist correspondent headquartered in Petersburg in winter 1865 fleshed out that which Dickinson hinted. His report echoed others' earlier observations in calling into question the commitment of Georgia Baptists to both the war effort and the mission enterprise. Ticking off a list of Georgia brigades that had neither a Baptist chaplain nor a missionary, and noting that Georgia soldiers were saying "very hard things about the Georgia Baptist Preachers not coming to the army," he found it difficult to defend his fellow Baptist ministers. The minister concluded by declaring, "Brethren, these things ought not to be."[75]

On the home-front, missionary J. M. Stansberry of the Southern Baptist Domestic Board in Virginia arrived in Macon and spent the month of January 1865 visiting and preaching to the hospitalized in the city, to soldiers in "five or six" artillery battalions in the vicinity, and at Camp Wright. The officers and soldiers were respectful and responsive, Stansberry reported. Preaching to Federal prisoners, he found them "glad...to hear preaching." During the month, the missionary preached ten sermons, attended twenty-four meetings,

---

[74] A. Van Hoose, "Army of Tennessee Correspondence," *Christian Index*, 26 January 1865, 1; A. E. Dickinson, "An Appeal," *Christian Index*, 26 January 1865, 1.
[75] J. W. J., "Our Army Correspondent," *Christian Index*, 2 February 1865, 1.

and distributed hundreds of Bibles, testaments, and religious newspapers in the Middle Georgia city.[76]

As spring approached, Van Hoose, now back in the mission field, reported to the *Index* from Cherokee Pond, South Carolina, near Augusta and far from the front lines. He ministered to a small group of soldiers whose activities consisted of twice daily drills. The Central Association missionary felt "awkwardly situated." Although ministering to soldiers who were receptive to his preaching, rations were so limited that he declined to dine with them, instead lodging a distance of 5 miles from the preaching point. "Nearly worn out" from the exertion of walking back and forth to the camps, he expected to return home soon. Far from the frontlines at a time when Confederate prospects looked ever bleaker, the lone army missionary appointed by the Central Association wearily nursed, by his own admission, a marginal ministry. Others shared Van Hoose's feelings. According to army colporteur A. D. Cohen, weariness consumed Georgia soldiers, who responded to the distribution of New Testaments with polite indifference.[77]

In short, by the last winter of the war, numerous accounts testified to the long-running lack of interest among Georgia Baptists, and specifically among Baptists of Middle Georgia, in serving as army missionaries and chaplains, or in financially supporting army mission efforts. The autonomous structure of Baptist church life may have contributed to the disinterest. Facing the same war-time financial struggles as Baptists, Southern Methodist support of army missionaries exceeded that of Baptists. While Methodists staked out one advantage by working with the Confederate government to supply chaplains, the denomination also benefited from its ecclesiastical structure as Methodist bishops traversed the South and directly solicited congregational support, both funding and

---

[76] M. T. Sumner, "Army Missions—The Domestic Board," *Christian Index*, 30 March 1865, 1.

[77] A. Van Hoose, "Letter from Bro. Van Hoose," *Christian Index*, 23 March 1865, 3; M. T. Sumner, "Army Missions—The Domestic Board," *Christian Index*, 30 March 1865, 1.

personnel, for army missions. Lacking bishops, Baptist appeals for support of army missions fell to the state convention, regional associations, and periodicals such as Samuel Boykin's *Christian Index*. Yet pastors and local congregations remained free to heed or ignore these voices from outside their church walls. The end result was the alienation of Baptists in uniform.[78]

Whereas the course of war unexpectedly suggested the spiritual weakness of Baptists and the South as a whole, leading to much self-reflection and a level of verbalized support that masked an astonishing lack of interest among ministers in serving among the army camps, the end of war witnessed a shift in terms of language as well as a new mission and purpose. The imagery of introspection remained, enjoined by lamentation and repentance as voiced by Central Baptists in 1865. "We have subdued our forest lands, worn out and desolated the soil, and spent the products in riotous living, and forgotten our responsibilities to God and our fellow men," an associational report declared. The sins of the South had not gone unnoticed by God, as the country stood in ruins, property confiscated by the enemy, and hopes crushed in the face of impending poverty. Past failures in mission efforts were cause for shame, although messengers expressed hope for a future revival of heart-felt religion. In the aftermath of the war, God revealed to Central Baptists a path to salvation, a new mission. Attempts to save the Confederate armies had ultimately failed. Although some soldiers found spiritual redemption, temporal defeat was not averted. In their defeat and desolation, God provided opportunity for Baptists and the South to be restored to His graces by helping lift the freedmen from their hapless circumstances and inherent vices of ignorance and idleness. "We devoutly recognize the Providence of God is the result of the late war which has emancipated the slave, and thus thrown upon the

---

[78] Bocke, Emory Stevens, ed. *The History of American Methodism*, 3 vols. (Nashville: Abingdon Press, 1964) 3:235–38.

churches a new measure of responsibility in regard to our colored populations."[79]

Their sure hopes of battlefield victory unrealized in the face of the failure of army mission efforts, Baptists of the Flint River Association traded ardent nationalism and an optimistic view of army morality for stoic realism. Offering no apologies for God or to man, demanding no explanation from God nor resorting to His Providence to explain how certain victory succumbed to utter defeat, Flint River Baptists accepted their lot and looked to the past for future direction. Although traditional Baptist mission fields lay in shambles, Flint River Baptists soon returned to their pre-war mission commitments to mission work among Native Americans and on foreign fields. Yet their sole official statement of 1865 regarding the war of the past four years could not veil the bitterness they felt: "In consequence of our recent national troubles, many of our churches are in a crippled state; many buildings of worship have been destroyed, and the folds of Jesus scattered; the ranks of the Ministry have been very much depleted, and thus there is an immense home work for us to do." Land and lives, shattered and broken, cried for help. Flint River Baptists called upon God to assist them in ministering to "our beloved countrymen." Victory, long ago assured, never materialized. God's sure help turned out to be anything but certain. Although Flint River Baptists seemed uncertain as to whether God could pick up the broken pieces of their land, verbalizing a commitment to familiar mission endeavors perhaps offered some semblance of hope.[80]

Not all Baptists, however, voiced or envisioned opportunity in the wake of defeat. Following Lee's surrender to Grant, Baptists of the Ebenezer Association faced the unexpected reality of vacant mission fields. Whereas Baptists of the Central Association quickly responded

---

[79] Minutes, Central Baptist Association, 1865, Special Collections, Jack Tarver Library, Mercer University, Macon GA.

[80] Minutes, Flint River Baptist Association, 1865, 6, Special Collections, Jack Tarver Library, Mercer University, Macon GA.

to Southern defeat by embracing ministry among freedmen, and thus snatching spiritual victory from the ashes of earthly defeat, Ebenezer Baptists, having placed faith in army missions, gave voice to confusion and uncertainty in the post-war era. With army missions suddenly shuttered and traditional mission opportunities long lost to the ravages of war, Ebenezer Baptists cast about for a new mission vision. Options appeared bleak. Southern Baptist foreign mission efforts were in disarray. The executive committee suggested that Native American missions be resumed, yet expressed reservations that such a plan would prove feasible. The mission committee turned to the possibility of missions to the "black race," requesting that the association study the viability of such efforts. A third committee, appointed to respond to the report of the mission committee, endorsed the mission report and encouraged churches to preach the Gospel to the freedmen. In the end, delegates eschewed specifics and instead agreed to a need to rebuild first a "missionary spirit" among member churches. Even as the coming of war hindered mission efforts and caused spiritual consternation, the end of the conflict disrupted mission efforts, snuffed out the great revivals in the armies, and left Baptists in the Ebenezer Association in spiritual disarray.[81]

The defeat of the Confederacy thus signaled an end to the short-lived but intense white Southern Baptist effort to construct a new mission paradigm. Surveying the ruins of the South, the abrupt end of army missions and the virtual non-existence of traditional mission fields, Baptists in Middle Georgia looked in divergent directions in an effort to identify new mission opportunities in the immediate post-war era. Baptists of the Central Association, failing to focus on responsibilities to slaves during the war, suddenly recognized mission potential among freedmen in the post-war era, absolving their past shortcomings and promising future renewal. Unrepentant Flint River Baptists returned to a focus upon Native American missions, while Ebenezer Baptists failed to identify a promising

---

[81] Minutes, Ebenezer Baptist Association, 1865, 3, 6, Special Collections, Jack Tarver Library, Mercer University, Macon GA.

mission field. By way of contrast, Primitive Baptists, never vested in missions, did not share in the collective spiritual soul-searching.

In broader perspective in the immediate years following the war, Middle Georgia Baptists grasped for new mission directives while white Southern evangelicals at large appropriated prior social arrangements and morality to create the civil religion that became the "Lost Cause" as articulated by Charles Reagan Wilson. Whereas Baptists of the pre-Civil War era led the way in terms of denominational growth, Presbyterians of the post-war era moved to the forefront in the shaping of the Lost Cause, through luminaries such as James H. Thornwell, the late General Stonewall Jackson, Benjamin M. Palmer, and Robert L. Dabney. Southern Baptists joined Southern Presbyterians in expressing no interest in national reunion. By way of contrast, some Methodists sought national reconciliation beginning in the 1870s. Meanwhile, Southern black Baptists and Methodists, aided by Northern missionaries streaming into the South, exercised their newfound freedoms and withdrew from white-led churches and formed their own autonomous congregations.[82]

Struggling through the war years and immediately thereafter, and in the face of unwanted Northern encroachment upon the home mission field, Southern Baptists at large finally refocused almost exclusively on foreign missions in 1877, emphasizing evangelism and targeting the nation of China. By the end of the century, the denomination's foreign missionary force reclaimed pre-war numerical levels as Baptists in central Georgia joined Baptists throughout the South in supporting roughly fifty missionaries in China and a lesser number elsewhere. Samuel Boykin's berating of Middle Georgia Baptists for insufficiently supporting army mission

---

[82] Charles Reagan Wilson, *Baptized in Blood: The Religion of the Lost Cause* (Athens: University of Georgia Press, 1980); Richard T. Hughes and C. Leonard Allen, *Illusions of Innocence: Protestant Primitivism in America, 1630–1875* (Chicago: University of Chicago Press, 1988) 188–204; Samuel S. Hill, "Religion and the Results of the Civil War" in Randall M. Miller, Harry S. Stout, and Charles Reagan Wilson, *Religion and the American Civil War* (New York: Oxford University Press, 1998) 360–82.

work during the war had proven to be a harbinger of things to come, as it took nearly four decades for Southern Baptists to recover the missionary fervor that had existed prior to the four-year conflict.[83]

---

[83] See Li Li, "Diversifying the Operation: Southern Baptist Missions in China at the Turn of the Century, 1890–1910," *Baptist History & Heritage Journal* 34/2 (Spring 1999); H. B. Cavalcanti, "Southern Baptists Abroad: Sharing Their Faith in Nineteenth-Century Brazil," *Baptist History & Heritage Journal* 38/2 (Spring 2003); F. Calvin Parker, *The Southern Baptist Mission in Japan, 1889–1989* (Lanham MD: University Press of America, 1991); Jesse C. Fletcher, *The Southern Baptist Convention: A Sesquicentennial History* (Nashville: Broadman & Holman, 1994).

CHAPTER 4

BAPTIST SOLDIERS:
FROM CHURCH TO BATTLEFIELD

While the moral challenges presented by army camps redirected missionary efforts of Baptists during the war years, Baptist soldiers from Middle Georgia experienced the same fears, hardships, and sufferings as did other Confederate soldiers. Church membership did not afford special privileges on the battlefield or in the camps, nor did religious faith offer protection from bullets or disease.

The story of Thomaston Baptist Church in Upson County provides some insight into the plight and journeys of soldier members and their families. In spring 1861, William Spivey watched two sons march off to war. John served in Company D of the 13th Georgia Regiment, while Charles fought with the Upson Sentinels of the 46th Georgia Regiment. T. S. and George Sharman (uncle and nephew) and H. H. Hartsfield joined John in serving in the 13th Georgia.[1]

While family members departed to distant battlefronts, the Thomaston congregation as a community publicly evidenced its support of the war and Confederacy. Spring and summer 1861 became a festive time as the church celebrated her soldier sons in a series of patriotic events, including a Fourth of July dress parade of the Upson Guards, a presentation of a Confederate flag by the ladies of Upson County to the Guards, and the formative meeting of the

---

[1] Minutes, Thomaston Baptist Church, Upson County, 1862, Special Collections, Jack Tarver Library, Mercer University, Macon GA, microfilm reel 95. Edwin L. Cliburn, *In Unbroken Line: A History of the First Baptist Church of Thomaston, Georgia* (Tallahassee FL: Rose Printing, 1979) 123–26; National Park Service Civil War Soldiers and Sailors System, http://www.itd.nps.gov/cwss/ (accessed 14 June 2011).

Ladies Relief Society for the benefit of soldiers. During this time, pastor J. H. Weaver enrolled as a volunteer chaplain for the 13th Georgia Regiment, following the Spivey brothers, Sharmans and Hartsfield. Upon his departure, the congregation solicited "Brother King to come and preach for us as often as he can during Brother Weaver's absence." Weaver served through 1862, at which time the army accepted his resignation and the preacher returned to pastor the congregation again. Weaver's military service, however brief, reflected a departure from the unwillingness of most Middle Georgia pastors to enroll in the military, as previously noted.[2]

The festivities in the opening months of war underscored the church's vested interest in the war, although fate would result in death only lightly touching the congregation. Only a single church member is known to have died as a result of the war. An opponent of secession who nonetheless remained loyal to the Southern cause, Edwin Dallas departed Thomaston as a sergeant and was quickly promoted to lieutenant. Writing from Richmond, Virginia, on 20 August 1861 with fall approaching, he asked for his overcoat to be sent with the fresh recruits that would soon be arriving from Upson. Former pastor J. H. Weaver had visited Dallas in his tent while the officer composed the letter, and had "informed me of his appointment." The two men from Thomaston Baptist no doubt were glad of one another's company. Dallas commented on Weaver, "ant you glad his health his good. There never was a clever[er] man." Despite high morale in his company, the officer expressed disappointment that "thar ar som in Thomaston that ought to be handcuffed and sent to war that is trying to get up feeling between the members of this company."[3]

Focusing on camp life rather than religious faith, Lieutenant Dallas further offered insights into the soldier's regimen and longing

---

[2] Minutes, Thomaston Baptist Church, 6 July 1861, Special Collections, Jack Tarver Library, Mercer University, Macon GA; Carolyn W. Nottingham and Evelyn Hannah, *History of Upson County, Georgia* (Macon GA: J. W. Burke, 1930) 631–38; Cliburn, *Unbroken Line*, 131.

[3] Cliburn, *Unbroken Line*, 122–23.

for family. "In the eating line the meat we get is not fit to eat," he noted. "Sometimes the flower is very bad. Shugar is blackes stuff you ever saw...the far is bad. Everything is hig. Butter is worth fifty cts.... Peaches is worth five cts a peace. I have thought of the froot in old Georgi often." Yet if the bad food weighed on his mind, the separation from his family was much worse. "Wife, my paper is getting skerce and i must say something about my little wones I have left behind. Tell them i think of them often. Sometimes i think i can never stande it to think that if I should be spared to return it will be so long before i shall see you all. Tell Anner i will send her a present.... Tell them all howdy and kiss Anner and Andy for me."[4]

Three months afterwards, suffering illness, Dallas wrote home again. Telling his wife that he had a "terifying" disease, the officer could not "get shet of irecepulus. It has spread all over me. I have to take salce everyday or calomel which of course has reduced me very much." His pants were wearing thin, and "what the sword does not destroy diseas will." Despite his condition, Dallas boasted of a victorious "fite" and declared his company could "whip for or five times" their number. Expressing a longing for home, he inquired about his crops (cotton and corn) and asked how the "poneys...look." "Give my love to the children," Dallas wrote, and "tel sis to save her kisses for me." Little did he know that when he closed that November letter with the words, "remaining your husband until death," he would soon be dead, killed far from home in the Battle of Antietam at Sharpsburg, Maryland, on 17 September 1862.[5]

Upon confirmation of Edwin Dallas's death, Reverend Weaver, having resigned from the chaplaincy and returning to the pastorate of Thomaston Baptist, drafted a church resolution commemorating the officer. Lamenting the "great loss" and the "sad and untimely death" of Dallas, the statement declared that "we will by Gods grace treasure up for our own imitation the many private and christian virtues

---

[4] Ibid.; minutes, Thomaston Baptist Church, April 1864, Special Collections, Jack Tarver Library, Mercer University, Macon GA.

[5] Cliburn, *Unbroken Line*, 123.

which he so ably discharged," and "we will continue to our supplications to him who maketh wars to cease unto the ends of the earth who breaketh the bow and cutteth the spear in sunder for that almighty interposition which will give to our nation a great an honorable and a permanent peace." The family Dallas left behind faced an uncertain future. "We tender to our bereaved sister and her orphaned children our sincere sympathy and condolence and earnestly commend them to the tender care of Him who tempers the winds to the shorn lamb."[6]

Edwin Dallas did not live to see home again, but other soldier members of Thomaston Baptist did. Present at the surrender at Appomattox, E. B. Thompson hitchhiked back to Georgia via wagon, then walked from Milner to Thomaston, only to discover that all his possessions had been destroyed in his absence. Worse yet, his father, left in charge of the Thompson's business, had fled to South America, and would never be heard from again. Peter C. King walked from Virginia to Thomaston, arriving with $100 in his pocket. On the town square, he traded his cash for "one pound of tobacco and ten yards of calico cloth."[7]

In contrast, perhaps no congregation in Middle Georgia experienced the war to a greater proportion than did Stone Creek Baptist Church in Twiggs County, a body closely studied by historian Billy Walker Jones. The largest congregation in the Ebenezer Association, the aforementioned Stone Creek Baptist Church had 307 members prior to the war. Membership was almost evenly split between whites and blacks, 156 to 151, respectively, including some free blacks. Following the formation of the Confederate States of America, Simeon Tharpe, a leader of the Stone Creek congregation, wrote a letter to Governor Joseph E. Brown expressing his reservations about the preparations for war. Dated 26 February 1861, the letter lamented the "deplorable conditions" of the Twiggs

---

[6] Ibid., 131–32.
[7] Ibid., 136. The Thompson and King stories were recounted by descendants of the two men in interviews conducted by Cliburn in 1961 and 1962.

Volunteers. Coming to the defense of families in his community, Tharpe told the governor that "the majority of the company are men of large families and no one to labor but themselves for support, yet I believe that the major part of them are at your command at any moment you may need their services; and I pray on you in behalf to let them remain at home to support said families until your excellency may need said Company." Hopeful that Brown could "supply the needs of the state" without them, Tharpe noted that "if not let us know and we will come forward at 2 or 5 days notice." Tharpe's observations indicate an underlying tension between loyalties to family and the Southern Confederacy. Portraying a reluctance to perform duty to country in the face of familial responsibilities, Tharpe's description of the Twiggs Volunteers prior to the declaration of war as "deplorable" and impoverished contrasts with Julia Stanford's description of Forsyth's Quitman Guards, based on letters received from soldiers, as "enjoy[ing] themselves superlatively" and having "had a pleasant route over Mountains and vallies" in the opening months of war.[8]

---

[8] Minutes, Ebenezer Baptist Association, 1860, 12, Special Collections, Jack Tarver Library, Mercer University, Macon GA, microfilm reel 1065; minutes, Stone Creek Baptist Church, Special Collections, Jack Tarver Library, Mercer University, Macon GA, microfilm reel 280; Billy Walker Jones, *History of Black and White Worship: Stone Creek Baptist Church, 1808–1874* (Dry Branch GA: Billy Walker Jones, 2003) 28–30; Simeon Tharpe to Governor Joseph E. Brown, 26 February 1861 (Confederate records, Department of Archives, Atlanta GA; copy shown to the author by Billy Walker Jones in his home in Bibb County, Georgia); Billy Walker Jones, "Antioch Baptist Church in the Civil War Era" (Dry Branch, GA: 2000); Julia A. Stanford, diary, Spencer King Papers, Special Collections, Jack Tarver Library, Mercer University, Macon GA, 5 July and 9 July 1861; Billy Jones, interview with Bruce Gourley, September 2004. Billy Walker Jones is a sixth-generation descendant of one of the leading families in the church during the Civil War era, the Tharpes, and author of several self-published volumes on the subject of Baptists in Twiggs County in the nineteenth century. The Tharpe letter is reprinted in Jones's "Antioch Baptist Church" manuscript. In addition, in the "Antioch Baptist Church" essay Jones refers to Simeon Tharpe as an ordained minister, but neither Stone Creek records nor Ebenezer associational records indicate that Tharpe was either ordained as a minister or licensed to preach (Associational records contain an annual listing of both ordained and licensed

Tharpe's letter also suggests homeland concerns as an underlying factor in the lives of the Twiggs Volunteers. While immediate duties beckoned at home and needed attention, soldiers stood ready to perform their duty in defending country and home. According to James McPherson's survey of 647 Union and 429 Confederate soldier diaries, defense of homeland and a sense of duty represented two of the initial motivations for fighting in the war. Despite hesitance in marching off to war, the Twiggs Volunteers reflected universal reasons for joining military ranks.[9]

Any initial resistance aside, many members of Stone Creek did march off to war. At least 76 of 156 members of the congregation served during the war in some capacity, representing the majority of white males. Eighteen died during the war. The eighteen soldier member deaths, occurring throughout the war years from the comfort of home and hearth in Georgia to the distant battlefields and hospitals of Virginia, reveal the scope of the personal impact of the war upon the families of the Stone Creek congregation. Reflecting war-time deaths at large, battles and disease claimed the most lives. Of the eighteen, six succumbed to disease: three in Richmond, Virginia, one while imprisoned by Union forces, one at Camp Bartow in Virginia, and one of typhoid fever in an unknown location. An equal number died while in battle, one each at Cold Harbor, Malvern Hill, Chickamauga, Jonesboro, and Atlanta, as well as one in an unknown battle. Three soldier members later lost their lives to wounds. One was "wounded in Virginia and later died from his wounds," one "died from his wounds while at home," and one died

---

ministers as reported by individual congregations.). However, Tharpe was clearly a leader within the Stone Creek congregation, serving as a delegate to the Ebenezer Association in 1864; see minutes, Ebenezer Baptist Association, 1864, 13, Special Collections, Jack Tarver Library, Mercer University, Macon GA, microfilm reel 1065.

[9] James W. McPherson, *For Cause and Comrades: Why Men Fought in the Civil War* (New York: Oxford University Press, 1997) 13. McPherson includes concepts of duty, honor, community pressure, and manhood in his mix of motivations for serving.

Diverging Loyalties

of wounds in an unspecified location. Details of the remaining three deaths are unknown: one died in service, one died on furlough, and the third died at home. The Jessup, Read, and Tharpe families each lost two members.[10]

The movements and activities of the remaining fifty-eight soldier members who survived the conflict reflect the horrors, valor, divided loyalties, and oddities of a war that consumed soldiers and soldiers' families throughout its duration. Following his initial resistance, Simeon Tharpe joined the Confederate Army as a corporal in Company I, 6th Georgia Infantry, on 27 May 1861. Promoted to lieutenant in December of that year, he was wounded at some point thereafter. Living at home in 1864, he represented the Stone Creek church at the annual meeting of the Ebenezer Association that October. In January 1865, the army dropped him from army rolls for "excessive absences." Whatever his wound may have been, it was not life threatening, as Tharpe lived until 1896.[11]

---

[10] Jones, "Roster of Confederate Servicemen Who Were Members of This [Stone Creek Baptist] Church" (typed manuscript, undated), in my possession; minutes, Ebenezer Baptist Association, Special Collections, Jack Tarver Library, Mercer University, Macon GA; National Park Service Civil War Soldiers and Sailors System, http://www.itd.nps.gov/cwss/ (accessed 11 November 2006). The eighteen soldier deaths total is as compiled by Jones. According to Ebenezer Association records, Stone Creek reported a total of eighteen deaths from 1861–1864, but did not report deaths in 1865. This indicates that in the Stone Creek church, most deaths during the war years were soldier deaths, offering some evidence that local church deaths as reported in associational records during the war years can be presumed to consist largely of war-related deaths. Stone Creek soldier members served in a number of different units, including the 4th Georgia, 6th Georgia, 12th Georgia, 30th Georgia, 48th Georgia, 2nd Georgia Battalion, 25th Georgia Battalion, state guard units, and militia reserves. Only two churches in Middle Georgia associations reported more than nine total deaths from 1861 to 1865: Liberty Baptist with nineteen deaths, and Blue Water Baptist with twelve deaths, both in the Ebenezer Association, as was Stone Creek. The reported deaths were not broken down into categories, and complete total death records do not exist for many Middle Georgia association churches.

[11] Jones, "Roster," National Park Service Civil War Soldiers and Sailors System, http://www.itd.nps.gov/cwss/ (accessed 14 June 2011); minutes,

Tharpe's initial ambivalence may have been shared by other Stone Creek soldiers. Enrolling in December 1861, Edmond Vann secured a discharge the following April, only to re-enlist in 1863. Private Stephen Jones enrolled in March 1862 but quickly secured a substitute and was discharged in July. Captain Ulysses Rice also enrolled in March 1862, only to resign, for unspecified reasons, one year later.[12]

Some Stone Creek families sent many men to the battlefront. Seven Tharpes served, while the Andrews and Ard families each contributed six to the military. Like Julia Stanford, Stone Creek families lived in ongoing anxiety, fearfully listening for rumors and news of distant battles fought by husbands, sons, fathers, and brothers. Spring and summer 1862 were filled with anxiety on the home-front as battlefield news from Virginia trickled back home to Twiggs County, Georgia. Private William Hinson was "shot through the right leg and permanently disabled" at Seven Pines on 31 May. On 27 June, Private William Kitchens was "wounded and permanently disabled" at Cold Harbor, although he managed to answer roll call as late as 30 April 1864. Also on 27 June, Private Newton Land was wounded at Gaines Mill. Land remained in the army, serving as an enrolling officer to the close of the conflict. Malvern Hill, in July 1862, was devastating for the Burkett family, as Private Solomon Burkett was killed in the battle and Lieutenant Joseph Burkett shortly thereafter resigned "due to ill health." Wounded at Malvern Hill, Private Wiley Clance remained in the army and in 1864 was placed on hospital duty in Richmond. Also wounded at Malvern Hill, Private Kennedy Manning remained in the service, but was hospitalized in Macon in 1864. Private Judson Tharpe died in July in Richmond from an unspecified disease.[13]

Ebenezer Baptist Association, 1864, 13, Special Collections, Jack Tarver Library, Mercer University, Macon GA.
   [12] Jones, "Roster," National Park Service Civil War Soldiers and Sailors System, http://www.itd.nps.gov/cwss/ (accessed 14 June 2011).
   [13] Ibid.

Virginia in spring and summer 1862 was but a prelude for much greater heartache and anxiety among Stone Creek's families. The following year in early July, many Stone Creek soldier members converged near the town of Gettysburg, Pennsylvania, as General Robert E. Lee pursued a bold offensive against Union forces that marked a high-water point for the Confederacy. When the armies withdrew from the bloodied battlefield, Corporal Joseph Rodgers was dead, having been killed on 2 July. Private Isham Andrews was a prisoner of Union forces. Never free again, he contracted an unspecified disease and died in captivity the following year. Wounded Sergeant John Bond also left Gettysburg a Union prisoner, remaining in captivity until his release on 16 June 1865, two months after the war's end. Corporal Russell Read lived through Gettysburg, but only after having his right arm amputated and being captured by the enemy, all on 3 July. In September of that year, Read secured his release in a prisoner exchange. Private William Read was also wounded at Gettysburg, avoiding capture only to die while home on furlough in 1864. Also wounded and captured, Sergeant Willis Epps remained imprisoned by Union forces until a prisoner exchange in 1865. Private William Ard was never heard from after Gettysburg, reported missing in action and presumed dead. Two Densons were wounded at Gettysburg. Wounded and captured, Private John Denson was released from a Baltimore hospital later that year and was at roll call in October 1864. Sergeant Elias Denson meanwhile was wounded but survived, only to be captured at Petersburg in 1865. Gettysburg, in short, was devastating for the soldier members of Stone Creek Baptist Church of Twiggs County, Georgia. That Stone Creek church records made no mention of Gettysburg, despite the tragedy and anxieties visited upon so many church families, yet two months later chronicled the acceptance of a single soldier into church membership, suggests that the congregation maintained a stoic attitude toward external war-time events, no matter how terrible. Members clearly continued to keep their religious and secular lives officially separate. Yet in all likelihood, never a meeting day passed when church families in private conversation did not share their own personal anxieties and tragedies with one another.[14]

The battlefield sacrifices continued for nearly two more years. Chickamauga claimed the life of Private William Jessup on 13 September 1863. Private Franklin Pierce died of wounds on 17 July 1864, at a place unknown. Sergeant Gabriel Parker died not far from his home, on the battlefield of Jonesboro, Georgia, on 1 September 1864, fighting Sherman's army for control of Atlanta. Private Jefferson Tharpe survived Jonesboro, albeit with wounds. Private William Read succumbed to death while home on furlough, 24 September 1864. Private John Smith was hospitalized with fever and diarrhea in October 1864, and received a furlough home the following month. Captain Jeremiah Sanders languished in a Richmond, Virginia, hospital as the war drew to a close. At least seven Stone Creek soldier members were discharged due to ill health, a bittersweet ending but perhaps a welcome relief to family members in Twiggs County. In addition, privates James Herring and Elam Hinson, Jr., returned home to defend Macon from Union advances in November 1864. Hinson was captured in the defense of Macon. Kennedy Manning may have wished to help in the defense of the city, but he was hospitalized in Macon from previous wounds.[15]

Other Stone Creek soldier members fought and survived for years in distant battlefields and camps, only to be captured in the closing months of war. Private William Edmonds was captured at Weldon Railroad, Virginia, on 21 August 1864. He obtained his freedom in a prisoner exchange on 14 February 1865. Private Hiram DeFore fought valiantly throughout the war, only to be wounded at Fort Steadman, Virginia, and captured at Richmond mere days before the war ended. While DeFore was being taken into captivity on 3 April 1865 in Richmond, Private Elias J. Denson was captured at Petersburg. Both men were released after the war ended.[16]

---

[14] Ibid.
[15] Ibid.
[16] Ibid.

Diverging Loyalties

In the end, only a handful of Stone Creek soldier members eluded death, debilitating illness, or capture to witness the end of the Civil War with weapons in hand. Present at Appomattox as Lee surrendered to General Ulysses S. Grant were privates James Ard, John Land, and William Phillips. In addition, the Stone Creek congregation was represented at Appomattox by several Confederate officers, one of whom was Captain Thomas Robertson. Having enrolled in 1861 as a private, Robertson was commissioned a corporal and then lieutenant in 1862, and finally a captain on 23 March 1863. To Robertson belongs the distinction of being the single known Confederate soldier from Stone Creek Baptist Church who accepted Christ and was baptized (by an army chaplain) during the war, thus meriting Stone Creek's only reference to distant soldier camps or battlefields.[17]

Also present at Appomattox was Lieutenant Colonel Edwin A. Nash. The most distinguished Confederate soldier from the Stone Creek congregation, Nash enrolled in the army on 25 April 1861 at the age of twenty-six. He served with distinction, earning promotions to first lieutenant, captain, major, and finally lieutenant colonel. Captured during the Wilderness Campaign on 10 May 1864, he "endured many prisoner hardships" before either being released or escaping captivity. When Lee surrendered, Nash was in charge of Cook's brigade. The distinguished veteran lived a long life after the war, dying in 1913, his final resting place a cemetery near Stone Creek Baptist Church.[18]

Stone Creek soldier members meanwhile contributed to the war effort in other ways. W. H. Bull, Elias Denson, Tullius Rice, and William Zachry all served as physicians or surgeons. Marcellus Tharpe enrolled in the army in 1861 but was transferred to the Confederate Navy in 1862, serving as coxswain aboard the Confederate ironclad *Virginia*. I. W. Wood stayed closer to home, serving as a prison guard at the notorious Andersonville Prison

---

[17] Ibid.
[18] Ibid.

Camp in Southwest Georgia. Finally, three slaves owned by J. A. Tharpe were pressed into the service of the Confederacy: Job (seventeen years old), Ivey (twenty-six years old), and Max (forty-seven years old). Counting Job, Ivey, and Max, a total of ten Tharpes served in the Confederate Army during the war.[19]

The Confederate service records of Stone Creek church members thus reveal that one congregation in Middle Georgia was well represented on the battlefields, tented fields, and in the coastal waterways of the war's eastern theatre. Individual soldier members in turn displayed a full range of human characteristics, from bravery, loyalty, and perseverance to ambivalence, despair, and disillusionment. Yet church records remained largely silent as soldier members basked in battlefield successes, suffered disease, illness, and battlefield wounds, were captured by Union forces and held in captivity, died while fighting on battlefields, or experienced death from injuries or illness. Acknowledging with joy and approval Thomas Robertson's newfound spiritual salvation on a distant tented field, Stone Creek Baptist Church otherwise opted to ignore the personal triumphs and defeats experienced by soldier members, and offered no church-wide endorsement of the Confederacy or war effort.[20]

Not all Baptist congregations in Middle Georgia experienced war as extensively as did Stone Creek Baptist. On the other hand, few congregations openly expressed emotional connections to their soldier sons as did Providence Baptist Church in Jasper County, a mid-sized congregation of 136 members. Whereas most soldier sons of Thomaston Baptist survived the war and war-related deaths of Stone Creek members took place throughout the conflict, three prominent young men in the Providence congregation died early in the war, each at the age of twenty-one. In a manner rare among Baptist churches in Middle Georgia, Providence in October 1862

---

[19] Ibid.

[20] Minutes, Stone Creek Baptist Church, 1861–1865, Special Collections, Jack Tarver Library, Mercer University, Macon GA.

formally recognized the wartime deaths of three soldier members, one of whom had been killed a year earlier, while the remaining two had died the previous summer. Plainly worded, the first memorial stated, "Thomas Green was born August 5th 1840, died in Virginia in the service of our Country Oct 18, 1861." Although the church had met regularly in the months following Green's death, his passing was not recognized until October 1862. Private Thomas W. Green had served in Company C, the Jasper Light Infantry of the 14th Georgia Infantry Regiment. Mustering on 9 July 1861, and dying far from home only months after the war began, Green never experienced major combat, his death apparently the result of camp diseases.[21]

The next death occurred the following summer: "Charles Bussey was born May 2 1841 died in Virginia in the service of our Country July 1st 1862." Private Charles D. Bussey served in Company H of the 44th Georgia Infantry Regiment. Company H consisted of recruits from Pike County, near Jasper County. Unlike Green, Bussey lived long enough to experience major combat. Serving under Robert E. Lee, Private Bussey and his fellow soldiers witnessed the emergence of Lee during the Peninsula Campaign in Southeastern Virginia from March through July 1862. The first large-scale offensive in the eastern theater, and an attempt by Union forces under Major General George McClellan to capture the Confederate capital in Richmond, the Peninsula Campaign ended with McClellan withdrawing his army from the vicinity of Richmond following an intense but inconclusive Confederate assault on his position at Malvern Hill. The offensive at Malvern Hill on 1 July 1862 marked the sixth and last of the Seven Days' Battles. Saving Richmond from Union forces despite gaining no

---

[21] Minutes, Providence Baptist Church, Jasper County, 1860–1862; minutes, Central Baptist Association, 1860, Special Collections, Jack Tarver Library, Mercer University, Macon GA; National Park Service Civil War Soldiers and Sailors System, http://www.itd.nps.gov/cwss/ (accessed 14 June 2011); "The Civil War in Georgia," http://www.researchonline.net/gacw/unit51.htm (accessed 14 June 2011); Georgia USGenWeb Archives, http://ftp.rootsweb.com/pub/usgenweb/ga/jasper/military/cvilwar/rosters/14c.txt (accessed 14 June 2011). In the last document, Green's name is incorrectly spelled "Greene."

ground on the Union army, the battle cost the Confederacy 5,300 casualties, of which Private Bussey was one.[22]

The third soldier commemorated by Providence Baptist Church also died in Virginia: "D. L. Davidson was born April 4, 1841 died in Virginia in the service of our Country July 7, 1862." Serving in the 14th Georgia Infantry Regiment, Company C, as had Greene, Private David L. Davidson survived the Seven Days' Battles only to die less than a week after Malvern Hill, possibly succumbing to battlefield injuries.[23]

The deaths of three young servicemen seemingly struck deep within the collective conscience of the Providence church, perhaps leading the congregation to take the unusual step of recording their deaths in church minutes. William Green and Charles Bussey, fathers of two of the dead young men, were notable lay leaders within the congregation, chosen by members to represent the church at associational meetings. Yet the loss of the young men hardly deterred the congregation from public support of the Confederacy. Months after the deaths of Green, Bussey, and Davidson, the Providence congregation in March 1863 voted to observe "a day of fasting & prayer" for the country.[24]

---

[22] Minutes, Providence Baptist Church, Jasper County, 1862, Special Collections, Jack Tarver Library, Mercer University, Macon GA; National Park Service Civil War Soldiers and Sailors System, http://www.itd.nps.gov/cwss/ (accessed 14 June 2011); Georgia USGenWeb Archives, http://www.research online.net/gacw/unit95.htm (accessed 14 June 2011); National Park Service CWSAC Battle Summaries, http://www.nr.nps.gov/hps/abpp/battles/va021.htm (accessed 14 June 2011).

[23] Minutes, Providence Baptist Church, Jasper County, 1862, Special Collections, Jack Tarver Library, Mercer University, Macon GA; National Park Service Civil War Soldiers and Sailors System, http://www.itd.nps.gov/cwss/ (accessed 14 June 2011); "The Civil War in Georgia," http://www.research online.net/gacw/unit51.htm (accessed 14 June 2011).

[24] Minutes, Central Baptist Association, 1860–1862, 14, Special Collections, Jack Tarver Library, Mercer University, Macon GA; minutes, Providence Baptist Church, Jasper County, 1860–1864, Special Collections, Jack Tarver Library, Mercer University, Macon GA.

In addition to grieving over the loss of soldier sons, in one notable instance the members of Providence Baptist were confronted with the prospect of accepting a soldier son into membership. In the waning weeks of summer 1863, nineteen-year-old soldier Peter B. Cardell, son of church member and family patriarch Peter Cardell, applied for church membership. Following a pattern common to active soldiers who experienced conversion while on the tented field, Cardell personally wrote a letter to the church congregation and included a certificate signed by his army chaplain. On 19 September, Providence Baptist took up the case of Cardell, as the congregation acknowledged his letter and "also a certificate from the Chaplain of his Reg. Certifying to his being baptized & recommending him to the Church for membership." Yet whereas the New Bethel congregation throughout the war routinely accepted into membership active soldiers who applied in this manner, the Providence Church was not easily persuaded. Despite the young Cardell's family status within the congregation, the "church refused to receive him" until "his experience was made known to the church." The church promptly appointed a committee to "request a full statement of the Christian experience in writing to be laid before the Church for action." A month later, no word had been received from Cardell, and the matter was deferred until the soldier contacted the congregation. Not until February 1864 did the congregation again take up the matter of Cardell's request, acknowledging that "written experience of P. B. Cardell was re'd." At that point, upon closer examination of the written personal testimony, the soldier son was received "as a member of this Church." Having lost three sons on distant battlefields, the congregation thus gained a new soldier member from afar.[25]

Meanwhile, Wilkinson County contributed Baptist sons to the fight for Southern independence. Joel Burke, Company F, 3rd

---

[25] Minutes, Providence Baptist Church, Jasper County, 1863–1864, Special Collections, Jack Tarver Library, Mercer University, Macon GA; "Soldiers and Sailors System," http://www.itd.nps.gov/cwss/ (accessed 14 June 2011).

Georgia, a member of First Baptist Church at New Providence, survived the conflict but nonetheless died at the young age of thirty-one in 1872. McInytyre Baptist's John C. Todd also survived the war, serving in the Georgia 13th Cavalry. At least four young men from New Providence Baptist served in the army. While James J. Collins served in Company I of the 3rd Georgia Infantry, the remaining three soldiered in the 57th Georgia Infantry: Eugenius E. Collins, James W. McCook, and Daniel Whalen.[26]

Collins, McCook, and Whalen were among many Middle Georgia young men who fought in the 57th Infantry Regiment. Also called the 54th Regiment, it was organized during spring 1862 and consisted largely of Middle Georgians. Commanded by Colonel William Barkuloo, Lieutenant Colonel Cincinnatus S. Guyton, and Major John W. Shinholser, many members of the 57th Georgia were recruited in Wilkinson, Troup, Peach, Montgomery, Oconee, Houston, Crawford, and Baldwin counties. Initially ordered to Chattanooga, followed by deployment to East Tennessee and Kentucky, the 57th Georgia then moved to Mississippi where it was assigned to T. H. Taylor's Brigade in the Department of Mississippi and East Louisiana. Fighting at Champion Hill, the regiment was captured in July 1863, at Vicksburg. Exchanged and placed in General Mercer's and J. A. Smith's Brigade, the regiment participated in numerous other conflicts through spring 1864, at which time it joined the Army of Tennessee. Involved in the Atlanta Campaign thereafter from 20 July to 1 September, the 57th reported fifty-four casualties. By December 1864, a total of 120 men remained in action. On 26 April in

---

[26] "Civil War Graves in Wilkinson County, Georgia," available online at http://www.georgiagenealogy.org/wilkinson/civilwarburialshome.html (accessed 14 June 2011). Names of Baptist soldiers cross-referenced with the National Park Service Civil War Soldiers and Sailors System, online at http://www.civilwar.nps.gov/cwss/ and http://ftp.rootsweb.ancestry.com/pub/usgenweb/ga/wilkinson/military/civilwar/rosters/d57.txt (all web sites accessed 14 June 2011).

Bennett's House (Durham Station), only a remnant surrendered, including Eugenius E.[27]

Students and graduates of Mercer University, the flagship school of Georgia Baptists, also joined Collins, McCook, and Whalen in service in the 57th Georgia. In particular, most members of Mercer's 1861 senior class enlisted. Nine of thirty-one classmates died in the service of the Confederacy by the end of the war. Among those who survived the war, Edwin T. Davis of Savannah dropped out of Mercer in December 1861 and served in Company A, enlisting as a sergeant in May 1862. In August, Davis was placed in charge of a pioneer corps repairing trails in advance of the army's movement through Kentucky's Cumberland mountains. Defeat at Vicksburg in July 1863 led to Davis's capture. Now a lieutenant, the former Mercer student later returned to action following a prisoner exchange. Almost exactly one year following the defeat at Vicksburg, Davis and the 57th Georgia bemoaned setbacks in the battle for Atlanta. Yet the young man openly declared the campaign thus far a victory in a letter he wrote to his hometown newspaper, the *Savannah Republican*. The Georgia troops conducted themselves in "splendid" fashion and the "impetuous valor" of officers and men led to the capture of thousands of prisoners and the routing of the enemy from entrenchments, Davis rejoiced. "Of the spirit and morale of the army I need say but little. It is large-spirited, determined, well-appointed, and fond of their new and great Commander-in-chief [Hood]. Under him, the pride of Texans and Georgians, they expect to be led to new fields of imperishable glory and renown." Davis's positive attitude continued through the fall of Atlanta and into the closing months of

---

[27] See http://www.colquitt.k12.ga.us/gspurloc/Cobbslegion/gasca/units/57th_gvi.htm, including links http://ftp.rootsweb.ancestry.com/pub/usgenweb/ga/wilkinson/military/civilwar/rosters/d57.txt, http://www.geocities.com/Heartland/Village/9340/57thgainf.html, and National Park Service Civil War Soldiers and Sailors System (all web sites accessed 14 June 2011).

war, as he was promoted to captain of Company B. At war's end, the former Mercer student held the rank of junior second lieutenant.[28]

Optimistic soldier reports such as those of Edwin Davis provided fuel for Samuel Boykin's editorials in the *Christian Index*. Davis's cheerfulness in the face of obvious adversity also reflected larger attitudes among Confederate soldiers, according to J. Tracy Power. Combing the letters and diaries of 400 Confederate officers and enlisted men in the Army of Northern Virginia from May 1864 to April 1865, Power concluded that Confederate soldiers, even in the face of obviously long odds late in the war, remained noticeably upbeat and seemingly certain of their eventual triumph. Power attributes the widespread optimism in part to Confederate soldiers' willingly believing the lie that Northern soldiers were in worse condition than those of the South. As such, Edwin Davis's self-delusion characterized a larger pattern that Power identifies as a primary reason why the war lasted as long as it did.[29]

Yet not all soldiers glossed over the difficulties that war entailed. Fellow Mercer graduate Alva Benjamin Spencer, born in Greene County and living in Dooly County in early 1861, experienced the same war as did Davis but offered a more nuanced perspective, recording his observations and thoughts in letters to his future wife Margaret and friends and family in Georgia. On 29 April 1861, the

---

[28] Spright Dowell, *A History of Mercer University, 1833–1953* (Macon GA: Mercer University Press, 1958) 110; Spencer B. King, *Sound of Drums: Selected Writings of Spencer B. King from His Civil War Centennial Column Appearing in the Macon Georgia Telegraph News, 1960–1965* (Macon GA: Mercer University Press, 1984) 242; Edwin Tralona Davis, "The Battle of Atlanta," *Savannah Republican*, 26 July 1864; National Park Service Civil War Soldiers and Sailors System (accessed 14 June 2011); Samuel H. Hawkins, diary, Digital Library of Georgia, http://dlg.galileo.usg.edu/hawkins/figures.php (accessed 14 June 2011). The Davis diary covers 12 December 1861 through 17 October 1862. See also Spencer C. King Papers, Special Collections, Jack Tarver Library, Mercer University, and Scott Walker, *Hell's Broke Loose in Georgia: Survival in a Civil War Regiment* (Athens: University of Georgia Press, 2005).

[29] J. Tracy Power, *Lee's Miserables: Life in the Army of Northern Virginia from the Wilderness to Appomattox* (Chapel Hill: University of North Carolina Press, 1998).

young man enlisted in Company C of the 3rd Georgia Regiment. By 13 May, Spencer was stationed in Virginia.[30]

Early on, Spencer realized the complexities brought about by war. "I hear a great deal of news," he wrote while stationed in Portsmouth 13 July, "but it is hard to separate the true from the false...I don't wish to write you any *lies*." At the same time, the early months of war proved far from strenuous. "We have bacon, fresh meat, and almost every kind of vegetables that we desire," Spencer noted. In August, not yet having engaged a battle, he lamented that "I should like it myself if I could be nearer the seat of war than I am," rather than being "stationed at the same old place...going through the same dull routine of duties from morning to night." Yet in the same letter, Spencer declared, "You have no idea of the fun I see here in Virginia every day. I have several days taken rides in boats with ladies up and down the Elizabeth river." Spencer's leisure activities continued into September, when on the eleventh day of the month he joined fellow soldiers in walking along the beaches and sailing near the coast of North Carolina's Outer Banks. "On the Sea beach we found a great variety of most beautiful shells." While on Nags Head Spencer "saw the Ocean in all its grandeur. The wind was blowing strong and the waves rolled high upon the beach." The pleasant days, however, did not last. In the following weeks, Spencer's desire to encounter the "Yankees" found fulfillment as his 3rd Regiment experienced a series of close encounters and small engagements on Roanoke Island along the North Carolina coast. War had arrived just before winter set in.[31]

Like many other soldiers who survived the Civil War, including members from Stone Creek Baptist, Spencer did not escape the long conflict without scars. On 19 April 1862, his "little finger" was struck by a "minnie ball." Although severely injured, the finger was not

---

[30] Clyde G. Wiggins III, ed., *My Dear Friend: The Civil War Letters of Alva Benjamin Spencer, 3rd Georgia Regiment, Company C* (Macon GA: Mercer University Press, 2007) 1–12.

[31] Wiggins III, ed., *My Dear Friend*, 13 July, 12 August, 11 September, 1 October, 10 November 1861.

amputated, and Spencer soon declared himself "harty" and in good health. Thoughts of his own well-being, however, took a back seat to larger concerns when in May he witnessed the evacuation of Portsmouth and Norfolk. "Since I left," the soldier confided, "the Merrimac has been blown to atoms" in order that it might not fall into enemy hands.[32]

Discouragement and destitution arrived December 1862 in form of bitter cold and the battle of Fredericksburg. Shortly after Spencer witnessed "snow storm in all its horrors.... came the horrors of the battle field." The storm initially crippled "several men in our division" with frostbite, but Fredericksburg was the worst event yet experienced by Spencer. "I visited the battle field the day after the battle, and I was so destitute of clothing that I robbed the dead Yankees of such clothing as I needed. I never thought I would be reduced to such extremity; but self preservation is the first law of nature."[33]

In between the monotony of camp life, the hardships of battle and distance from loved ones only grew worse. While in July 1863 fellow Mercerian Edwin Davis fought and was captured at Vicksburg, Spencer survived Gettysburg. "The loss in our brigade...was truly alarming," he noted. "I am truly thankful that I'm still alive, after having gone through so many hardships." In February 1864, Spencer passed the cold winter days by reminiscing of his "school-boy days" and "living in anticipation of the happy time" in which he would see his future wife. During the summer months, Spencer lay hunkered in the trenches of Petersburg. "I do wish this campaign would close," he declared in late July. "Tis very disagreeable, and very unhealthy, both from bullets and disease." Spencer worried about the distant battle for Atlanta. Although viewing General John Bell Hood as an "excellent officer," the Georgia native remained concerned that "the Yankeys are getting uncomfortably near my home and I'm extremely anxious they should

---

[32] Ibid., 4 May, 21 June 1861.
[33] Ibid., 31 December 1862.

be driven away as speedily as possible." While Davis offered a glowing report of Confederate forces near Atlanta in late July, from Petersburg Spencer remained somber. As Hood desperately sought to save Atlanta in August, "a great many think he will have to fall back," Spencer conceded. When the Georgia city finally fell to the enemy, it had a "demoralizing effect" upon Spencer and his fellow soldiers at Petersburg.[34]

Crestfallen over the loss of Atlanta while confined to the trenches of Petersburg, Spencer's hopes for the Confederacy dimmed while his personal enthusiasm for war waned. "Our cause now looks gloomy," he admitted. "Our armies are suffering defeats, and every thing looks anything but peaceful. Our many enemies are putting forth every energy to crush and annihilate the rebels." Seeking hope, the soldier turned to an infrequent subject: God. "I firmly believe tho' that a just God will not permit our cruel enemies to rule over us." Four months later, with the dawning of a new year, belief in a just God seemed distant. "Let our fate be what it may," he noted, "I wish the suspense to be done away with." In February 1865, his thoughts turned to a personal, rather than sovereign, God. Confessing "extremely wicked" but unnamed sins and petitioning that he might "still be permitted to live," Spencer hoped that he might be "happy again" one day. The following month, the soldier's last wartime letter acknowledged Sherman's victories but defiantly declared that "the people" could not be conquered, while yet holding out hope that the "unconstitutional and violently antagonistical" Confederate bill recruiting African Americans to fight for the Confederacy, would allow the army "another foray into Pennsylvania."[35]

The varied vignettes of these Baptist Confederate soldiers from Middle Georgia, in short, represents a Confederate or Southern narrative more than a Baptist or even Christian-specific narrative. While references to God and scripture periodically appear in their writings, observations of camp life and conditions, descriptions of

---

[34] Ibid., 17 July 1863; 19 February, 21 July, 19 August, 16 September 1864.
[35] Ibid., 24 September 1864; 10 February, 24 March 1865.

battles, longings for family and friends, and discussion of news and happenings at home typically occupied soldiers' thoughts. Church, revivals, and personal religious faith, while perhaps important to individual soldiers, occasioned less ink. Alva Spencer, for example, penned one religiously themed paragraph for the entirety of 1863. "I listened in the forenoon to a very good sermon," the Mercer graduate noted in May, "delivered by Rev. Mr. Potter from Ga., in Massapronax church. In the afternoon Mr. Crumley (from Ga.) delivered a sermon in camp. Prayer meetings have been in progress through the whole brigade...several have been baptized. Four from my company have or will join the church. The meetings are still in progress. Our Chaplains are doing all they can I think for the cause of religion." Nearly one year later, Spencer again returned to the theme of religion, reporting on prayer meetings and services held on a Confederate-appointed day of fasting and prayer.[36]

Stephen Woodworth's research indicates that the experiences of Edwin Dallas, Alva Spencer, Edwin Davis, and other Middle Georgia Baptist soldiers reflected broader trends within the Confederate Army. While Woodworth's extensive examination of soldier letters indicates that religion played a notable role in the private lives and belief systems of many Confederate soldiers, revivals and war-time religious experiences at large failed to alter the underlying cultural preconceptions that soldiers took to the battlefront. Religion, in short, assumed a subservient and supporting role within the larger narrative of the Confederacy, as well as within the Union. Nonetheless, the secondary attention paid to religious themes offers a contrast to Kent Dollar's analysis of Christian Confederate soldiers. Addressing the question of how the war affected Christian soldiers, Dollar selected nine individual soldiers, representing a cross-section of Southern society and religion, and traced their faith development throughout the war as addressed in letters and diaries. Dollar found that regular Bible-reading, fellowship with other Christians, attendance at religious services, and private devotion to God

---

[36] Ibid., 13 May 1863; 22 April 1864.

characterized the lives of all nine men throughout the war. While these religious themes, at least in part, likely reflected the war-time lives of many Baptist soldiers from Middle Georgia, this study suggests the level of open religiosity expressed by Dollar's nine chosen subjects may have been of an unusually high level.[37]

Indeed, if all Christian soldiers had visibly exhibited the high level of religiosity as those of Dollar's study, Samuel Boykin and other home-front Baptists would have had little cause to lament the immorality displayed among Christian soldiers, and somewhat less reason to be concerned about the lack of Baptist chaplains. Whether openly and daily reflecting their religion or not, the story of Baptist soldiers in Middle Georgia is a multi-faceted narrative of faith, sacrifice, mundane daily routines, small joys, duty to family and country, hope and despair, and death and disease portrayed against a backdrop of few Baptist spiritual leaders available to preach, counsel, console, reprimand, and perform the rites of death. To soldiers fell the burden of bearing their crosses without the support of a strong ministerial network. Although carrying their denominational identity to the battlefield and within the camps, Baptist soldiers' thoughts seemingly dwelled more upon family, friends, and home, underscored by a broad perception of their homeland as favored of God. In the end, while soldiers' emotions at large rose and fell with daily hardships and the larger fortunes of the Confederacy, and home remained a tangible if distant reality, the religious faith of some offered hope beyond battlefield defeat.[38]

---

[37] Steven E. Woodworth, *While God Is Marching On: The Religious World of the Civil War Soldiers* (Lawrence: University Press of Kansas, 2001); Kent T. Dollar, *Soldiers of the Cross: Confederate Soldier-Christians and the Impact of War on Their Faith* (Macon GA: Mercer University Press, 2005).

[38] The experiences of Baptist soldiers and families from Middle Georgia bears some resemblance to Virginia soldiers and families in Aaron Sheehan-Dean, *Why Confederates Fought: Family and Nation in Civil War Virginia* (Chapel Hill: University of North Carolina Press, 2007). Sheehan-Dean's thesis is that Virginia soldiers and their families perceived a personal and emotional association between the battlefield and the preservation of the home-front. The perception remained throughout the war, resulting in ongoing commitment to the

Sydney Romero, seeking to understand the larger impact of faith within military ranks, suggests that "the church was the single greatest institution in the maintenance of morale in the Confederate army." Within the roughly 20,000 Confederate letters, diaries, and manuscripts Romero examined, chaplains' voices find greater expression from Methodists and Presbyterians due to a shortage of Baptist chaplains, while soldiers' religious expressions and sentiments, when voiced, are typically done so without denominational specificity.[39]

In a similar fashion, among the ranks of Middle Georgia soldiers, more is known about Baptists as soldiers than soldiers as Baptists. While the Christian church at large may have indeed exercised tremendous influence upon the attitudes of Confederate soldiers, soldier records alone fail to demonstrate the full extent of Baptist thought and practice within the lives of individuals.

Confederacy on the part of common folk. Among Baptist soldiers in Middle Georgia, the tendency to discuss family and home-front more than personal religion suggests a similar dynamic.

[39] Sidney J. Romero, *Religion in the Rebel Ranks* (Lanham MD: University Press of America, 1983) 129. Romero attributes any denominational vagueness to a general harmony and common sense of mission shared by evangelicals at large in the South during the war years.

CHAPTER 5

PERSONAL MORALITY AND SPIRITUALITY:
PATTERNS IN GENDER AND RACE

While the Civil War brought theological tensions, a missions crisis, and soldiers' hardships to Baptists of Middle Georgia, the conflict also fostered spiritual challenges and evolution. On the home front, black members increasingly questioned the boundaries of their slave status within the church, even as whites ultimately failed in efforts to defend the morality and perceived biblical basis of African slavery. White women attained a greater role within local congregations through revival conversions and numerical superiority. Meanwhile, many Baptists fighting in defense of the Confederacy proved susceptible to the sins of army camp life. In turn, these interwoven themes among individual Baptists altered the dynamics of the Baptist community at large.

To the casual observer, Baptist congregations in Middle Georgia carried on during the war years much as they had prior to the initial shots upon Fort Sumter. Although many male members departed home and church to serve in the Confederate Army, few pastors left their pulpits. They continued to affirm the moral rightness of black slavery while preaching to integrated congregations. Few congregations discussed the Civil War in any official venue. Yet beneath the veneer of normalcy, internal tensions, fomented by war, threatened established patterns of gender and race.

In addition, discipline and revival, traditional checks and balances designed to constrain personal freedoms and ensure appropriate morality, proved to be of limited value during the war years as church records revealed changing social dynamics taking place within Civil War era Baptist congregations.

Central to congregation and society, slavery bisected themes of freedom and morality, placing Southern apologists, including white Baptists, on the defensive. Feigning innocence in spring 1863, *Christian Index* editor Samuel Boykin wondered why Confederates had not yet "discovered the reason why God has let this storm of war suddenly burst upon our fair land and create so much misery, cause so much distress, and carry devastation and ruin into so many quarters." That reason was slavery. The South stood "peculiarly situated," occupying "a station among the nations of earth totally unlike any other upon the face of the earth." Rooted in religion and expressed in the institution of slavery, this exceptionalism deserved blessings, not tribulations. "A christian people, we nurture the institution of slavery against which all the civilized world is arrayed. Democratic in government and sentiment, we are aristocratic socially.... dependent upon an inferior race for our prosperity."[1]

Baptists in the South had long welcomed slaves into their churches, accepting responsibility for their souls but not their bodies or minds. Refusing to believe that blacks could be considered human beings on the same level as white Europeans, Southern Baptists had joined other Christians in the South in equating the African race with descendants of Ham the Canaanite. In 1863, Baptist minister E. B. Teague interpreted the results of God's curse upon Noah's son Ham that took place following the flood in the book of Genesis. "The curse pronounced on Canaan, has never been removed; and, therefore, the children of Ham are in servitude to this day," Teague declared. "In Africa, they serve one another, most of them being slaves. In all ages and countries they have been a subject race, and the slave market for the world. In the United States, Cuba, and the West Indies, they serve the children of Japhet and Shem, in mind and person; and inferior must always serve superior races. The curse pronounced on the children of Ham consists in this: that God has made them inferior to the children of Japhet and Shem." Many thousands of years after the biblical story, white Baptists in the American South insisted upon

---

[1] "Cause of the War," *Christian Index*, 23 March 1863, 1.

their calling by God to recognize the timeless subservient status of Africans and their descendants, Christianizing them through the institution of slavery that properly perpetuated their racial inferiority.[2]

In the mind of Baptists, the biblical enslavement of Ham's descendents stood as the central issue of the war. "It cannot be denied," editor Boykin declared in summer 1861, "that the institution of slavery is the cause of the war." He further noted in December 1863 that, "Slavery is the only issue, the true issue between the North and South.... slavery and the South with it will live and triumph because it is of God." The *Index* editor recognized his sentiments were not universally accepted among the Baptist populace. Boykin fretted that the South's "public mind is not sufficiently convinced that slavery is of God," and determined to educate Baptists in the South to the scriptural, philosophical, moral, and historical rightness of the institution.[3]

A. C. Dayton, pastoring in Middle Georgia during the war years, echoed Boykin's fears that some younger white Baptists were not entirely committed to a slave society. "Many have been taught to look on slavery as a sin from early childhood," Dayton lamented. "This has been taught, not only in the North, but in the South. It is taught to-day, not by spoken words, but by books in many a Southern home." The books referred to by Dayton included Harriet Beecher Stowe's *Uncle Tom's Cabin*, an anti-slavery novel published in 1852 that became the second bestselling book of the nineteenth century,

---

[2] "Religion by Example," *Christian Index*, 3 June 1862, 4; Even as white Southerners, including Baptists, turned to the "myth of Ham" theology to sanction the racial social structures of the South, Sylvester Johnson argues that African Americans likewise sought legitimacy within the story of Ham. Black American Christians, seeking to establish their own roots in the larger biblical narrative, ironically reinforced their own illegitimacy in Southern culture by embracing Ham as the ancient father of their race. As such, the biblical story of Ham empowered as well as subjugated American blacks. See Sylvester A. Johnson, *The Myth of Ham in Nineteenth-Century American Christianity* (New York: St. Martin's Press, 2004).

[3] "The Moral Effect of the Present War," *Christian Index*, 28 August 1861, 1.

behind the Bible. While banned in the South, copies nonetheless sat on the shelves of many Southern homes. Boykin and Dayton's observations regarding a lack of uniformity on the issue of slavery lend credence to Eugene D. Genovese's argument that many Southern clergy in pre-Civil War years still harbored doubts as to the moral legitimacy of the South's "peculiar institution."[4]

Further complicating a decisive defense of slavery, Boykin understood the complexities inherent in maintaining the institution. Too many masters ignored their Christian responsibility to their slaves. "Neglect of the moral culture of our slaves, our subjecting the marriage tie among them too much to the will of man, our withholding too much from them the light of God's word—in short, our using them for our own aggrandizement rather than for carrying out the purpose of Jehovah, constitute sins for which it becomes us to grieve, and…amend as will procure the forgiveness of God and secure his favor," the editor pleaded to his audience. Not allowing formal marriages among slaves and in other cases breaking apart

---

[4] "The Moral Effect of the Present War," *Christian Index*, 28 August 1861, 1; "A. C. Dayton," 8 July 1862, 2; "Slavery," 25 November 1863, 1; Eugene D. Genovese, *A Consuming Fire: The Fall of the Confederacy in the Mind of the White South* (Athens: University of Georgia Press, 1998). Genovese argues that some Southern ministers were troubled over the manner in which slaves were treated by slaveholders. Religious slaveholders, for their part, struggled to reconcile the moral demands of Christianity with the socioeconomic interests vested in the institution of slavery. In addition, Daniel Stowell argues that Civil War-era Georgia Methodist minister John H. Caldwell, who reversed his proslavery stance in 1865, endured derision among white Southerners because they projected their own fears regarding slavery onto Caldwell. See Daniel Stowell, "'We Have Sinned and God Has Smitten Us!': John H. Caldwell and the Religious Meaning of Confederate Defeat," *Georgia Historical Quarterly* 78/1 (Spring 1994): 1–38. However, Boykin and Dayton, in their firsthand commentary regarding a lack of commitment to slavery among Baptists, do not limit the scope of their remarks to ministers and/or slaveholders. A second popular anti-slavery book was Hinton Helper's *The Impending Crisis: How to Meet It*, published in 1857. Helper was a poor white Southerner, and his economic argument against slavery enraged and alarmed Southern slaveholders.

slave families, in addition to not allowing slaves to read the Bible, were the worst of slaveholder sins identified by Boykin.[5]

In late 1864, devastation marred the landscape and God's blessings upon the South remained ever more elusive. From Atlanta to Savannah, Georgia reeled from Union General William Tecumseh Sherman's campaign of destruction, designed to cripple the South's military infrastructure and break the will of home-front Southerners. Baptists of Middle Georgia thus confronted a scenario none could have envisioned prior to the start of the Civil War: the prospect of freeing and arming slaves to fight on the side of the Confederacy. Amidst deepening national gloom and severe soldier attrition brought about by mounting battlefield losses, Southern politicians in fall 1864, desperate to recruit more men for the army, turned their attention to the hundreds of thousands of male slaves throughout the South.[6]

Discussion of incorporating slaves into the military frightened many, including Boykin. Writing from the relatively safe haven of Macon, he attacked the new military proposal by reiterating the firm Southern Baptist belief in the righteousness of slavery. "We believe," he declared, "that the institution of slavery as it exists among us is of Divine appointment." The holy sanctioning of slavery resulted from blacks being of "an inferior race." The lowly place of blacks among the peoples of the world evidenced itself in blacks being "indolent, thriftless and incapable of self-government." Lazy and directionless, blacks "left to themselves" had made "no advance in civilization" and

---

[5] "Slavery," *Christian Index*, 25 November 1863, 1.

[6] The Confederate debate over arming slaves anguished the South as white Southerner weighed the preservation of their liberty against granting liberty to slaves. Bruce Levine, in *Confederate Emancipation: Southern Plans to Free and Arm Slaves during the Civil* War (New York: Oxford University Press, 2005), argues that slaveholders were determined to give up their sons, husbands, and brothers to the Confederate army before offering up their slaves, and that those who supported employing blacks in the army did so in the hope of maintaining control over blacks once their freedom had been obtained. Also see Robert F. Durden, *The Gray and Black: The Confederate Debate on Emancipation* (Baton Rouge: Louisiana State University Press, 2000).

remained in paganism. Offering freedom to an inferior and untrustworthy race, even in return for fighting on behalf of the South, threatened both nation and Christianity.[7]

Nonetheless, white Baptists insisted that the institution of slavery resulted in great good for this otherwise worthless race of people. "We know it to be true," Boykin declared, "that with us they have become a semi-civilized people." Yet even more importantly, enslaved blacks "enjoy and appreciate the blessings of Christianity," the *Index* editor insisted. "Thousands" of slaves now existed among the ranks of Southern Christians, and "great benefits" to the black race were the providential "fruits of slavery." Furthermore, white Southerners stood "accountable to God" and under solemn "obligation" to maintain the "institution" of slavery ordained of God. To abolish slavery, "in part or wholly," would be a violation of a sacred trust because it would "remit the negro to his primary condition of paganism." Finally, opposition to slavery would negate the "witness" of the "ancient church" prior to the Reformation.[8]

In Baptist life in the South, the Christianization of slaves had taken place within the context of the local church. Prior to the war, slaves usually attended the same church as the slave owner. Within the context of the local church, race relations between whites and blacks—free citizens and slaves—affirmed the Southern status quo of slavery but assumed personal dimensions overshadowed by a concern for the salvation of souls. White Baptists in Middle Georgia, frequently framing the Civil War in spiritual terms, spiritualized race relations within the local church while affirming the legality of slavery. Considered "*property* under the protection of the laws," the slave was also "a *man* under the protection of Christianity."[9]

---

[7] "Arming the Negroes for Southern Defence," *Christian Index*, 18 November 1864, 2.

[8] Ibid.; *Christian Index*, "This War," 20 May 1864, 2.

[9] "Arming the Negroes for Southern Defence," *Christian Index*, 11 November 1864, 2. In 1823, Richard Furman of South Carolina defended slavery as a moral institution while defending the "religious privileges" of the enslaved. See Richard

Within the confines of the local Baptist church, master-slave relationships and attendant racial barriers during the war evidenced a modification not acknowledged in Southern society at large. Recognizing the distinction between body and soul, some local Baptist churches elevated slaves to a higher degree than found elsewhere in the South. W. J. Wellborn explained race relations within the local church by quoting from Galatians 3:28: "There is neither Jew nor Greek, there is neither bond nor free, there is neither male nor female, for ye are all one in Christ Jesus." He further observed, "We see that however men may vary in color, in condition, in their relations to one another, they are treated by the Lord their Saviour as brethren and equals *in the respect of their origin and of the Bible.*" Arguing from the basis of equality of souls, Wellborn positioned himself against a Confederate law prohibiting the instruction of reading to slaves, on the grounds that slaves should have access to the Bible. Samuel K. Talmage agreed with Wellborn, declaring his opposition to "withhold[ing] the revealed will of God, by law, from any human being," and blaming Southern wartime setbacks on the unjust law. Yet not all Baptists agreed with Wellborn and Talmage, and other Baptists published essays against appeal of the law in question. Such disagreements masked a continuing struggle to reconcile New Testament principles of human equality and dignity against Old Testament practices and interpretations conscripted to buttress a racially-tiered society.[10]

Wellborn's insistence on the equality of souls in the eyes of God also reflected a limited, but nonetheless significant, reality in local church life. Although central to the Baptist faith, theology infrequently played a direct role in church discipline cases, largely

---

Furman, *Exposition of the Views of the Baptists, Relative to the Coloured Population in the United States* (Charleston: A. E. Miller, 1838).

[10] "Shall We Not Permit Our Slaves to Read the Bible?" *Christian Index*, 30 March 1862, 2; Samuel K. Talmage, "Should the Law Be Repealed Prohibiting Teaching Our Slaves to Read the Bible?," *Christian Index*, 25 November 1862, 4; Philemon, "Instruction of Negroes in Letters," *Christian Index*, 30 September 1862, 3; Baptist, "Learning Slaves to Read," *Christian Index*, 30 September 1862, 3.

confined to situations in which church members attended or joined a church not of the Baptist and/or missionary faith. Church discipline theoretically buttressed Baptists' belief in a pure church of professed believers, ordered around common membership standards applied to all that framed personal freedoms and morality and held individuals accountable to the body at large. Reflecting the democratic nature of Baptist congregations, any member could theoretically bring charges against another member. Women and blacks, lacking voting rights in discipline cases, infrequently did so, however. Yet church members, both white and black, free and slave, in theory submitted to the same disciplinary standards, although slaves bore the additional burden of obedience to masters. Within Baptist life, church discipline occupied a central role on the Southern frontier, afterwards declining in prominence and largely disappearing in the twentieth century as Baptists in the South became more urban, educated, and socially mainstreamed. Accordingly, the Civil War era, including Reconstruction, arguably represents a near crest in the prominence of discipline in local Baptist congregations in the South.[11]

---

[11] The subject of discipline in local Baptist churches of the late eighteenth through nineteenth centuries has been explored in depth by Gregory A. Wills in his seminal *Democratic Religion: Freedom, Authority, and Church Discipline in the Baptist South, 1785–1900* (New York: Oxford University Press, 2003) and, to a lesser degree, by Randy J. Sparks in *On Jordan's Stormy Banks: Evangelicalism in Mississippi 1773–1876* (Athens: University of Georgia Press, 1994). Wills argues that church discipline existed in Baptist churches to "ensure pure belief as well as pure deportment" (84). Working from extensive local church records in the South, Wills concludes that women were one and a half times as likely to be excommunicated as were men, that social position sometimes influenced the outcome of discipline cases, and that discipline sometimes related to the upholding of Calvinistic theological tenets. Although Wills's focus on theology does not hold up in this study, his gender contention does: women were more likely than men to be excommunicated from Baptist congregations: in the period 1860–1865, 60 of 75 disciplinary cases (80 percent) involving females resulted in removal from the church, compared to 107 of 167 cases (64 percent) involving males. Wills also determined that slaves were sometimes allowed to bring charges against white church members, with disciplinary action rarely taken. No clear instances of such were found in this study. Finally, Wills concludes that church discipline declined in the late nineteenth century as Baptists in the South became

Individuals who voluntarily joined a Baptist congregation agreed to certain restrictions regarding personal freedoms and morality. Fewer than half of Southerners, however, held church membership and thus submitted themselves to such scrutiny, leaving some historians to conclude that church discipline played an insignificant role in the South at large. Bertram Wyatt-Brown argues that community and courts, not the church, served as the overarching arbiters of individual actions in Southern society. Yet Randy J. Sparks dissents from Wyatt-Brown, arguing that evangelical moral strictures played a disproportionate role in the larger frontier South of the early and mid-nineteenth centuries, influencing community codes and conduct outside the church house.[12]

Within the confines of church houses, Baptist congregations in Middle Georgia of the Civil War era (for purposes of this study, encompassing the years 1860-1865) excluded (or excommunicated) members for a variety of reasons, including repeat and unsatisfactory absences, issues of immorality, and attending other churches. Such infractions revolved around personal behavior. Viewed as a serious offense, non-attendance typically resulted in exclusion if the offender offered no satisfactory explanation following consecutive absences. Issues of morality typically involved drunkenness, profanity, sexual sins, gambling, involvement in inappropriate entertainment, and theft. In piestic and individualistic-oriented Baptist life in the South, personal morality (behavior) remained the primary concern, even as Baptists in the North prior to and during the Civil War projected a

---

more respectable in larger society and more averse to humiliate church members. Sparks's study of Methodists, Baptists, and Presbyterians in Mississippi posits a downward trend in discipline cases as early as the 1830s, reflective of modernizing trends in churches as a whole. Finally, Jean E. Friedman, in *The Enclosed Garden: Women and Community in the American South, 1830–1900* (Chapel Hill: University of North Carolina Press, 1985) in a study of churches in Southern seaboard states argues that discipline among Southern churches "declined during the Civil War and abated to an extent in the postwar years" (11).

[12] Bertram Wyatt-Brown, *Southern Honor: Ethics and Behavior in the Old South* (New York: Oxford University Press, 1982) xviii; Sparks, *On Jordan's Stormy Banks*, 149–50, 237.

growing awareness of larger social ills. These regional differences resulted in a widening ideological gap, highlighted in the issue of slavery. Finally, disciplinary actions against church members who attended other churches made little distinction in terms of denominations. Individual Baptists risked the wrath of their home congregation whether visiting Methodist or Presbyterian churches, or even Baptist churches holding differing views on missionary activity.[13]

Reflecting the commonness of discipline within local congregations, thirty-six of forty-four churches studied in Middle Georgia reported specific cases of discipline, excluding the frequent infraction of non-attendance. An issue largely confined to white members, non-attendance discipline cases indicated a basic dichotomy between black and white members who attended the same congregations. Whereas white members voluntarily chose to attend church services, or to not attend and face the consequences, black members attended services only by the will or permission of their masters. In few instances did congregations thus question non-attendance by black members; in no instances did churches cite slave owners for not allowing their slaves to attend services. In a similar fashion, cases involving attendance at other churches, all of which involved white members, reflected the inability of black members to make autonomous ecclesiastical decisions.[14]

Why, then, in the face of degrading racial structures and theologically reinforced subjugation on the one hand, as well as white ambivalence regarding church attendance by blacks on the other, did blacks join white Baptist congregations in the first place? Albert

---

[13] Middle Georgia Baptist's intolerance of church members visiting dissimilar congregations is echoed in Gregory Wills's *Democratic Religion*. For example, Wills traces tensions between missionary and anti-missionary Baptists to the early 1830s when Primitive Baptists refused to associate with missionary Baptists of the South (32).

[14] The lack of interest in holding slaveholders accountable for their slaves' church attendance appears reflective of the larger Civil War-era South, and echoes a lack of literature on the subject.

Raboteau argues that once slaveholders embraced the concept of Christianizing their chattel, recognizing that religion could be an additional tool for maintaining social control, they embraced a concentrated effort to convert blacks to American religion. While slaves initially resisted such efforts, Southern Methodists and Baptists, following the denominational schisms of the 1840s, expended considerable resources to convert slaves and incorporate them into their congregations. By the Civil War, Christianity, at least in terms of doctrine and symbols, was commonplace among slave communities. While William C. Johnson questions historical claims that as many as four million slaves were truly converted to Christianity by the Civil War era, Sandy Martin maintains that slaves identified with the evangelical emphasis on the immediacy of the one supreme God, a broad understanding widely reflected within the otherwise traditional African religious backgrounds of American slaves. While the concept of the individual's direct access to God permeated Protestant evangelicalism, the largely rural Baptist expression of Protestantism expressed in the mid-nineteenth-century American South placed strong emphasis on individual faith, avoided religious ritual, and esteemed vibrant oral proclamation. Thus by the Civil War, Middle Georgia and other Baptist congregations had become home to many black slaves, who, while chafing under white control, found in the Baptist faith an inherent appreciation of individualism lacking on the plantation. In Middle Georgia, white church leaders seemed more concerned with slaves' church membership, rather than enforcing church attendance.[15]

In theory, Baptists' respect for spiritual individualism within the congregational context transcended social structures grounded in the

---

[15] Albert J. Raboteau, *Slave Religion: The 'Invisible Institution' in the Antebellum South* (New York: Oxford University Press, 2004); Sandy Martin, "Black Baptists, African Missions, and Racial Identity, 1800–1915: A Case Study of African American Religion, *Baptist History & Heritage Journal* 35/3 (Summer/Fall 2000): 79–92. See also William C. Johnson, "A Delusive Clothing: Christian Conversion in the Antebellum Slave Community," *Journal of Negro History* 82/3 (Summer 1997): 295–311.

larger world. In practice, cultural norms infiltrated congregational life and spilled over into church member relations. Discipline cases involving personal morality provide a glimpse into the manner in which race relations impacted and evolved within the local church during the war years, in the process intersecting gender issues. While both free and slave were expected to adhere to certain behaviors understood to be central to the living out of the Christian faith, decision-making power remained firmly in the hands of white males, reflective of Southern culture at large.

Echoing other studies of nineteenth century church discipline in the South, men in Baptist congregations of Middle Georgia faced disciplinary charges more frequently than women. Far more than any other moral infraction, drunkenness demanded the repeated attention of local churches both prior to and during the war years. Sparks' study of Mississippi churches evidenced a significant decline in the percentage of alcohol-related discipline cases between the 1820s and 1860. At a time when most Baptist churches used alcohol when observing communion, however, and few considering drinking as a sin, the abuse of alcohol remained significant in the Civil War era, even as it garnered the wrath of church members.

Intoxication resulted in a significant exodus of men from church life. Of the sixty-four identified cases of drunkenness collectively identified in church records of Middle Georgia Baptist congregations for the years 1860–1865, no women were charged. Furthermore, only one instance involved a slave. Moreover, only twenty-two cases occurred during the war-time months, as many male members were away in the Confederate Army. In nearly all discipline cases, white males tried the cases and meted out punishment or forgiveness. Perhaps not surprisingly, male members were prone to forgive their own who abused alcohol: in twenty-eight of sixty-four instances, the offender was forgiven or acquitted upon making an appropriate apology or defense of his actions. Jean Friedman tentatively suggests that such leniency may also be a product of lower moral expectations for male members than female members.[16]

Occurring at a far lower rate than drunkenness, the specific sins of adultery/fornication, dancing, profanity, and stealing nonetheless garnered more ire on the part of local congregations. Adultery and fornication cases combined totaled more than any other type of offense other than drunkenness. Unlike intoxication, reported instances of the sins of the flesh largely involved women, with only eight of twenty-nine charges brought against male individuals. Whereas slaves rarely were charged with drunkenness, ten of the twenty-nine instances of adultery or fornication involved slaves.

---

[16] Local church discipline cases utilized in this study are comprised only of cases that are clearly identifiable in church records of Middle Georgia churches. The incomplete nature of many church records during the war years, coupled with sometimes otherwise sketchy record keeping, do not allow a full reconstruction of church discipline statistics. Each case represents one individual charged with a given offense(s). Few Baptist churches of the Civil War openly questioned drinking in and of itself. Two churches in the Mount Vernon Baptist Association voiced a progressive bent when in April 1860 each congregation passed resolutions against general alcohol use. Jackson Baptist Church in Washington County voted to "recommend" that members stop using alcohol (minutes, April 1860, Georgia Baptist Church Records, Special Collections, Jack Tarver Library, Mercer University, microfilm reel 552) while Bethlehem Baptist Church in Laurens County the same month voted in opposition to the "buying and selling" of "spirits" (minutes, 7 April 1860, GBCR, Mercer, microfilm reel 110). A third congregation, Antioch Baptist in Morgan County, in September 1865 considered the question of whether the church should "tolerate the making and selling of Ardent Spirits by its members," but decided to take no action on the matter (minutes, 10 September 1865, Special Collections, Jack Tarver Library, Mercer University, Macon GA, microfilm reel 372). Drunkenness, however, was not tolerated by Baptist congregations. Often accompanied by the sins of profanity and/or gambling, charges of drunkenness were frequent in church conferences. For Sparks's studies among Mississippi Baptists, see *On Jordan's Stormy Banks*, 153–71. Although studies of Middle Georgia churches of the Civil War era revealed no clear instances in which women were allowed voting power in discipline cases, Sparks's study of Mississippi Baptists revealed that women were allowed to vote in some Primitive Baptist congregations. Friedman (*Enclosed Garden*, 13, 138) cites two nineteenth-century Primitive Baptist congregations in North Carolina that allowed women to vote in discipline cases. On Friedman's expectations for males, see pp. 14 and 132.

While the sins of adultery and fornication demanded no further explanation as to their evil nature, the infraction of dancing sometimes brought forth further commentary. The members of Bethel Baptist Church in Jasper County voiced their opinion of dancing by declaring "that we the church at Bethel believe that dancing is an evil and contrary to religion & is only calculated to lead us from God." Cases of dancing exhibit a gender bias similar to that of adultery and fornication; thirteen of twenty-one instances involved women. As in drunkenness, however, local church records note only one instance of a slave dancing. Profanity, on the other hand, echoed patterns of drunkenness in regards to both gender and race. Of twenty-four reported instances of profanity, all but two involved men, and no slaves were charged with the offense. Thus, according to church records, white men proved almost exclusively susceptible to drunkenness and profanity, while white women were more likely to be charged with sexual sins and dancing. Blacks rarely stood before the local church charged with any of these sins aside from a few instances of sexual sins.[17]

The discipline-related gender trends in Middle Georgia exhibit both differences and similarities from earlier studies of other congregational groups throughout the South. While the prevalence of alcohol and profanity offenses among white males echoes Sparks's study of Mississippi evangelicals, white Baptist women in Middle Georgia were unlike white evangelical women two states to the West. While half again as many Middle Georgia white Baptist women faced accusations of sexual sins (twenty) over against dancing (thirteen), Sparks's study revealed that Mississippi white evangelical women were more than four times as likely to be accused of dancing (40.7 percent) than sexual sins (8.7 percent). On the other hand, Friedman's study of seaboard evangelicals in the South mirrors the experiences of Middle Georgia Baptist women: in terms of specific sins, sexual

---

[17] Minutes, Bethel Baptist Church, Jasper County, March 1863, Special Collections, Jack Tarver Library, Mercer University, Macon GA, microfilm reel 247.

offenses ranked uppermost at 44 percent. While there is limited overlapping between this study and Friedman's study (her sample of fifteen congregations included three Baptist churches in Georgia), the overall discrepancies between the three studies suggest localized factors, perhaps predicated upon denominational identity at the local level, may be reflected in the statistics.[18]

Meanwhile, among the most frequent offenses committed by church members, theft stood as the lone sin largely confined to slaves, as twenty-two of twenty-nine cases involved black members. While usually stated without explanation as to the item or items pilfered, church clerks in two instances reported details. In one case, Solomon was charged as an accomplice to stealing for "buying stolen flower [flour]" and expelled. On 14 April 1861, two days after the firing upon Fort Sumter, "Tom (a servant of Brother Lyne)" and a member of Antioch Baptist Church in Morgan County, "came forward stated to the church that he did take a small portion of syrup from his master at the mill when they first commenced making namely a little to eat was sorry he had ever done that & wished the church to forgive him." Tom was forgiven, one of only two slaves or freemen forgiven for stealing, but not without pastor J. M. Stilwell moralizing about what otherwise seemed a petty offense against slaveholder Lyne. "On motion he was forgiven and the Pastor made a few remarks to him cautioning him against a repetition of the same or any like offense." Forgiveness being the exception, the minister's remarks nonetheless served to reinforce church support of the master-slave relationship. Yet, in the end punishment for stealing was not reserved for slaves and freemen only. Reflecting a degree of egalitarian treatment among the races, only one of seven white members accused of stealing received forgiveness.[19]

---

[18] Sparks, *On Jordan's Stormy Banks*, 161. Friedman, *Enclosed Garden*, 14. Friedman's study focused on sexual sins in particular and did not include dancing offences.

[19] Minutes, Greensboro Baptist Church, Greene County, Special Collections, Jack Tarver Library, Mercer University, Macon GA, microfilm reel 491); minutes,

Other specific moral sins were much less common in local congregations, but collectively reflected the disconnect between the world of whites and blacks and the tendency toward male infractions. In Middle Georgia churches combined, two white members faced lewdness charges. A female member benefited from a verdict of forgiveness, while a male member was excluded. Seven white church members, all but one male, faced charges of gambling or card playing, five for fighting, one for mistreating his wife, and one for slander. One small church, Harmony Primitive Baptist in Pike County, bore more than its share of unusual church discipline cases. One congregant was found guilty for "maliciously killing" a hog belonging to a female member of the same church, resulting in expulsion. An acquittal resulted in a charge made against a member for cutting down a tree in the churchyard. And a third member received a sentence of expulsion for killing a man. In each instance, only white men were involved.[20]

Whereas certain discipline charges were confined to whites, other specific discipline cases remained exclusively in the realm of slaves and pertained to offenses committed by slaves against authority figures. Four slaves were charged with fighting and/or resisting their overseers, two slaves with running away, and three with leaving their master immediately following the war. Of the nine cases, three resulted in exclusion, five ended in forgiveness, and one case produced a dismissal for lack of evidence. A conviction rate of one-third, much less than that of white males charged with drunkenness, may have indicated white members' willingness to hear both sides of the story, or may have reflected openness to pleas of forgiveness. In one notable instance on 28 May 1865, three freemen, members of Smyrna Primitive Baptist Church in Monroe County, faced charges of previously "leaving their master and going to the

---

Bethesda Baptist Church, Greene County, Special Collections, Jack Tarver Library, Mercer University, Macon GA, microfilm reel 11.

[20] Minutes, Harmony Primitive Baptist Church, Pike County, August 1861, April 1865, 10 October 1863, Special Collections, Jack Tarver Library, Mercer University, Macon GA, microfilm reel 608.

Yankees." Having returned (whether voluntarily or not is unclear) Benny, Whitman, and Robert asked for forgiveness, which was granted by their fellow church members.[21]

Other less common disciplinary cases within local churches involved both whites and blacks. Of eight charges of lying, five involved slaves or former slaves. Two women, one a slave, were accused of not living with their husbands. In addition to specific sins, local churches often issued judgments on general charges of "misconduct," "disorder," "disorderly conduct," "contempt," "unchristian conduct" or "unchristianlike conduct." Of twenty-seven such cases, slaves were charged in eleven instances.

The story of Benny, Whitman, and Robert, representative of the frequent forgiveness extended to slaves in Middle Georgia Baptist churches, is at odds with patterns in the South at large. Sparks concludes that among Mississippi evangelical churches, slaves were punished with exclusion more often than whites, citing one congregation in which more than one in three black males on the 1860 church roll were excluded in the years following. Sparks's studies included a number of congregations that allowed blacks to discipline blacks, but records of Middle Georgia Baptist churches record few instances of that. Sparks also concludes that blacks usually received fair hearings comparable to those received by whites, and suggests that black members' higher discipline rates resulted from the difficulty of slaves successfully navigating the often contradictory moral codes of both the white evangelical community and the black community. Yet the experiences of Civil War era Middle Georgia Baptist churches suggest that white males may have recognized the racial dynamics of morality, evidencing a willingness to be lenient in their judgments.[22]

---

[21] Minutes, Smyrna Primitive Baptist Church, Monroe County, May 1865, July 1865, Special Collections, Jack Tarver Library, Mercer University, Macon GA, microfilm reel 85. Sparks's study echoes the prominence of charges of running away and theft targeted at slaves (p. 164).

[22] Sparks, *On Jordan's Stormy Banks*, 163–65.

In the broader picture, although some "sins" remained largely the exclusive domain of whites (drunkenness and profanity) and others strictly applied to blacks (theft and slave-specific offenses), discipline as a whole, including excommunication and forgiveness, cut across racial boundaries. That white Baptists in Middle Georgia seemingly embraced a degree of spiritual equality with their black "brothers" and "sisters" ran counter to prevailing notions among some Southerners. In South Carolina, leaders of the Society for the Propagation for the Gospel lamented that many slave owners prevented slaves from joining churches for fear that baptism would legitimize blacks as social equals. On the other hand, the Middle Georgia Baptist norm of mixed-race congregations differed from the Methodists of Charleston. By the end of the second decade of the nineteenth century, three-fourths of African-American members of the white Methodist churches had left their former congregations and joined the upstart American Methodist Episcopal Church. The majority of at least one of three AME congregations consisted of slaves. The absence of black-only Baptist churches in Middle Georgia both prior to and during the war suggests that slave members did not have the option of starting independent congregations.[23]

Despite the growing numbers of race-specific congregations in some areas of the South, including Savannah, the biracial composition of Middle Georgia Baptist churches, by no means unusual in larger evangelical circles, did serve to reinforce racial divisions. Clarence L. Mohr demonstrates that the predominance of mixed-race congregations in antebellum and Civil War-era Georgia reflected in part an effort by white evangelicals to frame the proslavery position

---

[23] Society for the Propagation of the Gospel, *Classified Digest of the Records of the Society for the Propagation of the Gospel in Foreign Parts 1701–1892* (London: Society for the Propagation of the Gospel, 1893) 16–17; Jason Poole, "On Borrowed Ground: Free African-American Life in Charleston, South Carolina, 1810–1861," in Kevin R. C. Gutzman, *Essays in History*, vol. 36 (Charlottesville: University of Virginia Press, 1994) 1–33. Among this study of Middle Georgia churches, some congregations allowed slave members to hold their own meetings, but only with the permission of and under the supervision of white church leaders.

as a way to improve the circumstances of the enslaved. Bertram Wyatt-Brown makes the same case concerning evangelicals throughout the South.[24]

While forced to remain within the confines of white Baptist life in Middle Georgia in the larger context of social racial control, slaves did not remain altogether powerless within the church house. According to Sandy Martin, evangelical religion, even that represented by slave-owning Baptists in the South, conveyed the characteristics of brotherhood/sisterhood, broad participation and inclusion, an immediacy of the divine realm, and some similarities with African traditional religions in terms of emotional and vibrant expressions of worship. For this reason, following the formation of the Southern Baptist Convention, many slaveholders resisted proslavery mission work among slaves on the plantation. Access to the Bible, whether directly or indirectly, provided slave members with hope for future liberation as they read or listened to the biblical stories of redemption from captivity. Although subject to punishment within the church upon violation of state slave codes, hope of future freedom remained.[25]

If limited spiritual equality did exist across racial lines in Baptist churches in Middle Georgia as evidenced by patterns of discipline, the war altered the larger portrait of discipline within the local church. As table 5.1 demonstrates, in 1860, the churches surveyed in this study dealt with sixty-six identifiable discipline cases, excluding matters related to absences. The following year, the number of cases remained largely steady at sixty-three. After that, church discipline

---

[24] Clarence L. Mohr, "Slaves and White Churches in Confederate Georgia," in John B. Boles, *Masters and Slaves in the House of the Lord: Race and Relations in the American South, 1740–1870* (Lexington: University of Kentucky, 1988) 153–72; Bertram Wyatt-Brown, "Modernizing Southern Slavery: The Proslavery Argument Reinterpreted," in *Region, Race and Reconstruction*, ed. J. Morgan Kousser and James M. McPherson (New York: Oxford University Press, 1982) 27–49.

[25] Martin, "Black Baptists, African Missions," 79–92.

plunged over the next three years to a low of twelve cases in 1864, only to rebound almost to pre-war levels in 1865.

Two factors contributed to the decline in discipline from 1862 to 1864. The loss of large numbers of white males to the military stood foremost. The disruption of many church meetings in the latter half of 1864 due to Sherman's activity in North Georgia further impacted some congregations in the northern portion of Middle Georgia. The number of instances of drunkenness, a sin confined almost solely to white males, further mirrors the wartime migration of that demographic from the pew to the battlefront. Only twenty-two of the sixty-four cases occurred during wartime, while thirty-eight instances of drunkenness took place from 1 January 1860 through 11 April 1861. Forty-seven of sixty-four total cases occurred in 1860 and 1861, while only seventeen were reported from 1862 to 1865, including none in 1864. Whereas local church records rarely reference church members serving in the Confederacy, the reported instances of drunkenness may offer some indication that a significant number of Baptists, the imbibers at least, fought in the war. Compared to the average number of cases of intoxication reported per month in 1860 and 1861 prior to the war, the monthly average plummeted 81 percent during the war. Assuming a correlation existed between drunkenness cases and the number of white male members attending church, one could conclude that as many as four of every five adult male members of Baptist churches in Middle Georgia served in the Confederacy. The actual percentage of members serving in the army was likely lower, however, when taking into account that only men of certain age typically served in the Confederate army (See tables 5.2 and 5.3.).[26]

---

[26] No actual statistics exist documenting the number of Baptists who fought in the Civil War (for either the Confederacy of the Union). As noted in previous chapters, local church records rarely discuss church members fighting in the war. Furthermore, male members enrolled in the army typically remained on church rolls, their absences (apparently) excused because of their military duty. As such, church membership statistics offer little to no insight into numbers of members on the battlefront. In addition, church records of the Civil War era are incomplete, rendering any compilation of discipline cases subject to available documentation.

Whereas cases of drunkenness in local Baptist churches prior to and during the Civil War hint at the extent of the war's impact upon congregations in terms of adult white male attendance, church discipline records also offer insights into race relations within Middle Georgia Baptist congregations during the same time. In the early months of war, as shown in table 5.4, discipline cases brought against blacks by whites increased significantly from pre-war levels, followed by continual decreases from 1862 to 1864 and another spike during the months following the surrender of the South.

The increase in the number of disciplinary cases brought against slaves in the weeks and months immediately following the beginning of the war suggests heightened tensions between blacks and whites. Although blacks could bring charges against blacks, war-time discipline cases involving black members always originated with complaints from white members, oftentimes slave owners. Yet beneath the tension lay complexity. Slave owners frequently, but not always, received resolution in their favor, but Baptist churches in Middle Georgia did not automatically exclude disruptive slaves during the opening months of the war. Two days after the firing upon Fort Sumter, for example, the congregation of Antioch Baptist Church in Morgan County dismissed a charge of stealing against the slave Gabriel. One month later, the same congregation unanimously adopted the resolution of the Georgia Baptist Convention in support of the Confederacy and slavery. Overall, of the sixteen charges brought against slaves in Middle Georgia Baptist churches in 1861 following Fort Sumter, in five instances the accused received forgiveness or the charges were dismissed. And for the remainder of the war, discipline cases against slaves were few. Of the sixteen

---

Few if any local churches actually met at every appointed meeting time. In addition to war-time disruptions in late 1864, inclement weather and temporary lack of pastoral leadership sometimes prevented meetings from taking place. Furthermore, records of Middle Georgia churches during the Civil War era are incomplete owing to factors that include documentation lost in the intervening years and damage to some remaining documents rendering unreadable text in some instances.

recorded cases from 1862 to Appomattox, five ended in forgiveness or the dismissal of charges. In short, white Baptists in Middle Georgia during the Civil War refused to take disciplinary action against slaves in approximately one-third of cases. Conflicted in some instances over whether or not to support the war effort and Confederacy, and how to do so, these white Baptists also expressed a willingness within the confines of their local congregations to side with slaves accused of wrongdoing and against slaveholders.[27]

Church discipline cases in 1865 following the cessation of hostilities between North and South bore witness to new tension and complexity. Confronting a world in which former slaves now stood free, white-led Baptist congregations struggled to deal with the new realities of black-white race relations. They proffered leniency far less often; only one of sixteen cases resulted in dismissal of the charges, and one resulted in forgiveness. Intensified discipline against blacks within churches proved temporary, but only because freedmen in the years following formed their own congregations independent of white supervision. Sparks concludes that the breakup of biracial churches contributed to a dramatic drop in discipline in white churches during Reconstruction and afterwards, reflecting white perception of blacks as less capable of exercising self-control.[28]

The new racial paradigm also impacted the language used to describe black-white relations. White Baptists in Middle Georgia now

---

[27] Minutes, Antioch Baptist Church, Morgan County, Special Collections, Jack Tarver Library, Mercer University, Macon GA, microfilm reel 372. Church records offer no indication that might explain why discipline cases against slaves decline steadily throughout the war. On the one hand, the decline appears counterintuitive: as Southern fortunes became ever bleaker during the last two years of the conflict, one might anticipate an increase in church discipline cases against slaves in order to maintain order and alleviate fears of slave uprisings. Yet the decrease in discipline within churches correlates with Sally E. Hadden's conclusion that slave patrols in Virginia and the Carolinas during the Civil War decreased in the face of hardships brought about by the war. See Sally E. Hadden, *Slave Patrols: Law and Violence in Virginia and the Carolinas* (Cambridge: Harvard University Press, 2001) 167–202.

[28] Sparks, *On Jordan's Stormy Banks*, 151.

Diverging Loyalties

struggled with how to refer to blacks, alternatively using the labels of "former slave," "freedman," "colored brother," and "colored sister." Others simply refused to recognize the freedom granted to former slaves. Providence Baptist Church in Jasper County and Mount Calvary Baptist Church in Pulaski County both continued to refer to their black members as "servants" months after the war ended. Mineral Springs Baptist Church in Washington County referenced black members as "belonging to" the former owner, while Houston Factory Baptist Church in Houston County continued to label blacks as "property." In May 1865, white members of Stone Creek Baptist Church in Twiggs County, refusing to recognize emancipation altogether, voted to expel "each and every colored member" of the congregation that deserted his or her owner and fled to the enemy. Yet by October 1865, even Houston Factory, perhaps then recognizing post-war realities, adopted the moniker "freedmen." Of these five congregations, only Providence Baptist had openly voiced formal support of the Confederacy and war effort, indicating a lack of direct correlation between approval of slavery and open support of the war.[29]

In addition to discipline cases, local church records reveal further insight into racial tensions within Middle Georgia Baptist congregations of the Civil War era. Theological acknowledgements of spiritual equality did not alleviate white concerns about the black race. In September 1860, white members of Antioch Baptist Church in Morgan County complained of "negroes lurking out sid" of the

---

[29] Minutes, Providence Baptist Church, Jasper County, August 1865, Special Collections, Jack Tarver Library, Mercer University, Macon GA, microfilm reel 77; minutes, Mount Calvary Baptist Church, Pulaski County, September 1865, Special Collections, Jack Tarver Library, Mercer University, Macon GA, microfilm reel 384; minutes, Mineral Springs Baptist Church, Washington County, September 1865, Special Collections, Jack Tarver Library, Mercer University, Macon GA, microfilm reel 524; minutes, Houston Factory Baptist Church, Houston County, August 1865, October 1865, Special Collections, Jack Tarver Library, Mercer University, Macon GA, microfilm reel 40; minutes, Stone Creek Baptist Church, Twiggs County, May 1865, Special Collections, Jack Tarver Library, Mercer University, Macon GA, microfilm reel 280.

building during monthly conferences. White members demanded that the troublesome blacks "go in said church" or be forced off the church property. On at least one occasion a Baptist church allowed the use of its house of worship for vigilante committee meetings. In August 1861, New Bethel Baptist Church in Washington County granted the "vigulens committee the use of the meeting house."[30]

Despite some Baptists' insistence on upholding slave laws established by the government, race relations inside the confines of the church meeting house, as noted by W. J. Wellborn and Samuel K. Talmadge, were of a more ambiguous nature. Looked upon in a different light than secular concerns, spiritual matters tested latent attitudes of whites toward blacks, intersecting national loyalties and private fears. Particularly perplexing to whites were instances in which blacks, whether slave or free, voiced a calling from God to preach the Gospel. When black Baptists in Middle Georgia asked white Baptists to grant them the right to preach, whites responded with utmost caution. In the year prior to the war, the two white-led congregations that received such requests ultimately refused to affirm the anointing of God upon their black brethren. On 21 July 1860, "Criffer, a servant of Sister McCoy," a member of Sandy Creek Baptist Church in Morgan County, applied for a "license to preach." His request was "indefinitely postponed." Less than two weeks after Sandy Creek's decision, Zion Baptist Church granted "colored brother" Sam Persall the "liberty to preach at our next meeting." The following month Sam was given permission to preach again in consideration of licensing him to the ministry, but in November the congregation "indefinitely declined granting a license to Sam."[31]

---

[30] Minutes, Antioch Baptist Church, Morgan County, Special Collections, Jack Tarver Library, Mercer University, Macon GA, microfilm reel 372; minutes, New Bethel Baptist Church, Washington County, Special Collections, Jack Tarver Library, Mercer University, Macon GA, microfilm reel 505.

[31] Minutes, Sandy Creek Baptist Church, Morgan County, July 1860, August 1860, Special Collections, Jack Tarver Library, Mercer University, Macon GA, microfilm reel 124; minutes, Zion Baptist Church, Newton County, September–

During the war, two other black Baptists asked for their white church brethren to grant them preaching privileges, and this time the requests were granted. Against the backdrop of Southern defeat at Gettysburg, on 18 July 1863, Bethel Baptist Church of Jasper County "licensed" Thomas Allen a "colored" man "to exercise in public his preaching gifts." Almost exactly a year later, and at a time of suspended discipline of black members of Middle Georgia congregations, New Hope Baptist Church in Greene County "granted brother Tincher a colored man leave to exercise his gifts" of preaching. The varied manner in which the four congregations responded to black members who sought to openly preach the Gospel immediately prior to and during the Civil War years echoed the lack of homogeneity in congregational responses to broader issues of nationalism and slavery during these same years. The four cases generally fit within a pattern of looser restrictions upon black members during the war years, however, than in the months leading up to war.[32]

Baptist congregations that allowed blacks to hold meetings separate from whites also exhibited caution and diversity during the war. Antioch Baptist in Morgan County and Thomaston Baptist in Upson County allowed black members to hold separate meetings from prior to 1860 until April 1861. The beginning of war hostilities put a halt to the practice, but in July 1863 Antioch "agreed to hold meeting on the afternoon of each regular meeting for the benefit of our Black Brethren." Also in 1861, High Shoals Primitive Baptist

---

November 1860, Special Collections, Jack Tarver Library, Mercer University, Macon GA, microfilm reel 315.

[32] Minutes, Bethel Baptist Church, Jasper County, July 1863, Special Collections, Jack Tarver Library, Mercer University, Macon GA, microfilm reel 247; minutes, New Hope Baptist Church, Greene County, July 1864, Special Collections, Jack Tarver Library, Mercer University, Macon GA, microfilm reel 473. In three of the four instances of black Baptists requesting a license to preach, only one expressly referred to the member in question as a slave.

Church in Monroe County in October voted to "partition a portion of the meeting house for the use of the colored people."[33]

Another Morgan County church, Madison Baptist, worked extensively and, according to church records, harmoniously in relating with black members during the final throes of the Confederacy and the months following the end of the war. In December 1863, as wartime hardships mounted in the South, Madison Baptist Church appointed "a committee to make arrangements for a place of worship for the blacks." Whether this was requested by black members or demanded by white members is unclear. The white membership two-and-a-half years earlier had endorsed the Georgia Baptist Convention resolution in support of the war and Confederacy, to the point of including a copy of the resolution in church minutes. In addition, in 1860 the congregation had considered naming deacons "among the blacks," only to decline to take action on the matter. Regardless of the motivations behind the decision to obtain a place of worship for black members, the action set in motion a chain of events that ultimately led to the foundation of a new congregation. In April 1864, white members voted to raise funding to buy or build a church building for black members. The building was apparently in place when, in September after the war ended, white members voted to support the "blacks" if they chose to organize as a separate congregation. The following day, "at a called conference for the blacks...that portion of the church signified their desire to organize a separate and independent church." The white membership granted letters of dismissal to the black members, and in November voted to allow the "Colored Baptist Church of Madison" to use the building previously constructed for black services, as long as the building was kept in "good repair." The freedmen agreed to

---

[33] Minutes, Antioch Baptist Church, Morgan County, Special Collections, Jack Tarver Library, Mercer University, Macon GA; minutes, Thomaston Baptist Church, Upson County, Special Collections, Jack Tarver Library, Mercer University, Macon GA; minutes, High Shoals Primitive Baptist Church, Monroe County, Special Collections, Jack Tarver Library, Mercer University, Macon GA, microfilm reel 301.

the conditions the following month. In short, in the case of Madison Baptist, despite the nationalistic sentiments of white members, blacks and whites ultimately bargained an agreement and parted ways by the end of 1865, although the white congregation remained, for the present, in ownership of the building housing the new black congregation.[34]

In a similar fashion, black members claimed newfound autonomy and departed First Baptist Church in Macon in the months following the end of the war. Prior to the war, black members, while ultimately remaining subject to white members, enjoyed more autonomy than in most biracial Baptist churches throughout the South. Meeting separately under the supervision of the pastor since 1845, black members by 1854 "had their own house of worship," conducted "their own services, under the direction of licensed ministers and deacons of their own color" and received and excluded "their own members." Ordinances, however, were "administered by the Pastor of the whole Church." Macon Baptist's black membership continued to grow, and by the end of the war years First Baptist Macon included three congregations, one white and two black, with the latter serving as arms or branches of the main congregation. Following the war, white members in September 1865 voted to dissolve their "connection with the colored church...provided they wish it." Both black congregations expressed their desire to be independent. First Baptist Macon became a white-only congregation as former black members obtained full autonomy.[35]

The seemingly amicable parting of ways of blacks and whites in the Madison and Macon churches belied deeper racial tensions in immediate post-war Middle Georgia. In addition to a few white

---

[34] Minutes, Madison Baptist, Morgan County, December 1863, April 1864, September 1865, November 1865, December 1865, Special Collections, Jack Tarver Library, Mercer University, Macon GA, microfilm reel 51.

[35] Minutes, First Baptist Church Macon; minutes, Rehoboth Baptist Association, 1854, Special Collections, Jack Tarver Library, Mercer University, Macon GA. Also see H. Lewis Batts, *History of the First Baptist Church of Christ at Macon* (Macon GA: Southern Press, 1969) 37–58.

Baptist churches continuing to refer to blacks as enslaved, others complained about the new attitudes of free people. In May 1865, Midway Baptist Church in Bibb County formed a committee to investigate "disorderly" blacks. Although the committee disbanded one month later, in September some members complained of blacks speaking aloud during preaching. Also in September, Mount Calvary Baptist Church in Pulaski County expelled a "servant" for nonattendance. Two months later white members voted to maintain the status quo with blacks by continuing the practice of not allowing "colored" members to have a voice in church conferences. Greensboro Baptist Church in Greene County delivered mixed signals to black members following the war. In August white members ordained "Bro Charles Sewell, colored" into the "office of ministry." Yet the following month whites voted to prohibit the "colored brethren" from using the church building without permission. Three months later white members approved the ordination of an unnamed "colored" member.[36]

Other congregations understood the inevitability of change but responded cautiously. Bethesda Baptist Church in Greene County offered little commentary on race relations prior to the end of the war. In December 1861, blacks were allowed to hold a funeral service in the church, and in September 1864 they were allowed to hold preaching services. Not until September 1865 did white members begin to address race relations in earnest, in light of blacks' freedom. Seeking to exercise their autonomy, black members sought the use of the church building for regular services, a request initially granted in September. The following month, a freedman named Derry declared to the church that God had called him to preach, and sought the approval of white members. In November, the white members of Bethesda licensed Denny to preach, and in December granted blacks

---

[36] Minutes, Midway Baptist Church, Bibb County, Special Collections, Jack Tarver Library, Mercer University, Macon GA, microfilm reel 69; minutes, Mount Calvary Baptist Church, Pulaski County; minutes, Greensboro Baptist Church, Greene County, Special Collections, Jack Tarver Library, Mercer University, Macon GA, microfilm reel 491.

ongoing rights to use the church building for services. Thus, over the course of the last four months of 1865, black members increasingly petitioned whites for more autonomy within the larger congregation as well as the recognition of leadership within their own ranks, requests granted in successive stages by whites.[37]

Baptist congregations in Middle Georgia that took intentional steps in post-war 1865 toward recognizing altered race relations were the exception rather than the rule. Madison Baptist and Macon Baptist quickly assisted their black members in the quest for independent, religious self-determination. Bethesda Baptist gradually allowed blacks greater latitude within the congregation. Greensboro Baptist maintained strict parameters on black worship yet ordained two freedmen. Otherwise, Baptist congregations displayed no noticeable progress in granting self-determination to blacks within the context of the local church. In the latter instances black members, evidencing religious bonds forged while slaves, did not conduct an immediate mass exodus from white-controlled congregations, but rather assessed their circumstances in the next few years. For their part, whites maintained paternalistic attitudes, voiced concern for the freedmen in the years immediately following the war, and declared that free blacks would best be served by remaining with their current congregations. Thus the hesitation of freedmen coupled with the defensiveness and assertiveness of whites ensured an uneasy status quo into 1866.

Meeting in September 1866, the Rehoboth Baptist Association openly addressed the question of "the religious status of the colored people and our corresponding obligations and duty." The report concluded that in relation to the "colored race.... it would not be best to separate from them in our church relations." Retaining the practice of integrated churches was desirable because whites would "have much to do in making them good citizens and valuable laborers." Ignoring the few instances in which blacks had formed their own

---

[37] Minutes, Bethesda Baptist Church, Greene County, Special Collections, Jack Tarver Library, Mercer University, Macon GA, microfilm reel 11.

congregations and exhibiting a paternalistic bent, the report declared, "they are not prepared to set up in churches for themselves.... we think it manifestly for the interest of both races that we should keep them with us, and exert over them a paternal, Christian influence." Encouraging churches to form Sunday schools for blacks, Rehoboth Baptists were also warned that "the time is not distant when the churches will be called upon to ordain colored men to the work of the ministry," an eventuality for which "few of them" were prepared. "Great caution should be exercised" in so doing, the report concluded.[38]

Thomaston Baptist Church of Upson County, a member of the Rehoboth Association, provided an example of the situation that the association assumed most churches faced a year and a half after the war. Although no longer under obligation to the leadership of whites and despite growing racial tensions, the black members of the congregation chose to remain in the white-controlled church. Not until summer 1866 did tension spill over. From June through August, whites and blacks voiced disagreement concerning the proposed ordination of a black man named John Beall. Church records do not record the outcome of the conflict, but two summers later the congregation's black members, although meeting separately from the whites, remained an official part of the church.[39]

In the cities of Macon and Milledgeville, however, some white Baptists recognized that black Baptists were ready to stand on their

---

[38] Minutes, Rehoboth Baptist Association, 1866, 3, 10–11, Special Collections, Jack Tarver Library, Mercer University, Macon GA.

[39] Minutes, Thomaston Baptist Church, Upson County, 1865–1868, Special Collections, Jack Tarver Library, Mercer University, Macon GA; also see Edwin L. Cliburn, *In Unbroken Line: A History of the First Baptist Church of Thomaston, Georgia* (Tallahassee FL: Rose Printing, 1979) 133–49. The focus of this work is on the years 1860–1865. Thomaston Baptist is cited as representative of a larger pattern of Baptist churches in Middle Georgia directly addressing reconfigured race relations later in the decade. The aforementioned Rehoboth Baptist Association statement reflects the position of member churches in late 1866, at that point beginning to grapple with new racial configurations within the local church setting.

own. Following a request "from certain colored brethren from Macon and Milledgeville, in relation to the organization of a new colored Association," white Baptist delegates at the 1866 Central Baptist Association meeting expressed commendation for blacks forming their own association, expressing hope that "the greatest success may attend their efforts" and offering to assist "where such ministry is acceptable to them." While the Rehoboth Association sought to keep freedmen close by under paternalistic watch, the Central Association offered to assist black Baptists in their move toward independence.[40]

In immediate post-war Middle Georgia, black Baptists thus exerted their new status in different ways. Few chose congregational independence in the early months following the war. In two instances of early disassociation, Madison Baptist and Macon Baptist, former slaves departed congregations whose white members had expressed open and ardent nationalistic beliefs. In 1866, other black Baptists sought to develop religious organizations outside the scope of the local church. On the other hand, the 1866 statement adopted by the largely rural churches of the Rehoboth Baptist Association fits a pattern in the larger South as identified by Alwyn Barr. White Christians sought to retain former slaves in their churches "as a means of control or influence." According to Barr, "efforts to retain black members persisted the longest in Congregational, Episcopal and Presbyterian churches." Nonetheless, the relative equality experienced by blacks in some Baptist churches prior to the Civil War ultimately equipped blacks for a successful transition to religious self-determination. As Samuel Hill notes, "the formation of independent black congregations and denominations...proved to be the most profound religious change brought on by the Civil War." Thus, post-war 1865 in Middle Georgia largely served as a pregnant pause leading to the ensuing years in which racial configurations in the

---

[40] Minutes, Central Baptist Association, 1866, 8–9, Special Collections, Jack Tarver Library, Mercer University, Macon GA.

local church setting would be examined and reexamined by both blacks and whites.[41]

In short, discipline, while negative by nature and painful in execution, served the purpose of maintaining a pure church, broadly cutting across racial and gender lines in the enforcement of individual morality. Yet in practice it also revealed, by case type, racial and gender divisions in Baptist churches. Black members, moreover, bore the burden of an additional layer of control as whites served as judges of the inner spirituality of slaves and freed persons. Championing spiritual equality in theory, church discipline in the Civil War era, when complemented by other means of control targeted at black members, echoed larger racial tensions prior to Reconstruction. During the war, even the lenient congregation of Macon First Baptist did not allow black members full autonomy in spiritual matters.

White women, understood as inferior to white men by virtue of their gender, were also prohibited from full participation in congregational life. Black men could and sometimes did serve as preachers, but during the Civil War era white women were not allowed the same privilege. Nor could they take up the duties of deacons or other leadership roles. Such prohibitions often left Baptist women silent. Nonetheless, white women, long numerically dominant within Southern evangelical churches, arose to even greater prominence as the war progressed. While church discipline trends reflected expanding (if hesitant) degrees of freedom for black members, the loss of white male members increased congregational reliance upon white women while reinforcing established gender

---

[41] Alwyn Barr, "Black Urban Churches on the Southern Frontier, 1865–1900," *The Journal of Negro History* 82/3 (Autumn 1997): 368; Samuel S. Hill, "Religion and the Results of the Civil War," in *Religion and the American Civil War*, ed. Randall M. Miller (New York: Oxford University Press, 1998) 366. Also see Janet Duitsman Cornelius, *Slave Missions and the Black Church in the Antebellum South* (Columbia: University of South Carolina Press, 1999). Cornelius argues that antebellum slave mission efforts prepared the way for the growth of independent African-American churches in the decades following the Civil War.

roles. This trend reflects conclusions reached by Jean E. Friedman, who explored Southern evangelicals in the broader nineteenth-century context. Women's responses to congregational revivals during the war ensured a prominent presence in the pew. Taking place in late summer and early autumn, Baptist revivals in Middle Georgia were planned events of both spiritual and social significance. Proscribed for the purpose of winning converts to the Gospel and adding new members to church rolls, revivals also provided opportunities for community and social interaction. Church records often recorded souls saved and new members secured during revival week, while offering no social commentary.[42]

Baptists understood the difference between a time set aside for revival and a time of revival. Revival preachers expressly sought to save souls. Revivals that did not result in the salvation of souls lacked evidences of success, other dimensions of the event notwithstanding. Furthermore, revivals in which only a handful of decisions were made, whether for salvation or church membership, indicated only a marginally successfully revival season. On the other hand, preachers and laity alike rejoiced during revivals in which souls filled the aisles of the church seeking forgiveness for sins and/or a new church home.[43]

---

[42] Friedman, *The Enclosed Garden*, 129–30. The revivalist concern for the salvation of souls, characteristic in local church records in Middle Georgia, differed from many Protestant revivalist emphases in the North. For an analysis of the manner in which Northern Protestant revivals displayed an increasing concern for society's ills in the antebellum era, see Timothy L. Smith, *Revivalism and Social Reform: American Protestantism on the Eve of the Civil War* (Eugene OR: Wipf & Stock, 2004).

[43] Scheduled revivals typically took place between July and October. Invariably, the time frames in which the most members joined Baptist churches in Middle Georgia coincided with revival season. For purposes of this study, in regards to statistical analysis, "revival" is defined as a two-month-or-less period in the life of a given church in which church records indicate that at least five persons joined by "experience" (i.e., initial converts asking for baptism). In addition, when counting the total number of decisions made in the above-defined revival, additions to the congregation are included. For example, in a given

With many male members in the army, congregational revivals that resulted in five or more new converts ebbed during the course of the war. Whereas a total of thirteen such revivals took place in 1860, only four occurred in the years 1861, 1862, and 1864, as shown in table 5.5. But 1863 witnessed eight revivals, following the agonizing losses at Gettysburg and Vicksburg. Following the end of the war, twelve revivals occurred in Middle Georgia. The number of new members resulting from these revivals followed a similar trajectory, with 1865 experiencing the greatest increase in church membership.

The revival trends evident among Baptist congregations in Middle Georgia of the Civil War era are consistent with broader church membership trends identified by historians of nineteenth-century religion. Roger Finke and Rodney Stark's research indicates that the percentage of churched Americans doubled between 1776 and 1850, reaching 34 percent in the latter year. Labeling this trend "the churching of America," Finke and Stark demonstrate that in the decade of the 1850s, church membership continued rising, to a total of 37 percent of the population by 1860. The Civil War, however, decimated the ranks of church members. By the end of the Civil War, Robert Wuthnow estimates that less than 20 percent of Americans remained in the nation's pews. Southern church attendance, evidencing a higher rate than in the North, experienced "a serious decline in adherence" during the war and the early years of Reconstruction, and stood at 35 percent in 1870, according to Finke and Stark. Despite Southern evangelical struggles into Reconstruction, the end of the war in 1865 thus marked the beginning of a second period of nineteenth-century church growth in America. Wunthrow's research indicates a doubling of churched Americans, from 20 percent to 40 percent, between 1865 and 1900. Finke and Stark paint a more optimistic figure, citing 1906 as the year in which church membership crossed the 50 percent divide in America. As such, the revivals that took place in Middle Georgia Baptist

---

revival, five persons may have joined by experience, and an additional two by "letter" (signifying changing membership to the new congregation).

congregations in the months following the cessation of national hostilities proved a foreshadowing of an extended national period of religious revival.[44]

As church membership evidenced dramatic decreases nationwide during the war, and revivals in Baptist churches in Middle Georgia waned, white women displayed a consistently greater propensity to respond to the church's call to salvation during revivals at a time when many white male members served in the Confederate Army. Despite the post-war return of Southern men to the home-front, the pattern of female responses to revivalist appeals continued in the months immediately following the end of war hostilities. Black Baptist responses to revivals, by contrast, dropped sharply in the early years of war, rose dramatically during the second half of the war, then returned to 1860 levels in 1865. In short, Baptist revivals in Middle Georgia during the Civil War era typically resulted in new converts primarily in the form of white women (see tables 5.6 and 5.7).

The number and results of revivals reinforce Civil War era patterns of male members serving in the Confederate army distant to their home churches. Accordingly, revival responses suggest the growing importance of women within local congregations both during and after the war. Conversations about and from Baptist women indicate that the growing number of women converts also corresponded with a heightened consciousness concerning women's role within the church.

In the second year of war, the Rehoboth Baptist Association, assessing the impact of the war upon Baptist congregations, formally acknowledged the need for women to assume greater leadership roles as well, albeit within the context of women's sphere. In the face of immense losses of the lives of young men in the war, "the

---

[44] Roger Finke and Rodney Start, *The Churching of America, 1776–1990* (New Brunswick NJ: Rutgers University Press, 1992; 1997) 15,16, 55; Robert Wuthnow, *The Restructuring of American Religion: Society and Faith Since World War II* (Princeton: Princeton University Press, 1998) 21–22.

education of the young for some time to come will devolve more than ever upon females," delegates ascertained. While Rehoboth Baptists recognized the growing importance of women in the spiritual and temporal caretaking of their children, the *Christian Index* recruited women to anonymously address Baptist men on the battlefront in a series titled, "Women's Words to the Soldiers." Reflecting the role of the female gender as guardians of morality, one unsigned editorial by a Baptist woman warned churchmen to avoid the wickedness of army camps. Christian men must be cautious and diligent while away from home and women's influence, the author insisted. Unrestrained freedoms and rampant immorality endangered male integrity. Temptations abounded in army camps, while a uniform was believed to allow "unlimited license in all the wickedness of this world." When church membership proved too distant to ensure righteous behavior, the memory of wives and mothers should cause wayward-prone men to remain faithful to religion and morals[45]

Utilizing women as a trump card in the battle for morality in the army camps, male *Index* editors did not hesitate to appropriate the image of Christian womanhood in their own writings. "Twelve months after this Revolution commenced," declared one writer in summer 1864, "a more ungodly set of men could scarcely be found than the Confederate army." Yet at the present, cursing was rare, religious songs common, and gratitude to God prevalent. The moral rectitude of wives and mothers on the home-front had helped turn the tide. The removal of sin from camp life assured the South of victory. The army, now comprised of "Christian patriots," realized the sacred object to be accomplished and trusted in their commanders. Such a righteous army, the writer insisted, "may be temporarily overpowered by vastly superior numbers, but they never can be conquered. Our armies, God being with us, are invincible." The presence of God in the camps, in this instance, could be

---

[45] Minutes, Rehoboth Baptist Association, 1862, 6–8, Special Collections, Jack Tarver Library, Mercer University, Macon GA; "Woman's Words to the Soldier," *Christian Index*, 12 August 1862, 1.

attributed in no small degree to the righteous influence of women. Furthermore, woe be to the man who tried to take advantage of wives and mothers on the home-front, as did one "Bro. Slade" who was reprimanded for "selling wheat to the wives of soldiers at $1.00 per bushel!"[46]

Army chaplains also turned to memories of wives and mothers in an effort to help their charges stay on the straight and narrow path. In Virginia, Chaplain Ivy W. Duggan of the 49th Georgia evoked such imagery as he reported on the revivals among the soldiers. "When we assemble here in the groves of Virginia," Duggan noted, "we seat ourselves upon the leaves that cover the ground, and sing the same old songs that we sang with you long ago. No sweet voice of mother, sister, or wife, softens our music here, but we trust that your voices mingle with ours in harmony at the mercy seat."[47]

Their moral aura honored by Baptist leaders on the home-front and within army ranks, churched white women seem to have willingly accepted their enhanced role as guardians of righteousness, even as they largely remained silent in church business affairs. In so doing, they remained within Friedman's "enclosed garden." In only a few instances, Friedman concludes, did white women challenge "the rule of silence." Female efforts to ensure the "purity of the church" typically found embodiment in influence, example and conversation, a pattern followed by white Baptist women in Middle Georgia.[48]

In short, while growth in numbers did not translate into equality with male members, it did provide a greater sense of participation in ensuring and propitiating the moral codes of the local congregation. Whether women owned their own voices while advocating the moral codes of male-led congregations is questionable. Articles and essays written by women remained subject to the approval of male editors and clergy, who also took the liberty to appropriate the community's

---

[46] "The Spirit of Our Country, of Our Women, and of Our Soldiers," *Christian Index*, 1 July 1864, 2; "Brief Mention," *Christian Index*, 6 November 1863, 1.

[47] Ivy W. Duggan, "From the Wilderness," *Christian Index*, 8 June 1863, 1.

[48] Friedman, *Enclosed Garden*, 13–14.

image of women as a tool for harnessing the morality of Baptist men serving in the military.

Yet white women in Baptist congregations had legitimate reason to be concerned about the army camps, for the camps proved to be the primary testing grounds in the lives of their men for challenging the bounds of morality. While Baptists on the home-front refused to allow government-sponsored chaplains for fear of breaching the separation of church and state, and the few Baptists serving as ministers among soldiers, as well as *Index* editor Samuel Boykin, grew increasingly frustrated over the lack of interest among home-front ministers in volunteering to serve as army chaplains and missionaries, the immorality of camp life elicited widespread verbal concern.

One chaplain observed that the wickedness of camp life drew him closer to God. Recognizing soldiers as both the hope and bane of the South, a January 1863 editorial praised the South's noble warriors and professed pride and exultation as weary and hungry soldiers faithfully stood between the enemy and the home-front. Yet the writer sharply chastised the South's heroes as "addicted to the vices of the camp." Recounting a now-standard litany of camp sins—sabbath-breaking, gambling, and profanity—the editorial added to the list "robbery and stealing."[49]

Often singled out by Baptists, the "hideous evil" of card playing and gambling, permeating the Confederate army and recognizing no difference between soldier and officer, solicited wrath from home-front observers. Unwilling to recognize the frequent boredom in camp as the cause of card playing, home-front Baptists justified killing in warfare as the will of God while identifying gambling as a horrendous sin and a sure mark of godlessness. "Most sickening is it to behold those who one day are reveling in a carnival of death—standing almost at the judgment bar of God to answer for unnumbered sins, yet saved by a merciful providence—and the next

---

[49] *Christian Index*, 26 August 1862, 2; "Our Duties to Our Enemies," *Christian Index*, 19 January 1863, 1.

day, forgetful of their danger and their escape—forgetful of the God who sheltered them—forgetful of the duty of repentance they owe to him, sitting down to play a sinful game of cards." Oblivious to the irony of sanctifying slaughter while reviling table games, the editorial sought to shame soldiers for their immorality. Card playing, the writer admonished, took bread from the mouth of hungry family members and deprived them of clothing and wood for warmth. Such behavior was unacceptable, for God demanded, and family expected, moral purity from the soldiers.[50]

Drunkenness also affected camp life. Pastor Ebenezer W. Warren of First Baptist Church in Macon reserved harsh words for intemperate soldiers and officials who allowed such behavior. "Winked at by the authorities" despite warnings from Confederate President Jefferson David, drunkenness risked bringing the wrath of the God upon the South. Warren insisted that the president should dismiss any officer who refused to abstain "from the use of intoxicating liquors." Lowering such rhetoric following Gettysburg, Baptist ministers nonetheless remained concerned about morality in the camps. Dancing and liquor plagued the camps of Virginia during the winter lull in fighting of 1864, with local liquor shops selling cheap alcohol to soldiers garnering particular criticism. One army correspondent claimed to have witnessed more instances of drunkenness in the past two months than in the previous year. The government refused to outlaw selling liquor to soldiers, to the ministers' consternation.[51]

Less frequently mentioned, the sin of dancing, an offense largely confined to women in local church life, evidenced itself in camp life in Virginia during the harsh winter of 1864. Military conflicts and maneuvers suspended because of the weather, officers sought entertainment to alleviate boredom. General Robert E. Lee,

---

[50] "Card Playing and Gambling in the Army," *Christian Index*, 16 March 1863, 1.

[51] W., "Army Correspondence of the Index," *Christian Index*, 26 February 1864, 1; W., "Army Correspondence of the Index," *Christian Index*, 4 March 1864, 1.

disapproving of some forms of entertainment, garnered the praise of at least one chaplain for rebuking his officers for "getting up a grand military ball" during the downtime of the winter months. "This is *not* 'a time for dancing,'" the chaplain noted. He also commended Lee for urging liquor shops to refuse sales to soldiers.[52]

Shifting blame for camp sins to the influence of cities represented an evolving construct that allowed Baptists, in the face of mounting battlefield losses, to praise the South's defenders without denying the evils of camp life. Noting that war naturally decreased morality in the lives of soldiers, one army correspondent pointed to city vices as especially troublesome. Yet arguing that Southern armies remained more virtuous than circumstances would indicate, the writer insisted that mission efforts among the South's soldiers had at least prevented morals from degrading further.[53]

In short, the Civil War posed challenges to Baptist understandings of morality and freedom. Within local congregations, disciplinary patterns evolved to reflect the absence of many white males and the changing reality of slavery. White men yet faced typical charges of intoxication and profanity, while white women remained the primary culprits for sexual sins. Intoxication in congregations became less of an issue during the war months. At the same time, the war brought a decrease in charges against black members. Less prone to disciplinary action, black members sought, successfully in some cases, to stretch the boundaries of their congregational freedoms. Meanwhile, white women gained a new sense of numerical prominence within their own sphere of church life, comprising a growing bulk of persons responding to revival calls for salvation and achieving greater recognition for their role in ensuring male morality and training young people. For their part, white male members serving in the military confronted, and often succumbed to, temptations outside the control of congregational

---

[52] W., "Army Correspondence of the Index," *Christian Index*, 4 March 1864, 1.
[53] STAR, "Correspondence from the Army of Tennessee," *Christian Index*, 6 May 1864, 1.

safeguards, causing great consternation from home-front church members.

Chapter 6

Local Church Responses

Long after the Civil War came to a close, a Georgia resident and survivor of the conflict recalled years of hardship. Born in 1852 and a child when her father marched off to war in the service of the Confederacy, Mary Mize witnessed his death from typhoid fever while he was at home on leave. "He left ma with six chilluns, three boys and three girls," she remembered. "I was the oldest and I had to help ma raise the chilluns, but we worked hard, everybody had to work hard then. I have seen people cry and beg for something to eat. But I took those chillun and sent them to school, and I made them help me when they got home. We did all kinds of field work. Mother and me had to make all our clothes, spin the cotton and weave the cloth. Child, we have had to sit at night, spin cotton and weave by a light'ood knot for light a many a time."[1]

Food was scarce, but nonetheless they shared what they could with neighbors. "We have had folks to come to our smoke house a many a time and get the dirt and boil it for salt," Mize recalled. "And we didn't have no sugar either. Ma never let the syrup barrel get empty, unless, she was cleaning it out to fill it again with fresh syrup. We sweetened pies, cakes and coffee and liked it as good as we like sugar today."[2]

---

[1] Mrs. W. W. Mize, "Life during Confederate Days," *American Life Histories: Manuscripts from the Federal Writers' Project, 1936–1940*, transcript online at http://memory.loc.gov/cgi-bin/query/r?ammem/wpa:@field(DOCID+@lit(wpa 112070108)) (accessed 14 June 2011). The 1939 interview took place in Athens GA. Mary V. Mize, age fifty-seven, is listed as the wife of William W. Mize of Clarke County GA in the 1910 United States census. A widow, still resided in Clarke County in 1930, and is presumably the interviewee.

[2] Ibid.

In spite of the direst of times in which survival itself hung in the balance, faith in God did not waiver. "My mother would never let us cook on Sundays, we had to cook enough Saturdays to last till Monday.... We was raised to go to church. I allus saw that my brothers and sisters had good enough clothes to go. You see my oldest brother was a preacher and a fine Baptist preacher he was. My mother's father was a preacher, she had three brothers and one son that was preachers. I ain't bragging but my people on both sides were good."[3]

Baptists, like others of the early and mid-nineteenth century, personally suffered when calamities and financial hardships pressed upon their families and lands. Yet within their local church communities, as within associational bodies, their collective voices prior to the Civil War rarely spoke to events occurring in the world beyond the doors of the church. Acknowledgement of the outside world, when discussed at all, tended to be framed in terms of the believers' duty to live righteous lives in a sinful world. Holy living, tied directly to personal morality, was of utmost importance. Drunkenness, gambling, adultery, fornication, and other worldly amusements were to be avoided and warranted punishment. Baptists in the South, unlike an increasing number of Baptists in the North, tended to avoid or ignore the larger social implications within the teachings of Jesus.[4]

Despite the reticence to formally engage worldly matters in local church records, Baptists and other evangelicals in the South became increasingly intertwined with the larger world as the Southern frontier gave way to modernizing influences. On the frontier, the evangelical expression of plain folk democracy,

---

[3] Ibid.

[4] For a discussion of the shaping of Baptist views in the South prior to the Civil War, see John B. Boles, *The Great Revival 1785–1805: The Origins of the Southern Evangelical Mind* (Lexington: University Press of Kentucky, 1972); John B. Boles, *The Great Revival: Beginnings of the Bible Belt* (Lexington: University Press of Kentucky, 1996); Christine Heyrman, *Southern Cross: The Beginnings of the Bible Belt* (New York: Alfred A. Knopf, 1997).

evidencing itself in a revolt against the wealthy and powerful, proved too pervasive for the elite to ignore. Politicians appealed to the popular ideals shaped by evangelicalism, revivals, and political rallies often mirroring one another. Yet the taming of the frontier resulted in both thriving towns and institutional religion, as evangelical sects grew numerically and transitioned into denominational entities. In the words of Randy Sparks, town churches became "fashionable" and less likely to challenge Southern society. Lay leadership gave way to top-down authority, city ministers embraced education and wealth, and city churches evidenced transformation in preaching, worship, and musical styles. Among urban congregations, revivalism, formerly expressed in camp meetings, gave way to less exuberant protracted meetings. In short, city evangelicals embraced modernism, while traditional rural evangelicals remained suspicious of society, wealth, and education.[5]

The growing disparity between rural and urban evangelicals in the decades prior to the Civil War left city Baptists increasingly detached from rural Baptists such as Mary Mize. While Baptists from all walks of life marched off to fight for the Confederacy, urban Baptist Samuel Boykin criticized rural Baptist churches in January 1864 for not joining their urban brethren in offering "prayer meetings for our country." While offering no analysis of his charge, Boykin's complaint concerning the lack of patriotic activity on the part of country congregations revealed a perception that disparity between urban and rural congregations found expression in attitudes toward the Confederacy and war.[6]

In an area of the state only lightly touched by enemy fire and cannon balls, Boykin's criticism of rural Baptists hinted at patterns of response to the war and Confederacy. Baptists of the region did share some similarities with congregations located on the battlefronts.

---

[5] Randy J. Sparks in *On Jordan's Stormy Banks: Evangelicalism in Mississippi 1773–1876* (Athens: University of Georgia Press, 1994) 78–114; Samuel S. Hill, ed., *Encyclopedia of Religion in the South* (Macon GA: Mercer University Press, 1984) 293–97.

[6] "The Situation—Baptistically Speaking," *Christian Index*, 8 January 1864, 2.

Losses of loved ones to warfare and sickness, increasing financial and emotional despair, and growing threat of Northern ideologies usurping the Southern way of life were shared by Baptists throughout the South. In a broader perspective, James McPherson argues that enlistment in the Confederate Army reflected such factors as individual initiative, regional loyalty, proslavery convictions, ideological beliefs, community pride, and family ties. These personalized themes embedded within regional consciousness impacted church life throughout the South. Yet while Baptist laity did their part in filling the ranks of regiments from Middle Georgia, local churches, reflecting their status as religious sanctuaries, offered little commentary on the enlistment and departure of their sons, fathers, husbands, and brothers.[7]

Weekly city services and monthly rural gatherings continued as prior to the war, with the exception of some disruptions during fall 1864 in the face of Sherman's presence in North Georgia. Ramouth Baptist Church in Putnam County proved a rare exception to the continuity, as on 6 July 1861 the congregation lamented "our beloved pastor...has gone to the war and we are left without a supply." Reflective of Middle Georgia churches at large, the twenty-six churches of the Central Association in 1863 were pastored or supplied by twenty men who had been serving prior to the war, some of whom led more than one congregation. The remaining six ministers, three of whom assisted established pastors, were new to the association. In short, few Baptist church worship services were curtailed for lack of pastoral leadership.[8]

---

[7] James W. McPherson, *For Cause and Comrades: Why Men Fought in the Civil War* (New York: Oxford University Press, 1997). See also Gardiner H. Shattuck, Jr., *A Shield and a Hiding Place: The Religious Life of the Civil War Armies* (Mercer University Press, 1987).

[8] Minutes, Ramouth Baptist Church, Special Collections, Jack Tarver Library, Mercer University, Macon GA, microfilm reel 197; minutes, Central Baptist Association, 1863, Special Collections, Jack Tarver Library, Mercer University, Macon GA. Records of other Middle Georgia congregations also indicate continuity in area pulpits. Although records of many congregations of the period have not survived intact, associational records offer no indication of a significant

Other patterns of Baptist interaction with the war and Confederacy reveal more complexity. Boykin's charge that rural congregations neglected prayer meetings on behalf of the country may have been genuine. From the opening months of war, denominational entities and leaders, as well as Confederate leaders, had expressly asked congregations to vocalize their support of the Confederacy and war. The Georgia Baptist Convention, meeting in April 1861, called upon all Georgia Baptist churches to pass resolutions in support of the new nation and the armed conflict. Other denominational directives followed as the war progressed. In late 1862, denominational leaders further called upon Baptist churches to evangelize Southern soldiers. Secular leaders made similar appeals. Confederate President Jefferson Davis repeatedly requested that churches hold days of fasting, prayer, and thanksgiving. Churches also asked to donate material goods in support of the Southern cause. In each instance, the pressure upon churches to take concrete action was public in nature, while the institution issuing the directive (whether religious or secular) did so in a manner of expectancy.[9]

---

reduction in church activities during the Civil War years, with the exception of the period that encompassed Sherman's presence in Georgia. In at least one instance (Thomaston Baptist Church in Upson County) a pastor departed to serve as a chaplain, only to return a short time later to resume his pastorate. Finally, historians debate about why men fought in the Civil War, with James M. McPherson's *For Cause and Comrades: Why Men Fought in the Civil War* (New York: Oxford University Press, 1997) widely recognized as the authoritative volume regarding soldier motives. McPherson analyzed 25,000 letters and 250 diaries, representing both Union and Confederate soldiers, determining that slavery, whether for or against, was the primary motivator of military service, rising above a host of lesser reasons.

[9] Minutes, Georgia Baptist Convention, 1861, 3–6, 28, Special Collections, Jack Tarver Library, Mercer University, Macon GA. In addition to the GBC call for fasting and prayer, the Confederate government passed at least four resolutions calling for days of fasting, thanksgiving, and/or prayer (See *Journal of the Confederate Congress*, 14 May 1861; 26 March 1863; 17 February 1864; 11 January 1865; available online in a searchable database at http://memory.loc.gov/ammem/hlawquery.html; accessed 14 June 2011.). In addition, the University of Virginia's "Valley of the Shadows" Civil War documentary project notes that

Meanwhile, the constant press of war news and rumors provided church communities in Middle Georgia ample opportunity to acknowledge the war by referencing, directly or indirectly, events associated with the war, including battles, and acknowledging directly or indirectly Sherman's presence in fall 1864. In short, congregations navigated the war years under pressures, both formal and informal, religious and secular, to openly voice support or acknowledgment of the Confederacy and war. Such unprecedented forces pressing upon congregational life posed challenges for churches that had historically refused to allow, or at least to acknowledge the influence of, political machinations of the outside world into their sanctuaries. As such, the war years became a referendum between precedent and innovation, and polity and politics. Minus a roadmap and existing independently of any outside ecclesiastical councils, local Baptist churches in Middle Georgia responded in a variety of patterns.

Choosing innovation over precedent, some congregations responded to the prompting of external pressures in a manner indicative of acquiescence to nationalistic pressures. Against the backdrop of directives from denominational structures and government officials to express unequivocal support of the war and the Confederacy, sixteen of forty-four local churches in Middle Georgia voiced nationalistic sentiments in the form of adopted resolutions and/or days set aside for fasting, prayer, and/or thanksgiving. Of these sixteen congregations, eight adopted the Georgia Baptist Convention resolution regarding the war and Confederacy and/or heeded the Convention's call for a day of fasting and prayer in June 1861, while eleven observed other days of fasting, prayer, and/or

---

Confederate President Jefferson Davis set aside 21 August 1863 as a day of fasting and prayer (the "Valley of the Shadows" project is available online only at http://valley.vcdh.virginia.edu/reference/timelines/   timeline1863.html [accessed 14 June 2011]). From the 22 July 1862 edition of the *Christian Index* onward, articles addressing the subject of army chaplains routinely appeared in print. Some local church and associational records from 1862 forward also discuss army chaplains.

thanksgiving. Four followed the requests of both ecclesiastical and state officials, adopting the GBC resolution and observing at least one day of fasting, prayer, and/or thanksgiving other than in June 1861.

Among the sixteen vocally supportive churches, none expressed more patriotic fervor than New Bethel Baptist of Washington County. Founded in 1841 and a member of the Mt. Vernon Baptist Association in 1861, the congregation's 105 members included 24 blacks. A mid-sized church prior to the war, New Bethel, like most Baptist churches in the antebellum South, had refrained from addressing secular issues, including politics. Yet after the declaration of war in spring 1861, and despite Baptists' traditional separation of church and state, New Bethel became one of eight Middle Georgia churches that passed the GBC resolution. Indeed, the first order of business in the church's monthly business meeting of 25 May 1861, following the customary call for new members, consisted of acting "according to a resolution to the Baptist Convention of Georgia" in setting aside "the first & second days of June next as days of fasting and prayer." Although the congregation did not echo the GBC rationale for supporting the war effort and words of affirmation for the new Southern nation, the congregation left little doubt as to its loyalties.[10]

Church records do not reveal whether any Middle Georgia congregations observed all of the many days of fasting and prayer as proclaimed at various levels of government. Yet none exceeded New Bethel's enthusiasm for petitioning God on behalf of the Southern Confederacy and the war effort. The same congregation that above all others in the region consistently discussed soldier members and army missions throughout the war, Washington County's New Bethel congregation routinely embraced the cause of the Confederacy. In addition to the observance of the victory at Manassas, in October 1861 the church voted to hold weekly prayer meetings, presumably for the nation. In March 1862, New Bethel again declared a day of fasting

---

[10] Minutes, New Bethel Baptist Church, Washington County, 1841–1861, Special Collections, Jack Tarver Library, Mercer University, Macon GA, microfilm reel 504.

and prayer, followed by a renewed call to weekly prayer meetings in April 1863. Accordingly, New Bethel evidenced a trend among some Baptist churches in Middle Georgia. In addition to observing at least some of the national calls to fasting and prayer, some congregations took upon themselves the responsibility of directing their own formal petitionary prayer efforts.[11]

Among Baptist congregations in Middle Georgia, New Bethel thus provided a model for innovation during the war years. While church members, responding to external requests that perhaps seemed reasonable given the circumstances, may not have viewed themselves as innovators, few other churches in Middle Georgia approximated the congregation's open and official support of the Confederacy and the war. Yet New Bethel did not stand alone in offering unwavering and ongoing support for the Confederacy's war effort. Poplar Springs North in Laurens County joined its sister Georgia Baptist church on 25 May 1861 in voting to support the Georgia Baptist Convention directive and setting 1 and 2 June 1861 "to fast and pray." As did New Bethel, Poplar Springs North in July of the same year celebrated the victory at Manassas with a special service of "prayers and thanksgiving." And in October the congregation took the unusual step of formally pardoning absences by members serving in the Confederate army.[12]

In addition to officially excusing church members in the service of the Confederacy, Poplar Springs North received two soldiers into congregational membership during the war. No other soldiers joined Poplar Springs North, but the congregation on two more occasions,

---

[11] Minutes, New Bethel Baptist Church, 1861–1865, Special Collections, Jack Tarver Library, Mercer University, Macon GA.

[12] Minutes, Poplar Springs North Baptist Church, Laurens County, 1861–1864, Special Collections, Jack Tarver Library, Mercer University, Macon GA, microfilm reel 447. Baptist churches in the nineteenth century meticulously enforced church attendance, as did all forty-four churches in Middle Georgia included in this study. However, most congregations in Middle Georgia granted implicit permission (through silence in regards to church attendance) for members serving in the Confederate Army to miss church services. Poplar Springs North was an exception.

November 1863 and March 1864, voted to observe days of "thanksgiving, fasting and prayer" for the country and war effort. In a last reference to the war, church members commented on Sherman's presence in Georgia in November 1864: "There was no Meeting or Conference in November on account of the excitement occasioned by the passing through the country of Sherman's Army."[13]

Antioch Baptist in Morgan County displayed a fervor similar to that of Poplar Springs North. A member of the Central Association, Antioch in 1861 boasted 175 members, positioning it as the fourth largest congregation in the association. With only forty white members, however, the congregation had an unusual ratio of slave members to white, indicating planter influence within the congregation. Among the few white members, enthusiasm for the Confederacy was evident on Saturday, 11 May 1861. Following Pastor J. M. Stillwell's sermon, Antioch Baptist "met in Conference" and "on motion the church unanimously adopted a Resolution...by the Georgia Baptist Convention for a day of Fasting and Pray[er] on the first Lords day and Saturday preceeding in June." Other days of fasting and prayer for the Confederate nation and war effort followed. In November of the same year, "on motion the church in compliance with the Proclamation of President Davis apointed Friday the 16th day of November as a day of Fasting and Prayer." Again on 12 May of the following year, Antioch "agreed to keep Friday as a day of Pray[er]."[14]

Church records do not indicate any days of fasting and prayer from 1863 to 1864, but during those years the congregation routinely read letters from soldiers. In October 1863, following battlefield losses during the summer months, the church voted to "correspond with all the Brethren who were absent in the army." A flurry of letter writing

---

[13] Minutes, Poplar Springs North Baptist Church, Laurens County, 1861, Special Collections, Jack Tarver Library, Mercer University, Macon GA, microfilm reel 447.

[14] Minutes, Antioch Baptist Church, Morgan County, 1861–1865, Special Collections, Jack Tarver Library, Mercer University, Macon GA, microfilm reel 372.

and reading took place in the following eight months. November witnessed the reading of one letter from a soldier, but no commentary offered. In December, four letters from soldiers were read and "lisen to with much pleasure and...attention." Following the reading of another letter in February, the Antioch congregation voted to continue "to correspond with our Brethren in the army." Single letters were read in March and April, and two in June, all with no commentary offered. Afterwards, the reading of letters ceased, with no explanation offered and no further indication that the church continued corresponding with soldiers.[15]

The soldier letters read to the congregation in June 1864 represented the last reference to the war or Confederacy in Antioch church records. Despite the silence during the last ten months of war, Antioch, like New Bethel, clearly supported the war effort, as evidenced by the adoption of the Georgia Baptist Convention resolution and the observance of days of fasting and prayer. In addition, the congregation, more than others, routinely read letters from soldiers. The pattern to these actions may indicate shifting sentiment among church members as the congregation expressed, in chronological order, unanimous ideological support of the war and Confederacy, interest in the lives of church members serving as soldiers, and then silence in the face of the growing certainty of defeat in summer 1864 onward.

The First Baptist Church of Christ in Macon joined New Bethel, Poplar Springs North, and Antioch as a fourth congregation expressing fervent support of the Confederacy and the war. The largest congregation in the Central Association, Macon First's membership of 760 was more than twice that of the next largest church. Founded in 1828, the church had experienced a period of notable growth during the decade prior to the war, paralleling the rise of Macon as the foremost town in the central portion of the state. During the 1850s, Macon First's membership grew from 394 to 687,

---

[15] Minutes, Antioch Baptist Church, 1863–1864, Special Collections, Jack Tarver Library, Mercer University, Macon GA.

with most additions coming by baptism. The congregation constructed three new buildings: two new church buildings, one each for white members and black members, and a mission chapel. By the end of the decade, the church held two services each Sunday and two weekly Sabbath Schools. Such activity was unmatched by other churches in Middle Georgia.[16]

The urban congregation thus stood apart from the New Bethel, Poplar Springs North, and Antioch churches, thanks in part to the prominent voices of Pastor Ebenezer Warren and Samuel Boykin. Led from a pulpit that early equated the Confederacy with the Kingdom of God, the Macon church openly embraced the Southern cause prior to the beginning of the war, as expressed in Warren's noted pro-slavery sermon. Following the beginning of armed hostilities, First Baptist of Macon on 31 May 1861 voted to obey the directives of the Georgia Baptist Convention, Southern Baptist Convention, and Confederate President Jefferson Davis: "Resolved: That we observe the 15th of June as a day of fasting and prayer for our country, in accordance with the proclamation of President Davis, and to observe the 1st and 2nd of June likewise at the request of the State Convention and the Southern Baptist Convention." For First Baptist members, the pulpit embodied the call of spiritual and secular leaders to support the Confederacy. External pressures thus internalized, the innovation of engaging the outside world was framed as continuity.[17]

The remainder of 1861 passed without the congregation discussing the war during business meetings, but by spring 1862 the conflict appeared to weigh especially heavily on members. In March, "prayer meetings for the country" were held on "Mondays, Wednesdays and Fridays at 4 o'clock." In April the church expressed its patriotism by offering to donate its 900-pound church bell to the Confederacy, to be melted into cannon. And in May "Bro. Warren

---

[16] Minutes, Macon First Baptist Church of Christ, Bibb County, 1850–1861, Special Collections, Jack Tarver Library, Mercer University, Macon GA, microfilm reel 51.

[17] Minutes, Macon First Baptist Church of Christ, Bibb County, 1861, Special Collections, Jack Tarver Library, Mercer University, Macon GA.

appointed as corresponding agent for the church to correspond monthly or oftener with the absent members of the church now in the army." In addition, the church that month voted to hold a "prayer meeting for the country." On 4 November 1864, in the wake of General Tecumseh Sherman's march through Georgia that led the First Baptist Church of Atlanta to temporarily relocate to Macon and share facilities with Macon First, the Macon congregation voted to hold a "series of prayer meetings...at sunrise." The Macon church's open patriotism thus continued into the final months of war.[18]

A fifth Middle Georgia congregation, New Hope Baptist in Greene County, passed the Georgia Baptist Convention resolution but did not otherwise officially endorse days of fasting and prayer during the war. A small rural congregation of 109 members, including 41 slaves, New Hope embraced the directives of the GBC with a seemingly unmatched enthusiasm: "Adopted the resolution passed by the Georgia Baptist Convention at their session at Athens," church records note, "that we will observe the first Sunday in June and Saturday before as days of humiliation fasting and prayer to Almighty God that the evils threatening our country may be averted." Yet despite the initial enthusiasm accompanying the start of war, church records are silent regarding the conflict for the next three years. Only when Union soldiers appeared in Middle Georgia in the wake of Sherman's March to the Sea did New Hope once again tersely acknowledge the war. "No meeting on account of the near proximity of the Yankees," church records declared in November 1864. Not until February 1865, at which point defeat was certain for the South, did the congregation vote to "correspond with our members in the army monthly." Seemingly reflective of the tardy nature of the decision to correspond with soldier members, the following month, and only weeks from Lee's surrender, "the

---

[18] Minutes, Macon First Baptist Church of Christ, Bibb County, 1861–1865, Special Collections, Jack Tarver Library, Mercer University, Macon GA. The government took receipt of the bell in late 1863.

committee report they have received no letter or any other communication from our members in the Army."[19]

For other openly supportive churches in Middle Georgia, direct discussion of the war and Confederacy ceased with the South's surrender at Appomattox. New Hope's records, however, added a unique footnote to the conflict. In August, veteran James H. Perkins stood up when "new business" was called for and addressed the congregation, speaking from his heart regarding his service in the Confederate Army. Perkins "came forward and confessed that while in the army he had fallen into temptation and broat reproach upon the cause of Christ felt sorry for it thought he had been forgiven and wished the church to forgive him and pray for him the church forgave him." Perkins's singular admission thus validated Baptist concerns regarding personal sins in the camp, even though, surprisingly, no other similar confessions are found among church records of Middle Georgia congregations.[20]

Although not as fervently supportive of the war effort and Confederacy as New Bethel, Poplar Springs North, Antioch, or Macon First, New Hope's records clearly portray a congregation loyal to the Southern cause. That loyalty was not without irony. Whereas church records initially framed the conflict in corporate terms of "the evils threatening our country" from without, the final statement regarding the war referenced personal evils resulting from Confederate camp life. The killing of foreign aggressors justified, no

---

[19] Thaddeus B. Rice, *History of Greene County Georgia* (Macon, GA: J. W. Burke, 1973) 108; minutes, New Hope Baptist Church, Greene County, 1861–1865, Special Collections, Jack Tarver Library, Mercer University, Macon GA microfilm reel 473. Stillwell pastored the congregation throughout the war. Membership statistics are cited for 1863. Minutes, Antioch Baptist Church, Morgan County, 1861–1865, Special Collections, Jack Tarver Library, Mercer University, Macon GA.

[20] Minutes, Antioch Baptist Church, Morgan County, 1865, Special Collections, Jack Tarver Library, Mercer University, Macon GA.

further explanation was needed. Yet succumbing to personal immorality required forgiveness from the church body.[21]

A sixth Middle Georgia congregation that affirmed the Georgia Baptist Convention resolution, Madison Baptist in Morgan County, boasted the third largest congregation in the Central Association. Enslaved members outnumbered whites 181 to 124. Pastor David E. Butler, like Warren and Boykin a leader among Baptists statewide, embodied from the pulpit calls to embrace the Confederacy and war. Under Butler's leadership, Madison Baptist voiced concern regarding political developments in fall 1860, and in 1861 approved the GBC preamble and resolutions, reproducing the document in its entirety in church records. Yet Madison Baptist did not clearly embrace the war during the remainder of the conflict, evidencing either the casual nature of recordkeeping of that era or a reluctance to further engage the outside world.[22]

---

[21] For a larger treatment of the theme of the historical centrality of personal morality in Southern Protestant life, see Samuel Hill, *Southern Churches in Crisis Revisited* (Tuscaloosa: University of Alabama Press, 1999).

[22] Minutes, Central Baptist Association, 1861, 8, 14; 1862, 6; 1863, 3, Special Collections, Jack Tarver Library, Mercer University, Macon GA; minutes, Madison Baptist Church, Morgan County, 1860, Special Collections, Jack Tarver Library, Mercer University, Macon GA, microfilm reel 383; Robert G. Gardner, *A Decade of Debate and Division: Georgia Baptists and the Formation of the Southern Baptist Convention* (Macon GA: Mercer University Press, 1995) 66, 87; Robert G. Gardner, *A History of the Georgia Baptist Association, 1784–1884* (Atlanta: Georgia Baptist Historical Society, 1996) 235; Harwell, *An Old Friend With New Credentials*, 99–104; William Cathcart, *The Baptist Encyclopedia,* 2 vols (Philadelphia: Louis H. Everts, 1881) 1:171–72. Prominent in associational affairs, Madison's most notable pastor during the war years, David E. Butler, preached one of the annual sermons and served as a delegate to the Georgia Baptist Convention. Prior to the war, Butler, a personal friend of Jesse Mercer, had composed and executed Mercer's will. A lawyer, merchant, and planter prior to the war, Butler nonetheless owned no slaves at the time he attended the founding of the Southern Baptist Convention in 1845 in Augusta. An agent for Mercer University at the founding of the SBC, Butler received ordination at the hands of the Madison congregation in 1860. An "eloquent speaker" with a "fine command of language," Butler's prominence peaked after the war, at which time he was considered a "ruling spirit" within the Central Association, serving as president of the Georgia Baptist Convention from

Yet another congregation voicing support of the action of the Georgia Baptist Convention was Union Baptist of Spalding County, founded in 1849 and a member of the Flint River Association. While making no direct reference to the GBC Resolution in May 1861, the congregation nonetheless "agreed to observe fasting and prare" as the GBC had requested, the only reference to fasting and prayer in church records. During the course of the war, one soldier joined the church in August 1863, Thomas J. Folds. Perhaps Folds wrote "the letter from the armmy" briefly noted in church minutes of January 1864. Yet one month after the war ended without acknowledgement from Union Baptist, Folds, rather than being heralded as a hero by his church family, faced scrutiny from the congregation when the church "appointed a Commity to Brother T. Folds" in regards to his "christian conduct." Weighing accusations of gambling and drinking leveled against the army veteran, "the Church withdrew fellowship from Brother Thomas Folds" in June 1865. By way of contrast, even while disciplinary procedures were underway for Folds, the church "received by letter from the Army" David L. Patrick. Remaining a faithful member of Union Baptist for the remainder of his life, Patrick became a deacon in 1867 and church clerk in 1868, the latter post of which he held for thirty-seven years. Thus, although voicing clear support for the war effort on at least one occasion, Union Baptist ultimately expressed more concern with the spiritual and moral life of soldiers than their sacrifices and service in the Confederate Army.[23]

A final congregation, Jackson Baptist Church, heeded the directive of the GBC in May 1861 when members "agreed to adopt

---

1872–1875, and occupying the position of editor of the *Christian Index* from 1874–1878.

[23] Harold Elston Graham, Sr., *A History of the Flint River Baptist Association, 1824–1974* (Executive Committee of the Flint River Association, 1974) 111–12; minutes, Union Baptist Church, Spalding County, 1861–1868, Special Collections, Jack Tarver Library, Mercer University, Macon GA, microfilm reel 595. The records of the Union Baptist congregation include a typewritten summary of some events in the life of the church from the 1850s to the 1880s. Folds's reception into the church is noted in the brief, but not his excommunication. Patrick's reception in the church and longtime service to the church is noted.

the resolution passed by the Georgia Baptist State Convention." Located in Washington County and a member of the Mt. Vernon Baptist Association, the overwhelmingly white Jackson Baptist congregation claimed only nine black members among total membership of forty-eight. The brief statement referencing the GBC remains the only instance in which the church community addressed the war or Confederacy.[24]

In short, among the eight congregations that responded affirmatively to external pressures advocating open support of the Confederacy and war effort, the innovation of welcoming the outside world into the church sanctuary arrived with caveats. For most of the innovative congregations, the nationalistic passions conjured from pulpits and in business meetings in spring 1861 failed to permeate church records throughout the entirety of the war. Furthermore, the resounding silence that greeted the defeat of the Confederacy suggests perhaps that by the end of the war, churches may have had second thoughts concerning the yoking of congregation to politics in the wake of the disappointment and despair that blanketed the South.

An additional eight congregations, although neglecting to affirm the Georgia Baptist resolution, nonetheless participated in at least one day of fasting and prayer for the Confederate nation and war effort during the course of the war. Directed at the political fortunes of a young nation, fasting and prayer, while longstanding rites in Baptist congregational life, were appropriated in a novel manner by both these eight churches and the eight congregations affirmative of the pro-Confederacy GBC resolutions.

Of the eight congregations who limited their corporate support of the Confederacy to fasting and prayer, Providence Baptist Church in Jasper County, the congregation previously noted for losing three soldier sons in the opening months of war, turned to fasting and prayer the most frequently. Pastored by Edgar Jewell and a member

---

[24] Minutes, Jackson Baptist Church, Washington County, 1861, Special Collections, Jack Tarver Library, Mercer University, Macon GA, microfilm reel 552.

of the Central Baptist Association, the Providence church on four occasions collectively appealed to God on behalf of the Confederacy. All such occurrences took place from 1863 onward, following the soldier deaths of 1861 and 1862. In March 1863 the church voted to observe "a day of fasting & prayer." In the anguish that followed the defeat at Gettysburg, in August 1863 the "church agreed by a vote to meet at the Methodist Church" for a joint service "in accordance with the proclamation from the President." As the fate of the Confederacy grew increasingly bleak, Providence Baptist also held days of fasting and prayer in March and May 1864.[25]

The Providence Baptist community, in other words, engaged the war and Confederacy extensively, and in a manner unique among Baptist churches in Middle Georgia. Confining war-related comments to a year-and-a-half span from October 1862 to May 1864, the church took the unusual step of commemorating the deaths of three soldier sons, followed by a period of repeated fasting and prayer interspersed with a refusal, noted previously, to accept a soldier son into membership until he had demonstrated his spiritual conversion.

In many respects, the congregation demographically reflected a broader portrait of Southern Baptist Middle Georgia churches examined in this study. Consisting of 136 members, the church was an average-sized congregation in a typically rural location and comprised of landowners and farm workers. Of the 136, 76 members were white, a roughly equal split of races not uncommon in Middle Georgia congregations. Socio-economically, common folk easily outnumbered wealthy landowners. In the case of Providence, one large landowner, North Carolina native Edmond J. Walton, exerted a significant financial and membership presence within the congregation. His assets included $22,950 worth of land within a total personal worth of $45,190. The only large slaveholder within the

---

[25] Minutes, Central Baptist Association, 1861, 14, Special Collections, Jack Tarver Library, Mercer University, Macon GA; minutes, Providence Baptist Church, Jasper County, 1861–1864, Special Collections, Jack Tarver Library, Mercer University, Macon GA, microfilm reel 77. The soldier deaths—Green, Bussey, and Davidson—are discussed in detail in chap. 4.

Diverging Loyalties

church, Walton owned seventy-eight slaves, who likely comprised the majority of the congregation's sixty slave members.[26]

Yet Walton, as a large landowner and slaveholder, stood apart from many of his wealthy contemporaries in one notable way—his age. At twenty-four years old, Walton possessed privileges of wealth usually associated with older family patriarchs. In Walton's case, wealth had its privileges, particularly in regard to military service. While the young trio of Charles B. Bussey, Thomas Green, and D. L. Davidson, sons of Providence Baptist, marched off to distant battlefields in service of the Confederacy and met untimely deaths, Walton safely served on the home-front as a member of the 6th Georgia Infantry (State Guards).[27]

The wealth gap between Walton and the families of the deceased three reflected the extent of Walton's influence. Charles F. Bussey, father of Charles B., held personal wealth of $13,000, while patriarch William M. Green's personal wealth of $5,000 included $1,500 in real estate holdings and family head Jack Davidson's total worth of $3,550 included $2,700 in real estate. The combined wealth of the families of the deceased trio totaled less than half that of Walton.[28]

---

[26] Minutes, Providence Baptist Church, Jasper County, 1862, Special Collections, Jack Tarver Library, Mercer University, Macon GA; 1860 US Census Jasper County, Georgia, microfilm reel M653–128, sheet 278; 1860 Slave Census Schedule Jasper County, Georgia (400). No other members of Providence Baptist owned forty or more slaves.

[27] Minutes, Providence Baptist Church, Jasper County, 1862, Special Collections, Jack Tarver Library, Mercer University, Macon GA; 1860 US Census Jasper County, Georgia, microfilm reel M653–128, sheet 278; National Park Service Civil War Soldiers and Sailors System, http://www.civilwar.nps.gov/cwss/ (accessed 14 June 2010).

[28] Minutes, Providence Baptist Church, Jasper County, 1862, Special Collections, Jack Tarver Library, Mercer University, Macon GA; 1860 US Census Jasper County, Georgia, microfilm reel M653–128, sheet 278; Jasper County Georgia Bible records, Newton Family, http://files.usgwarchives.org/ga/jasper/bibles/newton.txt (accessed 14 June 2011); Jasper County Georgia Bible records, Bogan Family, http://files.usgwarchives.org/ga/jasper/bibles/bogan.txt (accessed 14 June 2011).

In addition, the Bogans, the second wealthiest clan in the congregation, patriarch John and son Caswell P., representing an extended family of nine, totaled wealth significantly less than that of Walton. Farmers and South Carolina natives, John's personal worth stood at $23,900, while Caswell was worth $7,000. Like Walton, however, the Bogan family was not represented on distant battlefronts, as none were of military age.[29]

Of those families who did send sons to battlefronts, money mattered little. One of the common folk families in the church, the Cardell clan, farmers and farm workers native to Georgia and led by patriarch Peter, sent son Peter B. to the warfront. Like most church families, their income was so meager that their share of church dues totaled less than $2.00 in 1862. Census records attribute no land holdings or personal worth to Peter, yet the family likely felt richly rewarded when Peter B. returned home after the war.[30]

In short, Providence Baptist's expressed sorrow over the loss of soldier sons, hesitation in accepting a soldier son into membership, and ready observance of days of fasting and prayer took place in the context of a church membership comprised of one wealthy landowner and slaveholder, an additional relatively wealthy family, a handful of small landowners, and many common folk. Small landowners and common folk alike sent sons to the battlefront, while on the home-front disparate families united in faith mourned and prayed over sons lost, prayed and fasted for the Confederacy, and focused on spiritual matters in the midst of family struggles.

---

[29] Minutes, Providence Baptist Church, Jasper County, 1862, Special Collections, Jack Tarver Library, Mercer University, Macon GA; 1860 US Census Jasper County, Georgia, microfilm reel M653–128, sheet 274.

[30] Minutes, Providence Baptist Church, Jasper County, 1862, Special Collections, Jack Tarver Library, Mercer University, Macon GA; 1860 US Census Jasper County, Georgia, microfilm reel M653–128, sheet 299; National Park Service Civil War Soldiers and Sailors System, http://www.civilwar.nps.gov/cwss/ (accessed 14 July 2008). Soldier Peter is listed as Peter D. in the Civil War Soldiers and Sailors System database.

Providence did not stand alone in expressing concern for spiritual matters in the midst of warfare. Despite observing days of fasting and prayer and demonstrating less caution in accepting active soldiers into membership, County Line Baptist in Newton County, a member of the Stone Mountain Association, followed a similar pattern to that of the Providence congregation in regards to some indication of ambivalence regarding soldier members. For County Line, the reservations surfaced earlier in the war. With their pastor absent when the church convened in April 1862, the lay moderator led the congregation to agree to "meet on the 3rd Sabbath in each month...for the purpose of holding a prayer meeting especially for the soldiers that have went from this vicinity." The monthly prayer meetings were agreed upon on one condition: "if a sufficient number of the brethren will attend." Church records give no indication as to whether the prayer meetings ever took place.[31]

Regardless of the ambivalence over regular prayer meetings for soldiers, County Line repeatedly opened the church doors to receive new soldier members. The request of E. S. Eliot regarding membership procedures, indicating his apparent unfamiliarity with Baptist polity, offers further insight into the role that decorum played in the process of soldiers joining Baptist churches. In April 1863, the congregation "considered the request of E. S. Eliot who being in the armey disires som way to become identified with us as a member of this Church." The pastor was authorized "to inform him by Letter that we authorise any orderily Baptist Minister of our order who is in good standing to Baptise him upon a profesion of his faith and forward a certificate to us of the same and we will receive him." The church's invitation to Eliot, predicated upon a profession of faith and proper baptism, remained unanswered. In May 1864, however, the congregation extended membership privileges to Joseph E. Lowery,

---

[31] Minutes, County Line Baptist Church, Newton County, 1862, Special Collections, Jack Tarver Library, Mercer University, Macon GA, microfilm reel 399.

son of prominent member William J. Lowery and soldier in the Army of Tennessee, who met the requirements of the congregation.[32] The outlook for the Confederacy was ominous by the time Lowery joined County Line Baptist in spring 1864. The church cancelled the scheduled July gathering because "Yankee raids prevented us from meeting." Reassembling in August, the church voted to accept a second soldier as a member of the congregation: George R. Elliott. The following month the presence of Sherman's army again "prevented the Church from meeting." One month after the surrender in April 1865, soldier Joseph E. Lowery, received as a member one year earlier, returned home, occasioning the only direct account among Middle Georgia churches of a former soldier being formally received into a congregation following conversion, baptism, and membership acceptance while serving on the battlefront: "extended the right hand of fellowship to Joseph E Lowery who was previously received in this church by sertifacate from the Tennessee armey." County Line, meeting prior to Lowery's reception and mere days after the surrender at Appomattox, either declined to take official notice of the momentous event or had not yet received word

---

[32] Minutes, County Line Baptist Church, Newton County, 1863–1864, Special Collections, Jack Tarver Library, Mercer University, Macon GA. The exact identity of the two soldiers, E. S. Eliot and Joseph E. Lowery, is questionable. Church records give no indication as to Eliot's regiment or field of operation, and the closest matches in the National Park Service Soldiers and Sailors System (http://www.itd.nps.gov/cwss/ [accessed 14 July 2008]) are an E. Elliot who served in the 27th Georgia Infantry Regiment (comprised of recruits from Pike, Jackson, Taylor, Talbot, Appling, Quitman, and Clay counties) and an E. Elliott who served the 43rd Georgia Infantry Regiment (comprised of recruits from Cherokee, Pickens, Cobb, Hall, Forsyth, Jefferson, and Jackson counties). Although church records do place Joseph E. Lowery in the Army of Tennessee, a match within the Soldiers and Sailors System is also problematic. The closest matches are a Joseph T. Lowery of the 7th Georgia Infantry Regiment (comprised of recruits from Coweta, Paulding, DeKalb, Franklin, Fulton, Heard, and Cobb counties) and J. R. Lowery of the 40th Georgia Infantry Battalion.

of the surrender. Regardless, the safe return of a church son occasioned rejoicing in the midst of anguish.[33]

Whereas praying for and accepting soldiers indicated concern for the spiritual welfare of soldiers, County Line left little doubt as to their ongoing loyalties in the observance of days of fasting and prayer in March 1863 and April 1864. Meeting in March 1863, the church clearly voiced the origin of the first day of fasting and prayer observed by the congregation, two years after the beginning of the war: "agreed to meet on the 27 inst. for the purpose of humiliation fasting and prayer in compliance to the request of the President of the Confederate States." In March 1864, the congregation voted for a second time to observe a day "for humiliation fasting and prayer" on 8 April, offering no further explanation.[34]

For County Line Baptist, in short, the war began quietly only to surface tentatively among the community one year later in a decision to pray for the soldiers, on condition that enough interest existed among the fellowship. Two days of fasting and prayer and two new soldier members later, the defeat of the Southern cause elicited silence, followed by renewed hope when Joseph Lowery, hardened by years of war but now a new spiritual man than when he marched off to defend the South, walked through the doors of the church.

Other congregations voiced support of the Confederacy with less commentary. Two churches in Middle Georgia, both members of the Central Baptist Association, each observed two days of fasting and prayer for the Confederacy and were "in compliance" with the request of Confederate President Davis. Small rural, white-majority churches with memberships of fifty-five and sixty-six respectively, Salem Baptist of Jones County and Ramouth Baptist of Putnam

---

[33] Minutes, County Line Baptist Church, Newton County, 1864–1865, Special Collections, Jack Tarver Library, Mercer University, Macon GA. National Park Service Civil War Soldiers and Sailors System (http://www.itd.nps.gov/cwss/) database indicates a George R. Elliott served in the 53rd Georgia Infantry Regiment in Virginia.

[34] Minutes, County Line Baptist Church, Newton County, 1863–1864, Special Collections, Jack Tarver Library, Mercer University, Macon GA.

County, did not fit Samuel Boykin's stereotype of unsupportive country congregations. A third small, rural, and white-majority congregation in the Central Association, Bethel Baptist of Jasper County, in June 1862 voted to observe weekly prayer "on behalf of the soldiers of the Southern Confederacy and the Country at large." In fall 1863, the congregation received two soldiers as members and hosted an army missionary, collecting $13 for the purpose of supplying religious reading material to soldiers. Outside of the Central Association, Bethlehem Baptist in Laurens County and a member of the Hephzibah Association observed days of fasting and prayer in spring 1862. In addition, Thomaston Baptist Church of Upson County and a member of the Rehoboth Association donated the congregational bell to be "cast into cannon." Among Primitive Baptist congregations, Mt. Carmel stood alone in officially embracing days of fasting and prayer, responding to a request by President Davis in March 1864. The only other war-related notation concerned the departure of two church leaders to the war front in 1864, necessitating a replacement for representation at the annual associational meeting.[35]

---

[35] Minutes, Central Baptist Association, 1862, 13, Special Collections, Jack Tarver Library, Mercer University, Macon GA; minutes, Salem Baptist Church, Jones County, 1861–1863, Special Collections, Jack Tarver Library, Mercer University, Macon GA, microfilm reel 184; minutes, Ramouth Baptist Church, Putnam County, 1861–1863, Special Collections, Jack Tarver Library, Mercer University, Macon GA, microfilm reel 197; minutes, Bethel Baptist Church, Jasper County, 1861–1865, Special Collections, Jack Tarver Library, Mercer University, Macon GA, microfilm reel 247; minutes, Bethlehem Baptist Church, Laurens County, 1861–1865, Special Collections, Jack Tarver Library, Mercer University, Macon GA, microfilm reel 110; minutes, Thomaston Baptist Church, Upson County, 1862, Special Collections, Jack Tarver Library, Mercer University, Macon GA, microfilm reel 95. Edwin L. Cliburn, *In Unbroken Line: A History of the First Baptist Church of Thomaston, Georgia* (Tallahassee FL: Rose Printing, 1979) 125; minutes, Mt. Carmel Primitive Baptist Church, Crawford County, 1863, Special Collections, Jack Tarver Library, Mercer University, Macon GA, microfilm reel 317. Membership numbers are from 1862 as recorded in associational minutes. The records of both Salem and Ramouth churches are illegible after 1863.

While sixteen of forty-four Baptist churches in Middle Georgia thus expressed support of the Confederacy and war effort by either adopting the 1861 Georgia Baptist Resolution, heeding the initial GBC call for a day of fasting and prayer, and/or voting to observe a day or days of fasting and prayer other than that directed by the GBC, thirteen additional congregations engaged the war in spiritual terms only by supporting army missions and/or accepting soldiers (or ex-soldiers) into the membership of their respective churches.

Lebanon Baptist Church of Crawford County, a small rural congregation of only thirty-six members, acknowledged more widespread support of army missions than any other congregation in Middle Georgia. The church's unparalleled vocal support of ministry among the soldiers may have been spurred by the tragic death of twenty-five-year-old Owen M. McAfee, son of A. J. McAfee, at Yorktown, Virginia, on 11 September 1861. The place of young McAfee's death remained in the mind of the congregation. The following June, the church prayed for the battle then raging at Yorktown. Throughout the war, Lebanon Baptist repeatedly provided financial assistance for mission work among the soldiers.[36]

Siloam Baptist Church of Greene County also formally acknowledged the war from a purely spiritual vantage point. Similar to the Lebanon congregation, death struck the congregation at an early date. "Brother William T. Jackson...fell in battle about the firs[t] of July," the church lamented on 5 July 1862. In the ensuing years of war, the congregation pooled financial resources to support the evangelization of soldiers and accepted into their membership a

---

[36] Minutes, Lebanon Baptist Church, Crawford County, 1861–1865, Special Collections, Jack Tarver Library, Mercer University, Macon GA, microfilm reel 638; minutes, Rehoboth Baptist Association, 1862, 16, Special Collections, Jack Tarver Library, Mercer University, Macon GA; National Park Service Civil War Soldiers and Sailors System, http://www.itd.nps.gov/cwss/ (accessed 14 June 2011).

soldier whose soul had been saved under the administration of Chaplain W. L. Curry of the 50th Georgia Infantry Regiment.[37]

Among the remaining Middle Georgia congregations that acknowledged spiritual aspects of the Civil War, Bethesda Baptist Church of Greene County rejoiced over the conversion of a soldier son of a church member and financially supported army missions. Liberty Baptist Church of Wilkinson County accepted four soldiers into membership during the war, while Mineral Springs Baptist received three soldiers as members, and the Stone Creek congregation of Twiggs County and Zion Baptist Church of Newton County each extended membership to one soldier. Sandy Creek Baptist Church in Morgan County, Indian Creek Baptist Church in Henry County, and Midway Baptist Church of Bibb County took up offerings for army missions. Following the war in June 1865, Harmony Primitive Baptist Church in Pike County and Houston Factory Baptist Church of Houston County each "extended the right hand of fellowship" to singular former soldiers.[38]

---

[37] Minutes, Siloam Baptist Church, Greene County, 1861–1864, Special Collections, Jack Tarver Library, Mercer University, Macon GA, microfilm reel 523; National Park Service Civil War Soldiers and Sailors System, http://www.itd.nps.gov/cwss/ (accessed 14 June 2011).

[38] Minutes, Bethesda Baptist Church, Greene County, 1861–1865, Special Collections, Jack Tarver Library, Mercer University, Macon GA, microfilm reel 11; minutes, Bethlehem Baptist Church, Morgan County, 1861–1864, Special Collections, Jack Tarver Library, Mercer University, Macon GA, microfilm reel 377; minutes, Ebenezer Baptist Association, 1861, 13, Special Collections, Jack Tarver Library, Mercer University, Macon GA, microfilm reels 1069, 1270; minutes, Liberty Baptist Church, Wilkinson County, 1861–1864, Special Collections, Jack Tarver Library, Mercer University, Macon GA, microfilm reel 196; minutes, Mineral Springs Baptist Church, Washington County, 1864, Special Collections, Jack Tarver Library, Mercer University, Macon GA, microfilm reel 524; minutes, Zion Baptist Church, Newton County, 1863–1864, Special Collections, Jack Tarver Library, Mercer University, Macon GA, microfilm reel 315; minutes, Ebenezer Baptist Association, 1860, 12, Special Collections, Jack Tarver Library, Mercer University, Macon GA, microfilm reel 1065; minutes, Stone Creek Baptist Church, 1860–1865, Special Collections, Jack Tarver Library, Mercer University, Macon GA, microfilm reel 280; minutes, Sandy Creek Baptist Church, Morgan County, 1862–1864, Special Collections, Jack Tarver Library,

The composition of churches that offered spiritual support of the war effort but stopped short of formal endorsement of the Confederacy and war varied greatly. For example, the small 36-member Lebanon Baptist congregation and larger Liberty Baptist Church, claiming 169 members, were both primarily comprised of white members. On the other hand, nearly half of Stone Creek's 307 members were blacks, as were 65 of Houston Factory's 105 members. Large and small, rural and town, yeoman and planter-influenced, congregations that acknowledged spiritual dimensions of the war followed a pattern of personal interaction with formerly unsaved soldiers, grief over the death of soldier members, and/or a general concern for the salvation of Confederate soldiers.[39]

Whereas sixteen churches expressed nationalistic sentiments and thirteen congregations voiced spiritual war-time concerns only, fifteen churches opted for neither. The nine Georgia Baptist churches and six Primitive Baptist churches whose records offer no indication of support of the war at any level nonetheless include a handful of non-committal observations, such as the acknowledgement of the death of a soldier member, a passing reference to Sherman's army, or a note about hardships endured by a church family. Yet in most instances, a total silence pervaded the entire war-era records of the given congregation, with no indication, directly or indirectly, that the North and the South were at war with one another, or that the Southern Confederacy even existed.[40]

Mercer University, Macon GA, microfilm reel 124; minutes, Indian Creek Baptist Church, Henry County, 1863–1865, Special Collections, Jack Tarver Library, Mercer University, Macon GA, microfilm reel 41; minutes, Midway Baptist Church, Bibb County, 1864, Special Collections, Jack Tarver Library, Mercer University, Macon GA, microfilm reel 69; minutes, Rehoboth Baptist Association, 1861, 12, Special Collections, Jack Tarver Library, Mercer University, Macon GA.

[39] Minutes, Ebenezer Baptist Association, 1860–1861, Special Collections, Jack Tarver Library, Mercer University, Macon GA, microfilm reels 1069, 1270; minutes, Rehoboth Baptist Association, 1861, 12, Special Collections, Jack Tarver Library, Mercer University, Macon GA.

[40] Minutes, Bluewater Baptist Church, Laurens County, Special Collections, Jack Tarver Library, Mercer University, Macon GA, microfilm reel 500; minutes,

Baptists in Middle Georgia during the Civil War

Among the fifteen silent churches, the relatively large number of Primitive Baptist congregations represent the most visible correlation. Six of a total of eight Primitive Baptist churches in Middle Georgia remained silent regarding the war, a significantly high proportion. Within this subset of congregations, racial dynamics are difficult to

---

Emmaus Primitive Baptist Church, Upson County, Special Collections, Jack Tarver Library, Mercer University, Macon GA, microfilm reel 608; minutes, Fort Early Baptist Church, Dooly County, Special Collections, Jack Tarver Library, Mercer University, Macon GA, microfilm reel 196; minutes, Friendship Baptist Church, Dooly County, Special Collections, Jack Tarver Library, Mercer University, Macon GA, microfilm reel 171; minutes, Greensboro Baptist Church, Greene County, Special Collections, Jack Tarver Library, Mercer University, Macon GA, microfilm reel 491; minutes, Hawkinsville Baptist Church, Pulaski County, Special Collections, Jack Tarver Library, Mercer University, Macon GA, microfilm reel 32; minutes, High Shoals Primitive Baptist Church, Monroe County, Special Collections, Jack Tarver Library, Mercer University, Macon GA, microfilm reel 301; minutes, Lauren Hills Baptist Church, Laurens County, 1865, Special Collections, Jack Tarver Library, Mercer University, Macon GA, microfilm reel 370; minutes, Mt. Calvary Baptist Church, Pulaski County, 1865, Special Collections, Jack Tarver Library, Mercer University, Macon GA, microfilm reel 384; minutes, Mt. Calvary Primitive Baptist Church, Monroe County, Special Collections, Jack Tarver Library, Mercer University, Macon GA, microfilm reel 339; minutes, Mt. Calvary Baptist Church, Pulaski County, Special Collections, Jack Tarver Library, Mercer University, Macon GA, microfilm reel 384; minutes, Shiloh Primitive Baptist Church, Bibb County, Special Collections, Jack Tarver Library, Mercer University, Macon GA, microfilm reel 339; minutes, Shoal Creek Primitive Baptist Church, Newton County, Special Collections, Jack Tarver Library, Mercer University, Macon GA, microfilm reel 655; minutes, Smyrna Primitive Baptist Church, Monroe County, Special Collections, Jack Tarver Library, Mercer University, Macon GA, microfilm reel 85. Two of the fifteen silent churches addressed the war in a brief and detached manner, one directly and the other indirectly. Harris Springs Baptist Church in Newton County noted the deaths of two members in summer 1864, offering commentary on neither. One of the members was a soldier. "Bro. Wm. Hurst was killed in battle July 22nd 1864." Also in 1864, church records note that there was "no meeting in Nov. on account of Shermans Army passing through our State at that time." Emmaus Primitive Baptist Church in Upson County, a member of the Primitive Towalgia Association, was likely referring to the ravages of the war when on 21 May 1864 a church member "reported brother Britt & family to be in a destitute & afflicted condition, whereupon a collection was taken up of $21.00 & 14 Bushels of corn & 4 Bushels of wheat subscribed for their benefit."

discern, as the churches did not maintain racial breakdowns of membership. Generally speaking, membership totals tended to be small. The largest of the six congregations boasted a membership of 120, while the remaining 5 each claimed membership of 68 or less. The overall membership totals reflect the predominantly rural and/or small town nature of Primitive Baptists in Georgia as a whole.[41]

Seemingly isolationist in nature, Primitive Baptists tended not to engage the Christian or cultural mainstreams while maintaining strict separation of church and state. "Except in times of extreme crisis, the outside world might as well not have existed as far as Primitive Baptist church records were concerned," historian John Crowley notes. Crowley cites only a few examples of Primitive Baptist engagement in larger culture and society prior to the Civil War. Related to defending strict separation of church and state, in these rare instances of engagement Primitive Baptists expressed opposition to tax exemption for churches, favoritism of laws prohibiting clergy from serving in political offices, and support of the abolishment of congressional chaplains and state support of religious schools. Crowley finds no evidence that Primitive Baptists of Wiregrass Georgia took written positions on slavery during the 1850s, and few instances in which the Civil War intruded into church and associational records. Crowley calls into question, however, the oversimplification of congregations refusing to engage their larger surroundings, maintaining that the Primitive Baptist tradition included a pattern of fusing together spiritual and temporal issues under the rubric of ecclesiology. Identifying Primitive Baptists as historically informed persons who to view the larger world through

---

[41] The Primitive Ocmulgee Baptist Association, addressing the war at length in circular letters, is an exception to Primitive Baptist silence regarding the war. For an analysis of the dynamics of Primitive Baptists in rural Georgia, see Cushing Biggs Hassell and Sylvester Hassell, *History of the Church of God, from the Creation to A.D. 1885* (1886; reprint, Conley GA: Old School Hymnal Co., 1973); Julietta Haynes, "A History of the Primitive Baptists" (Ph.D. diss., University of Texas at Austin, 1959); Emerson Proctor, "Georgia Baptists, Organization and Division: 1772–1840" (M.A. thesis, Georgia Southern College, 1969).

decidedly biblical lenses, Crowley disputes long-held criticisms of church members as unsophisticated. Accordingly, silence in regards to the Civil War and Confederacy reflected both congregational choice and faith heritage.[42]

Yet the majority of Primitive Baptist congregations of Middle Georgia were not alone in opting for silence in regards to the war and Confederacy. Whereas 75 percent of Primitive Baptist congregations remained silent, 25 percent, or nine of thirty-six Georgia Baptist churches also chose to remain silent concerning both the war and Confederacy, compared to 42 percent (fifteen) of GBC congregations that expressed nationalistic sentiments. None of the four silent congregations for which full membership statistics are available had a majority black membership. In addition, total membership of the four was relatively modest, ranging from 64 to 107, compared to the average GBC Middle Georgia congregation membership of 131. In short, GBC congregations in Middle Georgia that remained silent during the war years tended to be smaller, plain folk congregations, echoing Samuel Boykin's observations of less patriotism among rural churches.[43]

Aside from geography, congregational size, and racial composition as partial indicators of nationalistic sentiments or silence, soldier deaths also offer some insights into Middle Georgia congregational attitudes regarding the war and Confederacy. While local churches did not address deaths equally or systematically,

---

[42] John G. Crowley, *Primitive Baptists of the Wiregrass South, 1815 to the Present* (Gainesville: University Press of Florida, 1998) 86–98. Crowley discusses the Civil War era, citing some instances in which Primitive Baptists in the North and South addressed, directly or indirectly, the presence of war. Primitive Baptists in Wiregrass Georgia, however, maintained an overall silence, and Crowley finds a level of detachment from the Confederacy among some church members.

[43] Membership statistics are available for only four of the nine Georgia Baptist congregations that remained silent during the war years. One of the four congregations, Lauren Hills Baptist of Lauren County, was evenly split in white-black membership, with thirty-two members being white and thirty-two black. For more information on membership statistics of the churches in this study, go to www.divergingloyalties.com.

factoring available statistical data in such a manner as to measure the average number of reported annual deaths against total church membership does yield some helpful correlation regarding silent churches. Of eight silent Middle Georgia associational churches for which death data exists for at least two years of the period 1861–1865, the average total annual deaths divided by total church membership equals 2.15. The average of four Middle Georgia associational churches that only addressed the spiritual concerns of war equals 2.25. Yet the average of nine nationalistic Middle Georgia associational churches equals 1.31. In short, the death data indicates that both silent and spiritually concerned congregations lost more members to death, relatively speaking, than did the congregations openly expressing nationalistic sentiments. Although no definitive explanation can be offered, a high probability exists that a significant number of total deaths in local churches during the years 1861–1865 were the result of the war, in turn suggesting that congregations with relatively high war-related losses tended to be silent or express spiritual concerns only, whereas congregations with relatively low battlefield losses tended to voice nationalistic sentiments. To be sure, caution is required in making this assertion, because black members are included in membership counts and three of the four largest GBC churches had more black members than white. No silent GBC congregation claimed more black than white members. In addition, the local church pattern of low battlefield losses translating into nationalism and high battlefield losses into silence and/or spiritual concerns is the opposite correlation suggested by positions taken by Middle Georgia associations in relation to total reported deaths, and by inference battlefield deaths, among all churches within a given association.[44]

---

[44] Despite the importance attributed to the meaning and interpretation of death during the Civil War era, church records are far from complete in terms of deaths. Although frequently reporting annual death totals to their respective associations, local churches nonetheless did not annotate causes of death. During the war years, reported death statistics in church and associational records are not quantified as war-related or otherwise. The reported statistics are not complete,

Drew Gilpin Faust's recent study of death during the Civil War offers parallels to the experience of Baptists in Middle Georgia. In *This Republic of Suffering: Death and the American Civil War*, Faust portrays both Union and Confederacy as initially unprepared for the reality of death and unable to maintain adequate records. The war destroyed the Victorian notion of a "Good Death" in which persons passed away in the presence of family and at peace with God. Gradually, Northerners and Southerners alike had to adjust to death as wholesale, impersonal, unpredictable, and ugly. Faust argues that this new death paradigm, accompanied by previously unimaginable suffering on the part of soldier and home-front families, posed new challenges to religious faith. At the local church level in Middle Georgia, Faust's thesis of unanticipated mass, ugly carnage, which she argues may have been the most powerful reality of the entire war, offers an explanation for the lack of nationalistic enthusiasm among congregations experiencing high ratios of death during the Civil War.[45]

While the correlation with the number of deaths offers some insight into nationalistic patterns among local Baptist congregations, churches of certain associations also tended to either nationalism or silence. All seven Central Association churches for which statistics are available expressed nationalistic sentiments. In contrast, three of four Ebenezer Association churches for which statistics are available

---

as some churches did not report statistics to their association during one or more years and some associations did not meet each year. The three large nationalistic Georgia Baptist churches reporting more black than white members were Macon (Bibb County, Central Association) with 760 members (435 black) Madison (Morgan County, Central Association) with 305 members (181 black), and Antioch (Morgan County, Central Association) with 175 members (135 black). The largest non-nationalistic church, Stone Creek (Twiggs County, Ebenezer Association) had 308 members (155 black). No Primitive Baptist churches reported racial breakdowns in membership records. All membership statistics are from 1861 associational records. For more information on church death statistics, go to www.divergingloyalties.com.

[45] Drew Gilpin Faust, *This Republic of Suffering: Death and the American Civil War* (New York: Alfred A. Knopf, 2008).

remained formally silent, while the remaining congregation discussed the war and Confederacy only in spiritual terms. These two associations were the lesser nationalistic associations of the four Middle Georgia GBC associations, with the Flint River and Rehoboth bodies voicing a higher degree of patriotic sentiment. The one Flint River congregation in this study vocalized support of the war and Confederacy, but three of four Rehoboth congregations addressed the war and Confederacy only in spiritual terms, while the fourth voiced nationalistic sentiments (See table 6.1.).

Accordingly, the relationship between Georgia Baptist associations and churches in Middle Georgia in regards to responses to the Confederacy and war reflects a disparity between the voices of regional religious institutions and member local congregations as well as a struggle between innovation and precedent. Each association, comprised of numerous local congregations both urban and rural, most of which participated in annual meetings, issued statements reflective of regional dynamics and sensitivities related to the varied local congregations. For example, whereas the Central Association (comprised of twenty-six churches) exercised relative caution in issuing nationalistic statements, the records of some individual congregations reflect no such reticence. Within the larger sphere of the sixteen churches that held membership in the four Middle Georgia Baptist associations, nine expressed nationalistic sentiments (innovation), whereas seven went no further than to formally voice spiritual concern regarding the war, consistent with the precedent of not engaging secular politics.[46]

Enlarging the analysis to include all churches included in this study, the mixed responses of congregations at large suggest further

---

[46] The sampling of regionally clustered congregations in this study is statistically similar to that of Sparks's sampling of Mississippi Baptist congregations (twenty-two) and Friedman's sampling of Baptist congregations along the eastern seaboard (twenty, a number representing her usage of church minutes, excluding Baptist women's missionary society records). See Minutes, Central Baptist Association, 1861, 14, Special Collections, Jack Tarver Library, Mercer University, Macon GA, microfilm reel 191.

nuances to the pattern of innovation and precedent. Fifteen of sixteen nationalistic congregations were Georgia Baptist churches, participants within the Georgia Baptist Convention, a denominational body that broke with the tradition of avoiding secular politics in directing its members to vocalize support for the Confederacy and war. Only Mt. Carmel Primitive Baptist was not a GBC congregation. Eschewing denominational structures beyond the local sphere, Primitive Baptists at large remained true to their heritage of not engaging the outside world while war raged across the South. In voicing support for the Confederacy and war, the Mt. Carmel congregation expressed innovation.

Yet among Georgia Baptist congregations, the influence of the GBC proved insufficient to convince all congregations of the necessity of innovation even as the requests of Confederate officials were met with receptivity by some congregations. Any influence the GBC held over cooperating but autonomous congregations remained limited to the powers of suggestion and persuasion. That only eight of thirty-seven Georgia Baptist congregations in Middle Georgia were persuaded to either adopt the 1861 GBC resolution in support of the Confederacy and the war, or observe the GBC-declared day of fasting and prayer in early June, indicates the overall ineffectiveness of denominational persuasion in local church life. On the other hand, some Georgia Baptist churches evidently were capable of persuasion by voices other than from within their own denominational structures, as seven of the fifteen nationalistic GBC congregations ignored the suggestions of the Georgia Baptist Convention only to respond positively to calls from the Confederate government to observe days of fasting and prayer.

While death statistics provide some correlation with the war-time voices of local congregations, and associational affiliations of Georgia Baptist congregations offer little insight into nationalistic sentiments, the unanimity of Central Association churches merits further examination. No other Middle Georgia GBC association was represented more than once among the fifteen nationalistic churches.

Of the two non-Central Middle Georgia GBC churches, Union Baptist in Spalding County held membership in the Flint River Baptist Association, while Thomaston Baptist of Upson County participated in the Rehoboth Association. Five of the remaining six churches were members of associations whose geographical boundaries included some central Georgia counties, but were not confined to the region: the Mt. Vernon, Appalachee, Stone Mountain, and Washington associations. The remaining church, Poplar Springs North, left no records as to associational affiliation. The Central Association, in other words, is of paramount importance in understanding the fifteen GBC congregations who supported the Confederacy and war effort.[47]

The solidarity expressed by Central Association churches stands against the background of the prominent voices of Ebenezer Warren and Samuel Boykin, both active in the association and vocal proponents of the Confederacy. Former *Christian Index* editor and pastor of the most prominent church in Middle Georgia, Warren's proslavery and pro-Confederate views on the eve of the war received widespread attention. During the war, Warren assumed a prominent leadership role within the association. By virtue of his position as *Index* editor, Boykin's editorials were widely read among Baptists in Macon and the surrounding area. In addition, Boykin promoted the *Index* by visiting churches of the Central Association and speaking at association meetings. While the editor sometimes also promoted his paper at other associations, his presence at the Central meeting was unfailing. Unique in his relationship with the Central Association was Boykin's purchase of full-page advertisements within the printed minutes of the annual meeting that received distribution within local congregations. Boykin's presence and voice apparently were

---

[47] The Appalachee, Stone Mountain, and Washington Baptist associations each contained churches within one or more counties that overlapped into the counties represented by Middle Georgia associations, yet none of their congregations were located in Bibb County or a county adjacent to Bibb County.

manifested more fully within the churches of the Central Association than elsewhere.[48]

While echoing Boykin in supporting the Confederacy and war, the seven Central Association churches also collectively differed from the association at large and evidenced nuances among themselves. Boykin's urgings notwithstanding, the Central Association as a whole was the least nationalistic of all four Georgia Baptist associations in Middle Georgia. Expressing initial pro-Confederate sentiments that disappeared by the second half of the war, Central Baptists transitioned from early nationalism to concern for soldiers' souls. The nationalistic voices of the seven member churches for which records remain appear to be more reflective of the early associational voice. Yet the impetus for innovation reveals a divergence among the seven. While three congregations' nationalistic expressions came about in response to the Georgia Baptist Convention in passing the 1861 GBC resolution, the remaining four supported the Confederacy via fasting and prayer, but not in response to the GBC. The three GBC-responsive congregations—Macon Baptist in Bibb County, Madison Baptist in Morgan County, and Antioch Baptist in Morgan County—were three of the largest congregations in the association, with membership totals of 760, 305, and 175, respectively. Conversely, the four congregations that ignored the GBC resolution—Providence Baptist in Baldwin County, Bethel Baptist in Jasper County, Ramouth Baptist in Putnam County, and Salem Baptist in Jones County—were all smaller congregations, with memberships of 136, 80, 62 and 55, respectively. These statistics suggest a correlation between congregational size and the influence of the Georgia Baptist Convention upon local churches.

---

[48] Boykin's advertisements within the printed minutes of the Central Association seemingly promoted his name as much as they did the *Christian Index* newspaper. For example, his name appeared twice within the advertisement in the 1863 program, in large bold print as publisher of the *Index* and a second time in soliciting "letters" and subscription requests addressed to "SAMUEL BOYKIN, Macon, Ga."

A second statistical correlation also emerges from congregational data in relation to responses to the GBC from Central Association churches. Each of the three large, GBC-responsive churches had more black members than white members, whereas each of the four small, non-responsive churches was comprised largely of white members. In other words, planter-dominated churches tended to yield to the directives of the Georgia Baptist Convention, whereas plain folk congregations generally ignored the state convention. The loyalty of large, planter churches to denominational entities beyond the local level may reflect the fact that from its inception in 1845, Southern Baptist Convention meetings were attended by Georgia Baptist individuals who collectively owned a larger percentage of slaves than did the average Georgia slaveholder. Likewise, Georgia Baptist Convention gatherings consisted largely of men of means, including a disproportionably high percentage of slave-owners within the state.[49]

What, then, was the source of the pro-Confederate views of the smaller, plain folk churches? Or, stated another way, to whom were these congregations responding? Two of the four congregations—Providence Baptist and Salem Baptist—responded directly to appeals of the Confederate government to observe days of fasting and prayer. The other two congregations—Bethel Baptist and Ramouth Baptist—voted to observe days of fasting and prayer without indicating the influence of any outside agency. None of the four congregations observed a day of fasting and prayer prior to June 1862. Although the motivations of the latter two churches are ultimately unknowable, the available stated motivations of the non-GBC responsive, small, yeoman congregations point to a desire to follow government appeals.[50]

---

[49] See Robert G. Gardner, *A Decade of Debate*, 2, 29–30.

[50] No clear patterns emerge to indicate the motivating source for observance of days of fasting and prayer by the Bethel and Ramouth churches. The four Central Baptist Association congregations that did not respond to the Georgia Baptist Convention resolution of 1861 voted in the following months to observe days of fasting of prayer: Bethel (June 1862), Providence (March 1863, August

Accordingly, at least within the Central Baptist Association, the data suggests that the voice of the Confederate government counted for more in small, plain folk churches than did the voice of Baptist leadership. Conversely, to large, planter-dominated churches, the voice of the denomination seemingly carried more, or at least similar, weight than did the voice of the government. Only two of the three GBC-responsive churches (the Macon and Antioch churches), according to church records, also observed days of fasting and prayer as requested by the Confederate government. In short, patterns of nationalistic voices within the seven Central Association churches suggest that the Baptist denomination played a dominant role in shaping the pro-Confederate voices of large, planter-dominated churches, whereas the Confederate government played a more significant role in shaping the nationalistic voices of small, plain folk-oriented congregations.

On another level, the local presence and voice of *Christian Index* editor Samuel Boykin, expressed in his support both of the denomination and the Confederate government, may have served to bridge nationalistic responses in both large and small congregations of the Central Association. Farther from the offices and routine personal presence of Boykin (and to a lesser extent Warren), patterns of nationalistic rhetoric evidenced disparity with that of Central Association churches. The remaining two nationalistic congregations from Middle Georgia associations, Union Baptist (Flint River) and Thomaston Baptist (Rehoboth), suggest that congregational size and socio-economic composition are not fully reliable indicators of the sources of nationalistic rhetoric. The Union church, a small congregation of sixty members with a majority white population, joined the large, planter-dominated congregations of the Central Association in responding to the directives of the Georgia Baptist Convention in May 1861. Nonetheless, Union Baptist remained the only compliant church that did not actually endorse the GBC

1863, March 1864, May 1864), Ramouth (September 1862, March 1863), and Salem (August 1862, April 1863).

Diverging Loyalties

resolution, nor indicate that the setting aside of June 1 that year as a day of fasting and prayer was in response to the directive of the GBC. Acquiescence to the wishes of the state convention, in other words, remained implicit rather than explicit. On the other hand, the 144-member Thomaston church did not respond to the GBC resolution, nor do church minutes indicate the setting aside of days of fasting and prayer.[51]

Furthermore, a pattern of small, plain-folk-dominated churches supportive of the Georgia Baptist resolution existed outside Middle Georgia associations. Among the seven churches that were affiliated with associations other than the four Middle Georgia GBC associations, six were Georgia Baptist congregations. Of the four for which membership data is available, three expressly voiced support of the 1861 GBC resolution. New Bethel Baptist Church in Washington County (105 members), New Hope Baptist Church in Greene County (90 members), and Jackson Baptist in Washington County (48 members), all passed resolutions in support of the GBC directives. Contrary to patterns among Central Association churches, in all three instance white members outnumbered black members. For New Hope and Jackson, support of the Confederacy and war consisted only of following the directives of the GBC. New Bethel, on the other hand, evidenced continual support of the war, observing days of fasting and prayer, one expressly in response to the call of President Davis. The fourth congregation, County Line Baptist Church in Newton County, observed days of fasting and prayer, but did not embrace the GBC resolution. Smaller than New Bethel and New Hope, County Line counted only fifty-one members, including a mere eight slaves. As such, patterns evident among churches of the Central Association did not hold among churches of other Middle

---

[51] Minutes, Union Baptist Church, Spalding County, 1861, Special Collections, Jack Tarver Library, Mercer University, Macon GA.

Georgia associations or among churches in Middle Georgia claiming membership in non-Middle Georgia associations. [52]

In sum, a survey of nationalistic Georgia Baptist churches suggests the possibility that localized factors trumped congregational size and racial composition. Death rates and the immediacy of Samuel Boykin and the *Christian Index* both correspond with general patterns of nationalism and silence. More proportionally impacted by wartime deaths, the fifteen congregations remaining silent were generally small and rural in nature. In addition, Boykin's 1863 observation that rural churches were not observing days of fasting and prayer for the country may have reflected frustration over the limits of his influence in the face of higher illiteracy rates in rural areas of the state. Yet frustration often flowed from the pen of the *Index* editor. Although sixteen congregations evidenced patriotic sentiments and actions, and an additional thirteen offered support of army missions, Boykin in the second half of the war continuously scolded home-front Baptists for not supporting army missions. Ultimately, the edicts of denomination and government and the urgings of the editor of the nation's largest Baptist newspaper, while evidencing a degree of effectiveness, nonetheless proved unable on a large scale to overcome tradition in terms of avoidance of formal

---

[52] Minutes, New Bethel Baptist Church, Washington County, 1861–1865, Special Collections, Jack Tarver Library, Mercer University, Macon GA, microfilm reel 504; minutes, New Hope Baptist Church, Greene County, 1861–1865, Special Collections, Jack Tarver Library, Mercer University, Macon GA, microfilm reel 473; minutes, County Line Baptist Church, Newton County, 1861–1865, Special Collections, Jack Tarver Library, Mercer University, Macon GA. Membership statistics are from 1861. The fourth congregation, Bethlehem Baptist Church in Laurens County, was active in three different associations (Hephzibah, Ebenezer, and Mount Vernon) during the nineteenth century, although none of the three associations include the congregation in church summaries during the war years. In 1866, Bethlehem is listed as a member of the Mount Vernon Baptist Association, although church statistics for this study are not included because racial composition of Baptist churches shifted following the war. See Minutes, Mount Vernon Baptist Association, 1866, 7, Special Collections, Jack Tarver Library, Mercer University, Macon GA.

engagement in secular political matters in local Baptist congregations in Middle Georgia.

Finally, while Baptists as a whole only partially responded to calls for patriotic engagement, one lone congregation voiced formal criticism of the Confederate government. A congregation of 138 members, 86 of whom were white, Antioch Baptist Church of Washington County, a member of the Washington Baptist Association, appeared similar to other mid-sized churches in Middle Georgia. Antioch's only reference to the Civil War, however, is one of complaint. On 4 October 1862, the congregation appointed a committee to petition "Congress to relieve our soldiers from duty on the Sabbath." For the members of Antioch Baptist, religion remained more important than unbridled patriotism, and proper observance of the Sabbath was not to be defiled even for the good of the country.[53]

A lone congregational voice of limited opposition, Antioch nonetheless expressed the conundrum facing all Baptist congregations in the South during the Civil War: the demands of a nation dependent upon theological justification and the blood of saints, contrasted with the heritage of a religious people long defined by distinctions drawn between worlds secular and sacred. Caught between the pull of these two poles, Baptist churches gravitated toward one or the other in patterns that ultimately evidenced the primacy of decision-making at the local congregational level.

---

[53] Minutes, Washington Baptist Association, 1861, 13, Special Collections, Jack Tarver Library, Mercer University, Macon GA, microfilm reel 1246; minutes, Antioch Baptist Church, 1862, Special Collections, Jack Tarver Library, Mercer University, Macon GA, microfilm reels 375, 503.

CONCLUSION

The Civil War era evoked a variety of responses among Baptists of Middle Georgia. While historians as diverse as Samuel Boykin in the 1880s, David Chesebrough in the 1980s, and Daniel Stowell in the 1990s portrayed Baptists in the South as monolithic in their support of the Confederacy and war effort, this study of Baptists in Middle Georgia, a plantation region not known for Union sympathizers, suggests that Baptist voices and actions in the South during the Civil War were frequently complex and sometimes contradictory.[1]

While the war drew men from Middle Georgia's Baptist churches into the service of the Confederate army, Baptists remaining in Middle Georgia offered mixed messages regarding the conflict consuming the South. Baptist elites in Georgia officially addressed the national conflict. Meeting in April 1861, the Georgia Baptist Convention, comprised of leading Baptist figures in the state, including numerous slaveholders, passed a resolution strongly endorsing the Confederacy and the war, and asked local churches in Georgia to affirm the statement. In addition, the GBC requested that churches set aside a day of fasting and prayer. Yet only seven of the thirty-six Middle Georgia GBC churches studied endorsed even a portion of the resolution. The churches that did respond to the GBC resolution tended to be larger and urban, congregations more likely to send representatives to the Georgia Baptist meetings, and more likely to count large slaveholders among members, than were smaller, rural churches. Among the remaining Baptist congregations at large, thirteen during the course of the war addressed the national

---

[1] Samuel Boykin, *History of the Baptist Denomination of Georgia*, 2 vols. (Atlanta: Jas. P. Harrison, 1881) 1:225–35; David B. Chesebrough, "A Holy War: The Defense and Support of the Confederacy by Southern Baptists," *American Baptist Quarterly* 17/1 (March 1987): 17–31; Daniel W. Stowell, "The Ways of Providence: Baptist Nationalism and Dissent in the Civil War," *Baptist History & Heritage* 32/3,4 (July/October 1997): 7–20.

conflict on a spiritual level, while fifteen offered no observations regarding the war and Confederacy. While denominational affiliations reveal clear-cut patterns (expressed in nationalism being much more common in GBC-related churches than in Primitive Baptist congregations), congregational dynamics such as racial composition, geographical location, and battlefield deaths of soldier members offer some clues regarding patterns of nationalism, spirituality, and silence.

In addition, the responses, or lack thereof, of Baptists to the Civil War and Confederacy took place within the context of the diversification of broader patterns in Baptist life that encompassed cultural, political, theological, and structural dynamics. Identification with Southern culture, secession, and war led Baptists to repeatedly revisit and reshape accepted Calvinistic understandings of providence, evidencing a lack of consensus concerning the knowing of God's will. The war also challenged traditional Baptist views of the separation of church and state. In addition, when the war devastated established evangelistic and mission venues among Baptists, associations and churches struggled to craft new mission philosophies and fields of service. Although army missions became an overarching focus of Baptists during the war, many Baptists on the home-front nonetheless remained aloof to mission work among soldiers. Meanwhile, Baptists serving in the army often found little denominational support and exhibited nominal denominational identity. When the South's defeat threw Baptist mission efforts into chaos yet again, Baptist groups responded to this second missions crisis in decidedly differing fashions.

The war years also reshaped discipline, gender, and racial norms in Baptist congregations and associations. Discipline patterns shifted during the war years. In the face of the absence of significant numbers of male members, women found new empowerment within church life, yet were unable and seemingly unwilling to challenge the traditional male-dominated social structures that defined internal ecclesial hierarchies. Meanwhile, as racial tensions increased throughout the South, black church members increasingly confronted white power structures in biracial congregations, in turn eliciting varied responses at the local church level, and in general attaining various levels of autonomy in the months immediately following the end of the war.

Unable to fashion a unified front during the war, much less assure Southern victory, the post-war Baptist landscape in significant ways looked noticeably different than in pre-war years. While most preachers remained in the pulpit from beginning to end, Baptist congregations, associations and individuals in Middle Georgia navigated divergent spiritual and temporal paths during the war years, emerging from their wilderness experience with frayed political and cultural ideologies, less cohesive theological foundations, twice-shattered missionary paradigms, a greater proportion of female church members, and the fragmentation of biracial congregational life.

The effects of the Civil War permeated Baptists in the South for decades, paralleling the struggles of the region at large. In some cases, the changes wrought by the Civil War became a fixture in Baptist life in the South well into the twentieth century. In other instances, war-era transformations ultimately provided the underpinnings that empowered Baptists in the South of the twentieth century to expand their reach.

Resenting the presence of Northern Baptists who seized opportunities to minister in the South following the war, many Baptists in the South nonetheless found themselves dependent upon Northern Baptist organizational stability and religious literature until the last decade of the century. Upon finally wresting Southern churches away from the influence of Northern Baptists at the turn of the century, Southern Baptists created a centralized organization that engendered greater loyalty to denominationalism and ultimately propelled the Southern Baptist Convention into a roll as a dominant political force in the South in the latter half of the twentieth century. At the same time, the trajectory of Southern Baptists expanded geographically. When many white Southerners migrated northward in search of jobs in the first half of the twentieth century, the Southern Baptist Convention began a systematic march into Northern states, becoming a national organization by the decade of the 1960s.

Theological changes also resulted from the Civil War-era transformation of Baptists. While Primitive Baptists retained Calvinistic theology and an isolationist attitude, for Southern Baptists the Calvinism that underscored assurance of God's providential blessing during the war declined in the decades following, virtually disappearing from public theological discourse by the turn of the century, only to return in the late twentieth century. The waning of Calvinistic discourse did not indicate a period of disinterest in the tenets of Calvinism, but rather an absorption of providence and sovereignty into a heightened embrace of human free will at a time of human progress as evidenced in the spread of democracy and freedom worldwide. Yet following the cultural and social revolutions of the 1960s and 1970s, and in the midst of the subsequent rise of fundamentalist-modernist struggles within Southern Baptist life, Calvinist theology reemerged in public discourse. Some conservatives of the late twentieth century, spearheaded by the Calvinistically-reoriented Southern Baptist Theological Seminary, appropriated the language of providence from Baptist life of the 1850s and 1860s in an effort to legitimize their current cultural positions and seek purity of theology.

Of broader interest among Baptists, the trajectory of missions was also influenced by the failures of the Civil War years. Not until the 1880s did Southern Baptist missionary activity finally experience notable recovery, thanks to the efforts of women. Although yet regulated to traditional roles of limited power within local churches, women experienced increased numerical influence within church life after the Civil War. Seizing an initiative that men failed to address adequately, women in the 1880s used their numerical clout to develop funding mechanisms for missionaries at home and abroad. In the ensuing years, women's support has remained critical to the success of Baptist mission work, while their influence on the mission front has enabled women to assume increased, formal leadership roles, including pastoral positions, in Baptist churches throughout the South, despite resistance from fundamentalist Baptists.

Meanwhile, freedmen, abandoning white Baptist churches during Reconstruction, by the turn of the century established their own missionary and educational structures that continued to grow and prosper in the ensuing years. Freed from the constraints of white paternalism, black Baptists by the late twentieth century experienced rapid growth even as Southern Baptist growth peaked in the 1950s. Southern Baptist efforts to recruit black members in the latter decades of the twentieth century produced limited progress. Even as the newly fundamentalist-led SBC at the turn of the twenty-first century routinely garnered public attention for both sectarian and secular political activities amid denominational numerical decline, the National Baptist and Progressive National Baptist Conventions, both African American, experienced significant numerical and organizational growth. While most Baptist congregations yet remain segregated, as they were in the years immediately following the war, African-American Baptists today are arguably more influential than Southern Baptists in the South, reflecting a juxtaposition of the racial dynamics of Civil-War era Baptists.[2]

---

[2] For a summary of Baptist life in America from Reconstruction through the end of the century, see Leon McBeth, *The Baptist Heritage: Four Centuries of Baptist Witness* (Nashville: Broadman Press, 1987) 392–463, 717–22. A 2008 joint conference, the New Baptist Covenant Celebration held in Atlanta, of moderate white Baptists and African-American Baptists offers a glimpse into the current influence of African-American Baptists. Comprised primarily of African-American Baptists, the meeting, attended by some 15,000, represented a majority of Baptists throughout North America.

WORKS CITED

Primary Sources

Unpublished Sources
"A Calm Appeal," 1845. Special Collections, Jack Tarver Library, Mercer University, Macon, Georgia. Catalogued with 1845 SBC *Proceedings*.
Antioch Baptist Church records, Morgan County, Georgia. Georgia Baptist Church Records. Special Collections, Jack Tarver Library, Mercer University, Macon, Georgia, reel 372.
Antioch Baptist Church records, Washington County, Georgia. Georgia Baptist Church Records. Special Collections, Jack Tarver Library, Mercer University, Macon, Georgia, reels 375, 503.
Bethel Baptist Church records, Jasper County, Georgia. Georgia Baptist Church Records. Special Collections, Jack Tarver Library, Mercer University, Macon, Georgia, reel 247.
Bethesda Baptist Church records, Greene County, Georgia. Georgia Baptist Church Records. Special Collections, Jack Tarver Library, Mercer University, Macon, Georgia, reel 11.
Bethlehem Baptist Church records, Laurens County, Georgia. Georgia Baptist Church Records. Special Collections, Jack Tarver Library, Mercer University, Macon, Georgia, reel 110.
Bethlehem Baptist Church records, Morgan County, Georgia. Georgia Baptist Church Records. Special Collections, Jack Tarver Library, Mercer University, Macon, Georgia, reel 377.
Bluewater Baptist Church records, Laurens County, Georgia. Georgia Baptist Church Records. Special Collections, Jack Tarver Library, Mercer University, Macon, Georgia, reel 500.
Carmel Primitive Baptist Church records, Crawford County, Georgia. Georgia Baptist Church Records. Special Collections, Jack Tarver Library, Mercer University, Macon, Georgia, reel 317.
Central Baptist Association minutes. Georgia Baptist associational records. Special Collections, Jack Tarver Library, Mercer University, Macon, Georgia.
County Line Baptist Church records, Newton County, Georgia. Georgia Baptist Church Records. Special Collections, Jack Tarver Library, Mercer University, Macon, Georgia, reel 399.
Ebenezer Baptist Association minutes. Georgia Baptist associational records. Special Collections, Jack Tarver Library, Mercer University, Macon, Georgia.

Diverging Loyalties

Ebenezer Primitive Baptist Association minutes. Georgia Baptist associational records. Special Collections, Jack Tarver Library, Mercer University, Macon, Georgia.

Echoconnee Primitive Baptist Association minutes. Georgia Baptist associational records. Special Collections, Jack Tarver Library, Mercer University, Macon, Georgia.

Emmaus Primitive Baptist Church records, Upson County, Georgia. Georgia Baptist Church Records. Special Collections, Jack Tarver Library, Mercer University, Macon, Georgia, reel 608.

Flint River Baptist Association minutes. Georgia Baptist associational records. Special Collections, Jack Tarver Library, Mercer University, Macon, Georgia.

Fort Early Baptist Church records, Dooly County, Georgia. Georgia Baptist Church Records. Special Collections, Jack Tarver Library, Mercer University, Macon, Georgia, reel 196.

Friendship Baptist Church records, Dooly County, Georgia. Georgia Baptist Church Records. Special Collections, Jack Tarver Library, Mercer University, Macon, Georgia, reel 171.

Georgia Baptist Association minutes. Georgia Baptist associational records. Special Collections, Jack Tarver Library, Mercer University, Macon, Georgia.

Georgia Baptist Convention minutes, 1840–1867. Georgia Baptist Church Records. Special Collections, Jack Tarver Library, Mercer University, Macon, Georgia.

Greensboro Baptist Church records, Greene County, Georgia. Georgia Baptist Church Records. Special Collections, Jack Tarver Library, Mercer University, Macon, Georgia, reel 491.

Harmony Primitive Baptist Church records, Pike County, Georgia. Georgia Baptist Church Records. Special Collections, Jack Tarver Library, Mercer University, Macon, Georgia, reel 608.

Harris Springs Baptist Church records, Newton County, Georgia. Georgia Baptist Church Records. Special Collections, Jack Tarver Library, Mercer University, Macon, Georgia, reel 596.

Hawkinsville Baptist Church records, Pulaski County, Georgia. Georgia Baptist Church Records. Special Collections, Jack Tarver Library, Mercer University, Macon, Georgia, reel 32.

Hephzibah Baptist Association minutes. Georgia Baptist associational records. Special Collections, Jack Tarver Library, Mercer University, Macon, Georgia.

High Shoals Primitive Baptist Church records, Monroe County, Georgia. Georgia Baptist Church Records. Special Collections, Jack Tarver Library, Mercer University, Macon, Georgia, reel 301.

Houston Factory Baptist Church records, Houston County, Georgia. Georgia Baptist Church Records. Special Collections, Jack Tarver Library, Mercer University, Macon, Georgia, reel 40.

Indian Creek Baptist Church records, Henry County, Georgia. Georgia Baptist Church Records. Special Collections, Jack Tarver Library, Mercer University, Macon, Georgia.

Jackson Baptist Church records, Washington County, Georgia. Georgia Baptist Church Records. Special Collections, Jack Tarver Library, Mercer University, Macon, Georgia, reel 41.

Julia Stanford diary. Spencer King Papers. Special Collections, Jack Tarver Library, Mercer University, Macon, Georgia.

Lauren Hills Baptist Church records, Laurens County, Georgia. Georgia Baptist Church Records. Special Collections, Jack Tarver Library, Mercer University, Macon, Georgia, reel 370.

Lebanon Baptist Church records, Crawford County, Georgia. Georgia Baptist Church Records. Special Collections, Jack Tarver Library, Mercer University, Macon, Georgia.

Liberty Baptist Church records, Wilkinson County, Georgia. Georgia Baptist Church Records. Special Collections, Jack Tarver Library, Mercer University, Macon, Georgia, reels 71, 638.

Macon First Baptist Church records, Bibb County, Georgia. Georgia Baptist Church Records. Special Collections, Jack Tarver Library, Mercer University, Macon, Georgia, box CH 4.

Madison Baptist Church records, Morgan County, Georgia. Georgia Baptist Church Records. Special Collections, Jack Tarver Library, Mercer University, Macon, Georgia, reel 383.

Midway Baptist Church records, Bibb County, Georgia. Georgia Baptist Church Records. Special Collections, Jack Tarver Library, Mercer University, Macon, Georgia, reel 69.

Mineral Springs Baptist Church records, Washington County, Georgia. Georgia Baptist Church Records. Special Collections, Jack Tarver Library, Mercer University, Macon, Georgia, reel 524.

Mount Calvary Baptist Church records, Pulaski County, Georgia. Georgia Baptist Church Records. Special Collections, Jack Tarver Library, Mercer University, Macon, Georgia, reel 384.

Mount Calvary Primitive Baptist Church records, Monroe County, Georgia. Georgia Baptist Church Records. Special Collections, Jack Tarver Library, Mercer University, Macon, Georgia, reel 339.

New Bethel Baptist Church records, Washington County, Georgia. Georgia Baptist Church Records. Special Collections, Jack Tarver Library, Mercer University, Macon, Georgia, reel 504.

Diverging Loyalties

New Hope Baptist Church records, Greene County, Georgia. Georgia Baptist Church Records. Special Collections, Jack Tarver Library, Mercer University, Macon, Georgia, reel 473.
Notes, Civil War Centennial Column. Spencer King Papers. Special Collections, Jack Tarver Library, Mercer University, Macon, Georgia.
Ocmulgee Baptist Association minutes. Georgia Baptist associational records. Special Collections, Jack Tarver Library, Mercer University, Macon, Georgia.
Palmyra Baptist Church minutes, Lee County, Georgia. Georgia Baptist Church Records. Special Collections, Jack Tarver Library, Mercer University, Macon, Georgia.
Providence Baptist Church records, Jasper County, Georgia. Georgia Baptist Church Records. Special Collections, Jack Tarver Library, Mercer University, Macon, Georgia, reel 77.
Ramouth Baptist Church records, Putnam County, Georgia. Georgia Baptist Church Records. Special Collections, Jack Tarver Library, Mercer University, Macon, Georgia, reel 197.
Rehoboth Baptist Association minutes. Georgia Baptist associational records. Special Collections, Jack Tarver Library, Mercer University, Macon, Georgia.
Salem Baptist Church records, Jones County, Georgia. Georgia Baptist Church Records. Special Collections, Jack Tarver Library, Mercer University, Macon, Georgia, reel 184.
Sandy Creek Baptist Church records, Morgan County, Georgia, reel 124.
Shiloh Primitive Baptist Church records, Bibb County, Georgia. Georgia Baptist Church Records. Special Collections, Jack Tarver Library, Mercer University, Macon, Georgia, reel 339.
Shoal Creek Primitive Baptist Church records, Newton County, Georgia. Georgia Baptist Church Records. Special Collections, Jack Tarver Library, Mercer University, Macon, Georgia, reel 655.
Siloam Baptist Church records, Greene County, Georgia. Georgia Baptist Church Records. Special Collections, Jack Tarver Library, Mercer University, Macon, Georgia, reel 523.
Smyrna Baptist Church records, Monre County, Georgia, reel 85.
Southern Baptist Convention Proceedings, 1845–1866. Georgia Baptist Church Records. Special Collections, Jack Tarver Library, Mercer University, Macon, Georgia.
Stone Creek Baptist Church records, Twiggs County, Georgia. Georgia Baptist Church Records. Special Collections, Jack Tarver Library, Mercer University, Macon, Georgia, reel 280.
Tharpe, Simeon to Governor Joseph E. Brown, 26 February 1861. Confederate Record. Georgia Department of Archives and History, Atlanta, Georgia.

Thomaston Baptist Church records, Upson County, Georgia. Georgia Baptist Church Records. Special Collections, Jack Tarver Library, Mercer University, Macon, Georgia, reel 95.
Towaliga Primitive Baptist Association minutes. Georgia Baptist associational records. Special Collections, Jack Tarver Library, Mercer University, Macon, Georgia.
Union Baptist Church records, Spalding County, Georgia. Georgia Baptist Church Records. Special Collections, Jack Tarver Library, Mercer University, Macon, Georgia, reel 595.
Washington Baptist Association minutes. Georgia Baptist associational records. Special Collections, Jack Tarver Library, Mercer University, Macon, Georgia.
Zion Baptist Church records, Newton County, Georgia. Georgia Baptist Church Records. Special Collections, Jack Tarver Library, Mercer University, Macon, Georgia, reel 315.

Newspapers
American Baptist Register (Philadelphia), 1851.
Augusta (GA) *Chronicle and Sentinel*, 1845.
Christian Index (Macon GA), 1845, 1855–1866.
Georgia Journal and Messenger (Macon GA), 1860.
Macon (GA) *Telegraph*, 1860–1865.
Religious Herald (Richmond VA), 1845.
Savannah (GA) *Republican*, 1864.

Published Sources

Bennett, William W. *A Narrative of the Great Revival which Prevailed in the Southern Armies during the Late Civil War between the States of the Federal Union*, 1877. Reprint, Penn Laird VA: Sprinkle Publications, 1989.
Boykin, Samuel. *History of the Baptist Denomination in Georgia*. 2 volumes. Atlanta: Jas. P. Harrison, 1881.
Brown, Joseph. "Gov. Joe Brown's Reply to Alabama's Commissioner," 5 January 1861. Http://members.aol.com/jfepperson/jbrown-AL.htm, accessed 2 August 2008.
Campbell, Jesse H. *Georgia Baptists Historical and Biographical*. Macon GA: J. W. Burke, 1874.
Cates, V. T. *Conference Minutes of the Bethesda Baptist Church, Union Point, Greene County, Georgia*. Alto: East Texas Genealogical Society, 1991.
Cathcart, William. *The Baptist Encyclopedia: A Dictionary of the Doctrines, Ordinances, Usage, Confessions of Faith, Sufferings, Labors and Successes, and the General History of the Baptist Denomination in All Lands*. 2 vols. Philadelphia: Louis H. Everts, 1885.

Classified Digest of the Records of the Society for the Propagation of the Gospel in Foreign Parts, 1701–1892. London: Society for the Propagation of the Gospel, 1893.

Colquitt County Schools. "57th Regiment, Georgia Infantry." Http://www.colquitt.k12.ga.us/gspurloc/Cobbslegion/gasca/units/57th_gvi.htm, accessed 7 July 2008.

Digital Library of Georgia. "Samuel S. Hawkins Diary." Http://dlg.galileo.usg.edu/hawkins/figures, accessed 28 July 2008.

Eastern Digital Resources, "Georgia 14th Infantry Regiment." Http://www.researchonline.net/gacw/unit51.htm, accessed 1 November 2006.

———."Georgia 49th Infantry Regiment." Http://www.researchonline.net/gacw/unit100.htm, accessed 1 November 2006.

Furman, Richard. *Exposition of the Views of Baptists Relative to the Coloured Population in the United States in Communication to the Governor of South Carolina.* Charleston SC: A. E. Miller, 1838.

Georgia Division of the United Daughters of the Confederacy. "Diary and Official Correspondence Concerning Edwin Tralona Davis," in *Confederate Reminiscences and Letters, 1861–1865.* Atlanta: Georgia Division of the United Daughters of the Confederacy, 1999.

Hassell, Cushing Biggs and Sylvester Hassell. *History of the Church of God, from the Creation to A.D. 1885.* 1886. Reprint, Georgia: Old School Hymnal Company, 1973.

Hillyer, S. G. *Reminiscences of Georgia Baptists: Together with a Study of the Author's Life Written by His Daughter.* Atlanta: Foote & Davies, 1902.

Jasper County Georgia Bible Records. *Bogan Family.* Http://files.usgwarchives.org/ga/jasper/bibles/bogan.txt, accessed 14 July 2008.

———. *Newton Family.* Http://files.usgwarchives.org/ga/jasper/bibles/newton.txt, accessed 14 July 2008.

Library of Congress, *Journal of the Congress of Confederate States of America,* 1861–1865. Http://memory.loc.gov/ammem/amlaw/lwcc.html, accessed 2 August 2008.

Knight, Luican L. *Georgia Landmarks, Memorials and Legends,* Volume 2. Atlanta: Byrd Printing, 1914.

Mell, P. H., Jr. *Life of Patrick Hues Mell: By His Son.* Louisville KY: Baptist Book Concern, 1895.

Mercer, Jesse. *History of the Georgia Baptist Association.* Washington GA: Georgia Baptist Association, 1838.

Memoirs of Georgia: Concerning Historical Accounts of the State's Civil, Military, Industrial and Professional Interests, and Personal Sketches of Many of Its People. Atlanta: Southern Historical Association, 1895.

Mize, W. W. "Life during Confederate Days," in *American Life Histories: Manuscripts from the Federal Writers' Project, 1936–1940*. Http://memory.loc.gov/cgibin/query/r?ammem/wpa:@field(DOCID+@lit (wpa112070108), accessed 2 August 2008.

Sherwood, Julia L. *Memoir of Adiel Sherwood, D. D.: Written by His Daughter*. Philadelphia: Grant & Faires, 1884.

Tucker, Henry H. *God in the War. A Sermon Delivered Before the Legislature of Georgia, in the Capitol of Milledgeville, on Friday, November 5, 1861*. Milledgeville GA: Boughton, Nisbet & Barnes, 1861.

Wiggins III, Clyde G., editor. *My Dear Friend: The Civil War Letters of Alva Benjamin Spencer, 3rd Georgia Regiment, Company C*. Macon GA: Mercer University Press, 2007.

Wilkinson County Georgia History and Genealogy, "Civil War Graves in Wilkinson County, Georgia." Http://www.georgiagenealogy.org/wilkinson/civilwarburialshome.html, accessed 2 August 2008.

Books

Batts, Lewis H. *History of First Baptist Church of Christ at Macon*. Macon GA: Southern Press, 1969.

Beringer, Richard, Herman Hattaway, Archer Jones, and William N. Still, Jr. *Why the South Lost the Civil War*. Athens: University of Georgia Press, 1987.

Boles, John B. *The Great Revival: 1785–1805: The Origins of the Southern Evangelical Mind*. Lexington: University Press of Kentucky, 1972.

———. *The Great Revival: Beginnings of the Bible Belt*. Lexington: University Press of Kentucky, 1996.

Brinsfield, John W. *Faith in the Fight: Civil War Chaplains*. Mechanicsburg PA: Stackpole, 2003.

Burch, Jarrett. *Adiel Sherwood: Baptist Antebellum Pioneer in Georgia*. Macon GA: Mercer University Press, 2003.

Cliburn, Edwin L. *In Unbroken Line: A History of the First Baptist Church of Thomaston, Georgia*. Tallahassee FL: Rose Printing, 1979.

Connelly, Thomas L. *The Marble Man: Robert E. Lee and His Image in American Society*. Baton Rouge: Louisiana State Press, 1977.

Cornelius, Janet Duitsman. *Slave Missions and the Black Church in the Antebellum South*. Columbia: University of South Carolina Press, 1999.

Crowley, John G. *Primitive Baptists of the Wiregrass South: 1815 to Present*. Gainesville: University Press of Florida, 1998.

Durden, Robert F. *The Gray and Black: The Confederate Debate on Emancipation*. Baton Rouge: Louisiana State University Press, 2000.

Faust, Drew Gilpin. *Creation of Confederate Nationalism: Ideology and Identity in the Civil War South*. Baton Rogue: Louisiana State University Press, 1988.
———. *This Republic of Suffering: Death and the American Civil War*. New York: Knopf, 2008.
Flanders, Ralph B. *Plantation Slavery in Georgia*. Chapel Hill: University of North Carolina Press, 1933.
Flynt, Wayne. *Alabama Baptists: Southern Baptists in the Heart of Dixie*. Tuscaloosa: University of Alabama Press, 1998.
Freehling, William W., and Craig M. Simpson. *Secession Debated: Georgia's Showdown in 1860*. New York: Oxford University Press, 1992.
Friedman, Jean E. *The Enclosed Garden: Women and Community in the Evangelical South, 1830–1900*. Chapel Hill: University of North Carolina Press, 1985.
Gardner, Robert, Charles O. Walker, J. R. Huddlestun, and Waldo P. Harris III. *A Decade of Debate and Division: Georgia Baptists and the Formation of the Southern Baptist Convention*. Macon GA: Mercer University Press, 1995.
———. *A History of the Georgia Baptist Association, 1784–1984*. Atlanta: Georgia Baptist Historical Society, 1996.
Genovese, Eugene D. *A Consuming Fire: The Rise and Fall of the Confederacy in the Mind of the White South*. Athens: University of Georgia Press, 1998.
Goen, C. C. *Broken Churches, Broken Nation: Denominational Schisms and the Coming of the American Civil War*. Macon GA: Mercer University Press, 1985.
Graham, Harold E. *A History of the Flint River Baptist Association, 1824–1974*. Atlanta GA: Executive Committee of the Flint River Association, 1974.
Hadden, Sally E. *Slave Patrols: Law and Violence in Virginia and the Carolinas*. Cambridge: Harvard University Press, 2001.
Harline, Craig. *A History of the First Day from Babylonia to the Super Bowl*. New York: Doubleday, 2007.
Harrell, David E. *Varieties of Southern Evangelicalism*. Macon GA: Mercer University Press, 1981.
Harwell, Jack U. *An Old Friend with New Credentials: A History of the* Christian Index. Atlanta GA: Executive Committee of the Baptist Convention of the State of Georgia, 1972.
Harvey, Paul. *Redeeming the South: Religious Cultures and Racial Identities among Southern Baptists, 1865–1925*. Chapel Hill: University of North Carolina Press, 1997.
Heyrmann, Christine. *Southern Cross: The Beginnings of the Bible Belt*. New York: Alfred A. Knopf, 1997.
Hill, Samuel, Jr. *Southern Churches in Crisis*. New York: Holt, Rinehart and Winston, 1967.
Iobst, Richard W. *Civil War Macon: The History of a Confederate City*. Macon GA: Mercer University Press, 1999.

Johnson, Sylvester A. *The Myth of Ham in Nineteenth-Century American Christianity*. New York: St. Martin's Press, 2004.

Jones, Billy Walker. *History of Black and White Worship: Stone Creek Baptist Church, 1808–1865*. Dry Branch GA: self-published, 2003.

Jordan, Isabella S. *A Century of Service: First Baptist Church, Augusta, GA*. Augusta GA: self-published, 1921.

King, Spencer B. *Sounds of Drums: Selected Writings of Spencer B. King from His Civil War Column Appearing in the (Macon Telegraph News, 1960–1965)*. Macon GA: Mercer University Press, 1984.

Lawless, Chuck. *In Search of Robert E. Lee*. Conshohocken PA: Combined Books, 1996.

Lester, James A. *A History of the Georgia Baptist Convention, 1822–1972*. Atlanta: Baptist State Convention of Georgia, 1972.

Levine, Bruce. *Confederate Emancipation: Southern Plans to Free and Arm Slaves during the Civil War*. New York: Oxford University Press, 2006.

Mahan, Joy R. *Our Kith and Kin: The Ancestry and Descendants of George Washington Waldrep*. Roswell GA: W. H. Wolfe Associates, 1994.

Mathis, James R. *The Making of the Primitive Baptists: A Cultural and Intellectual History of the Antimission Movement, 1800–1840*. New York: Routledge, 2004.

McLoughlin, William H. *The American Evangelicals, 1800–1900*. Gloucester MA: Peter Smith Publisher, 1985.

McPherson, James M. *For Cause and Comrades: Why Men Fought in the Civil War*. New York: Oxford University Press, 1997.

Monroe County Georgia: A History. Forsyth GA: Monroe County Historical Society, 1979.

Montgomery, William H. *Under Their Own Vine and Fig Tree: The African-American Church in the South, 1865–1900*. Baton Rouge: Louisiana State University Press, 1994.

Mosteller, James. *A History of the Kiokee Baptist Church in Georgia*. Ann Arbor MI: Edwards Brothers, 1952.

Newman, A. H. *A Century of Baptist Achievement*. Philadelphia: American Baptist Publication Society, 1901.

Nolan, Alan T. *Lee Considered: General Robert E. Lee and Civil War History*. Chapel Hill: University of North Carolina Press, 1991.

Noll, Mark A. *The Civil War as a Theological Crisis*. Chapel Hill: University of North Carolina Press, 2006.

Nottingham, Carolyn W., and Evelyn Hannah. *History of Upson County, Georgia*. Macon GA: J. W. Burke, 1930.

Phillips, Jason. *Diehard Rebels: The Confederate Culture of Invincibility*. Athens: University of Georgia, 2007.

Power, Tracy L. *Lee's Miserables: Life in the Army of Northern Virginia from the Wilderness to Appomattox*. Chapel Hill: University of North Carolina Press, 1998.

Reed, John Shelton and Edwin M. Yoder. *The Enduring South: Subcultural Persistence in Mass Society*. Chapel Hill: University of North Carolina Press, 1986.

Rice, Thaddeus B. *History of Greene County Georgia*. Macon GA: J. W. Burke, 1973.

Robertson, James I. *Stonewall Jackson: The Man, the Soldier, the Legend*. New York: Macmillan, 1997.

Robinson, Robert L. *History of the Georgia Baptist Association*. Union Point GA: self-published, 1928.

Romero, Sidney J. *Religion in the Rebel Ranks*. Lanham MD: University Press of America, 1983.

Rubin, Anne S. *A Shattered Nation: The Rise and Fall of the Confederacy, 1861–1868*. Chapel Hill: University of North Carolina Press, 2005.

Shattuck, Gardiner H. *A Shield and Hiding Place: The Religious Life of the Civil War Armies*. Macon GA: Mercer University Press, 1987.

Sheehan-Dean, Aaron. *Why Confederates Fought: Family and Nation in Civil War Virginia*. Chapel Hill: University of North Carolina Press, 2007.

Silver, James W. *Confederate Morale and Church Propaganda*. New York: W. W. Norton, 1957.

Smith, E. E. *The History of Education in Monroe County*. Forsyth GA: Monroe Advertiser, 1934.

———. *History of First Baptist Milledgeville*. Atlanta: Cherokee Publishing Company, 1976.

Smith, Timothy L. *Revivalism and Social Reform: American Protestantism on the Eve of the Civil War*. Eugene OR: Wipf & Stock, 2004.

Sparks, Randy J. *On Jordan's Stormy Banks: Evangelicalism in Mississippi, 1773–1876*. Athens: University of Georgia Press, 1994.

Stampp, Kenneth. *The Imperiled Union: Essays on the Background of the Civil War*. New York: Oxford University Press, 1981.

Starr, Edward C. *A Baptist Bibliography*. Chester PA: American Baptist Historical Society, 1954.

Sullivan, Buddy. *A State History of Georgia*. Mount Pleasant SC.: Arcadia Publishing, 2003.

Thomas, Emory M. *Robert E. Lee: A Biography*. New York: W. W. Norton, 1995.

Walker, Scott. *Hell's Broke Loose in Georgia: Survival in a Civil War Regiment*. Athens: University of Georgia Press, 2005.

Wetherington, Mark V. *Plain Folk's Fight: The Civil War and Reconstruction in Piney Woods Georgia*. Chapel Hill: University of North Carolina Press, 2006.

Williams, David. *Rich Man's War: Class, Caste, and Confederate Defeat in the Lower Chattahoochee Valley*. Athens: University of Georgia Press, 1988.

Wills, Gregory A. *Democratic Religion: Freedom, Authority and Church Discipline in the Baptist South, 1785–1900*. New York: Oxford University Press, 2003.

Wyatt-Brown, Bertram. *Southern Honor: Ethics and Behavior in the Old South*. New York: Oxford University Press, 1982.

Articles

Barr, Alwyn. "Black Urban Churches on the Southern Frontier, 1865–1900," *Journal of Negro History* 82/4 (Fall 1997): 368.

Berends, Kurt O. "Wholesome Reading Purifies and Elevates the Man: The Religious Military Press in the Confederacy." In *Religion and the American Civil War*, edited by Randall Miller, 131–66. New York: Oxford University Press: 1998.

Chesebrough, David B. "A Holy War: The Defense and Support of the Confederacy by Southern Baptists," *American Baptist Quarterly* 17/1 (March, 1987) 1987): 17–31.

Fletcher, Jesse. "Effects of the Civil War on Southern Baptist Churches," *Baptist History & Heritage* 32/Nos. 3-4 (July/October 1997): 32–46.

Foster, Gaines M. "Guilt over Slavery: A Historiographical Analysis," *Journal of Southern History* 56/4 (November 1990): 665–94.

Gourley, Bruce T. "John Leland: Evolving Views of Slavery, 1789–1839," *Baptist History & Heritage* 40/1 (Winter 2005): 104–16.

Harvey, Paul. "'Yankee Faith' and Southern Redemption: White Southern Baptist Ministers, 1850–1900." In *Religion and the American Civil War*, edited by Randall Miller, 167–86. New York: Oxford University Press: 1998.

Hill, Samuel H. "Religion and the Results of the Civil War." In *Religion and the American Civil War*, edited by Randall Miller, 360–82. New York: Oxford University Press, 1998.

Jones, Billy Walker. "Antioch Baptist Church in the Civil War Era." Dry Branch GA: self-published, 2000.

———. "Roster of Confederate Servicemen Who Were Members of This [Stone Creek Baptist] Church." Typed manuscript, undated. In author's possession.

Martin, Sandy D. "Black Baptists, African Missions, and Racial Identity, 1880–1915: A Case Study of African-American Religion," *Baptist History & Heritage* 35/3 (Summer/Fall 2000): 79–92.

Mitchell, Reid. "Christian Soldiers?: Perfecting the Confederacy." In *Religion and the American Civil War*, edited by Randall Miller, 297–309. New York: Oxford University Press, 1998.

Mohr, Clarence L. "Slaves and White Churches in Confederate Georgia." In *Masters and Slaves in the House of the Lord: Race and Relations in the American South, 1740–1870*, 153–72. Lexington: University of Kentucky, 1988.

Poole, Jason. "On Borrowed Ground: Free African-American Life in Charleston, South Carolina, 1810–1861." In *Essays in History*, volume 36. Charlottesville: University of Virginia Press, 1994.

Shurden, Walter B. and Lori Redwine Varnadoe. "The Origins of the Southern Baptist Convention: A Historiographical Study," *Baptist History & Heritage* 37/1 (Winter 2002): 71–96.

Snay, Mitchell. "American Thought and Southern Distinctiveness: The Southern Clergy and the Sanctification of Slavery," *Civil War History* 35/4 (December 1989): 311–28.

Stowell, Daniel W. "The Ways of Providence: Baptist Nationalism and Dissent in the Civil War," *Baptist History and Heritage* 32/3-4 (July/October 1997): 7–19.

———. "'We Have Sinned and God Has Smitten Us!' John H. Caldwell and the Religious Meaning of Confederate Defeat," *Georgia Historical Quarterly* 78/1 (Spring 1994): 1–38.

Wilson, Charles Reagan. "Overview: Religion in the U.S. South." Http://www.southernspaces.org/contents/2004/wilson/1a.v2.htm, accessed 2 August 2008.

Wyatt-Brown, Bertram. "Church, Honor, and Secession." In *Religion and the American Civil War*, edited by Randall Miller, 89–109. New York: Oxford University Press, 1998.

———. "Modernizing Southern Slavery: The Proslavery Argument Reinterpreted." In *Region, Race and Reconstruction*, edited by J. Morgan Kousser and James M. McPherson, 27–49. New York: Oxford University Press, 1982.

Electronic Databases

National Park Service. *Civil War Soldiers and Sailors System.* http://www.itd.nps.gov/cwss/, accessed 2 August 2008.

Dissertations and Master's Theses

Haynes, Julietta. "A History of Primitive Baptists." Ph.D. dissertation, University of Texas at Austin, 1959.

McMahone, Martin L. "Liberty More than Separation: The Multiple Streams of Baptist Thought on Church-State Issues, 1830–1900." Ph.D. dissertation, Baylor University, 2001.

Proctor, Emerson. "Georgia Baptists, Organization and Division: 1772–1840." Master's thesis, Georgia Southern College, 1968.

Appendixes

Table 5.1. Annual Discipline Cases (Excluding Absences) among Baptist Churches in Middle Georgia

Year	# of Discipline Cases
1860	66
1861	63
1862	25
1863	31
1864	12
1865	54
TOTAL:	185

Sources: The total number of cases only includes instances, other than absences, in which the offense can be identified or the offense is undetermined but the sentence is recorded. Excluded are stated cases of absences, cases for which no resolution could be determined, cases carried over from 1859 into 1860 records, and cases initiated in 1865 but not resolved by December 31 of that year. Frequently, a single case took place over a number of months in the following pattern: (1) the presentation of a charge of sinful behavior, (2) the formation of a committee to explore the charge, (3) an opportunity for the accused to respond to the accusations, and (4) a verdict from the church body. Other factors sometimes contributing to the length of time involved in deciding a given case included cancelled monthly meetings (typically the result of inclement weather) and an inability (or failure) to contact the accused.

Table 5.2. Number of Drunkenness Cases
Reported by Churches in Middle Georgia

Year	# of Drunkenness Cases
1860	20
1861	27
1 January–11 April	18
12 April–31 December	9
1862	7
1863	3
1864	0
1865	7
1 January–17 April	3
18 April–31 December	4
TOTALS:	64
Pre-War	38
Post-War	4
Total Pre-/ Post-War	42
Total Wartime	22

Sources: Church records of Baptist churches in Middle Georgia from 1860 to 1865.

Table 5.3. Statistical Comparison of Drunkenness
Cases before and during the War

Year	# Cases	Monthly Average	(% Change from Period 1 January–11 April 1861)
1860–1861 Pre-War	38		2.48
1861 War	9		1.05 (–58%)
1862	7		.58 (–77%)
1863	3		.25 (–90%)
1864	0		— (Infinity)
1865 War	3		.85 (–66%)
WAR TOTALS:	22		.46 (–81%)

Sources: Church records of Baptist churches in Middle Georgia from 1860 to 1865. The number of drunkenness cases refers only to instances in which a case is resolved, and includes repeat offenders when involved in multiple cases. For 1 January 1860 to 11 April 1861, the number of drunkenness cases is divided by 15.3 months. For 1 January 1865 to 17 April 1865, the number of drunkenness cases is divided by 3.55 months. The cumulative war months' percentage is derived by dividing by 48.18 months. Incomplete records of the ages of church members does not allow any conclusive factoring out of older, service-exempted men from drunkenness statistics. In short, the 81 percent drop in the number of drunkenness cases is likely a significantly higher percentage than that of Baptist men who fought in the Confederacy. Other factors contributing to the 81 percent figure could be a temporary decline in interest in church discipline in the face of war pressures, hinted at by the continual drop in percentages of drunkenness cases reported as the war progressed from the beginning through 1864, and cancelled church meetings during the latter half of 1864, a partial factor in no instances of drunkenness reported for that year.

Table 5.4. Discipline Cases Brought against Slaves/Freemen	Year Total # of Cases
1860	7
1861	18
1 January–11 April	2
12 April–31 December	16
1862	9
1863	6
1864	0
1865	17
1 January–17 April	1
18 April–31 December	16
TOTALS:	
1 January 1860– 11April 1861	9
During the War	32
18 April 1865–31 December 1861	16

Sources: Church records of Baptist churches in Middle Georgia from 1860 to 1865. Only discipline cases in which the accused is identified as black are included. In all but one instance prior to the end of the Civil War, all blacks referenced in discipline cases were referred to as "slave," "servant," or "property of."

Table 5.5. Breakdown of Revivals and Results by Year

Year	# of Revivals	# of New Members
1860	13	163
1861	4	38
1862	4	50
1863	8	81
1864	4	44
1865	12	214

Sources: Church records of Baptist churches in Middle Georgia from 1860 to 1865.

Table 5.6. Gender Breakdown of Revival Converts

Year	Female	Male	% Female
1860	55	56	49.5
1861	24	21	53.3
1862	39	11	78.0
1863	55	26	67.9
1864	29	15	65.9
1865	113	72	61.0

Sources: Church records of Baptist churches in Middle Georgia from 1860 to 1865. Totals include both conversions and transfers of church memberships. Annual totals do not match total revival decisions because of a lack of full reporting in church records. In some instances, the gender of converts cannot be accurately determined.

Table 5.7. Racial Breakdown of Revival Converts

Year	White	Black	% Black
1860	92	28	23.3
1861	36	2	5.2
1862	44	6	12.0
1863	67	14	20.8
1864	30	14	31.8
1865	140	45	24.3

Sources: Church records of Baptist churches in Middle Georgia from 1860 to 1865. Totals include conversions and transfers of church memberships. Annual totals do not match total revival decisions because of a lack of full reporting in church records. In some instances, the race of converts cannot be accurately determined.

Table 6.1. Associational and Congregational Civil War Sentiment

Association	Sentiment	LC* Nationalist	LC Spiritual	LC Silent
Flint River	More Nat.	1	0	0
Rehoboth	More Nat.	1	3	0
Ebenezer	Less Nat.	0	1	3
Central	Less Nat.	7	0	0
Totals:		9	4	3

Sources: Compiled from Middle Georgia associational and local Baptist church records utilized in this volume. Only churches that were members of the Flint River, Rehoboth, Ebenezer, or Central Baptist associations are included. Records are housed in Special Collections, Jack Tarver Library, Mercer University, Macon, Georgia. Note: * abbreviation for "Local Church."

INDEX

2nd Georgia Battalion 140
3rd Georgia Infantry 68, 123, 149, 152, 251
4th Georgia Infantry 140
6th Georgia Infantry 27, 103, 140, 216
9th Georgia Infantry 100, 110
12th Georgia Infantry 45, 67, 140
13th Georgia Calvary 149
13th Georgia Infantry 134, 135
14th Georgia Infantry 119, 146, 147
19th Georgia Infantry 103
23rd Georgia Infantry 103
25th Georgia Battalion 140
27th Georgia Infantry 68, 103, 219
28th Georgia Infantry 103
30th Georgia Infantry 140
31st Georgia Infantry 111
32nd Georgia Infantry 67
34th Georgia Infantry 121
43rd Georgia Infantry 219
44th Georgia Infantry 146
45th Georgia Infantry 108
46th Georgia Infantry 134
48th Georgia Infantry 118, 148
49th Georgia Infantry 102, 118, 124, 194
50th Georgia Infantry 120, 223
53rd Georgia Infantry 220
57th Georgia Infantry 149, 150
88th Georgia Infantry 110
Abolitionism 22, 53, 54, 56, 59, 84, 85
Adkins, D. J. 119
Adultery 170, 171, 200
Alabama 17, 38, 85, 86, 249, 252
Alcohol 114, 169-171, 196. *See also* Drinking and Drunkenness
Allen, Thomas 182
African Americans 3, 6, 14, 19, 25, 43, 56, 57, 82, 90, 94, 95, 98, 99, 101,

154, 159-160, 168, 175, 176, 189, 243, 253, 255. *See also* Slavery
American Baptist Antislavery Convention 84
American Baptist Antislavery Society 85
American Baptist Home Mission Society 85
American Methodist Episcopal Church 175
Andrews, Isham 142
Andrews, J. D. 120
Antietam, Battle of 121, 136; *Also see* Sharpsburg
Anti-missions Baptists 7, 9, 88, 167
Antioch Baptist Church (Morgan County) 172, 178-183, 207-209, 211, 229, 233, 235, 245
Antioch Baptist Church (Twiggs County) 138
Antioch Baptist Church (Washington County) 72, 238, 245
Appalachee Baptist Association 232
Appomattox 50, 81, 118, 124, 137, 144, 179, 211, 219
Ard, James 144
Ard, William 142
Arminianism 31
Army Camps 4, 13, 30, 48, 63, 66, 67, 76, 79, 96, 97, 99-103, 105, 106, 108-110, 112, 115, 125, 126, 128, 129, 134, 143, 144, 156, 193, 195, 196
Army of Northern Virginia 108, 109, 126, 151, 253. *See also* Lee, Robert E.
Army of Tennessee 111, 126, 127, 149, 197, 219
Athens, Georgia 199, 210

Atlanta, Campaign 13, 139, 143, 149, 150, 153, 154, 162
Atlanta, Georgia 13, 41, 90, 96, 126, 139, 143, 149, 150, 151, 153, 154, 162, 210, 243
Augusta, Georgia 22, 59, 86, 128, 212
Avarice 34, 77
Baker, Joseph S. 21-23, 108-110, 118
Baldwin County 7-10, 149, 180, 233
Barkuloo, William 149
Barr, Alwyn 188, 189, 255
Barrett, E. B. 33, 102, 108
Battlefield 12, 25, 28, 32, 37-41, 46, 47, 50, 51, 61, 62, 64, 74, 78, 79, 105, 106, 112, 115, 124, 130, 134, 139, 141-145, 147, 148, 156, 162, 197, 207, 216, 228, 240
Bennett, William W. 104, 105, 113, 249
Berends, Kurt 4, 12, 96, 101, 108, 113, 255
Beringer, Richard 43, 44, 251
Bethesda Baptist Church (Greene County) 85, 122-125, 173, 185, 186, 223, 245, 249
Bethlehem Baptist Church (Laurens County) 170, 221, 237, 246
Bethlehem Baptist Church (Morgan County) 120, 121, 223. 246
Bethsaida Baptist Church (Fayette County) 103
Bethel Baptist Church (Jasper County) 25, 89, 119, 120, 171, 182, 221, 233, 234, 245
Bibb County 5-10, 121, 138, 185, 209, 210, 223-225, 229, 232, 233, 247, 248
Bible 19, 43, 47, 49, 53, 54, 56, 61, 89, 98-101, 109, 110, 128, 155, 161, 162, 164, 176, 200, 216, 250-252. *See also* Scripture
Bogan, Caswell P. 217
Bogan, John 217
Bond, John 142

Boykin, Samuel 1, 6, 11, 12, 14, 16, 17, 20, 22-25, 28, 29, 31-33, 35, 37, 39, 45, 46, 48, 50, 52, 60, 68, 69, 76, 78, 79, 89, 90, 103, 104, 107, 112, 113, 116, 126, 129, 132, 151, 156, 159-163, 195, 201, 203, 209, 212, 221, 227, 232, 233, 235, 237, 239, 249
Bribery 34
Brinsfield, John W. 11, 12, 66, 69, 70, 114, 251
Brittain, James M. 110
Brown, Joseph E. 80, 137, 138, 248, 249
Bull, W. H. 144
Burke, Joel 148
Burkett, Joseph 141
Burkett, Solomon 141
Bussey, Charles D. 146, 147, 216
Bussey, Charles F. 216
Butler, David E. 212
Butts County 7-10
Camp Bartow, Virginia 139
Campbell Abner B. 100
Campbell, Jesse H. 77, 78, 100-102, 249
Cardell, Peter 148, 217
Cardell, Peter B. 148, 217
Cards, Playing 74, 76, 196
Calvinism 18, 21, 31, 35, 36, 42, 46, 62, 65, 103, 104, 165, 240, 242
Cathcart, William 17, 22, 23, 43, 116, 118, 121, 122, 212, 249
Central Baptist Association 8, 9, 12, 23, 25, 31, 36, 37, 63, 67-69, 74, 86-91, 93, 94, 106, 107, 114, 116, 119, 120, 126, 128-131, 146, 147, 188, 202, 207, 208, 212, 215, 220, 221, 229-236, 245, 264
Champion Hill, Battle of 149
Chaplains 4, 11, 12, 14, 65-70, 72, 77, 78, 81, 95, 96, 100-104, 109-114, 118, 119, 121, 124, 125, 127, 128, 135, 136, 144, 148, 155-157, 194, 195, 197, 203, 204, 223, 226, 251
Chattanooga, Tennessee 101, 149
Cherokee Baptists 6

Index

Chesebrough, David A. 2, 239, 255
Chickamauga, Battle of 139, 143
Christian Index, 1, 10, 15-17, 20, 21-25, 28-30, 32, 33, 37-50, 52, 57, 60-62, 66-70, 73-79, 86, 87, 89, 95-97, 99-104, 107-114, 117, 120, 122, 125-129, 151, 159-164, 193-197, 201, 204, 213, 232, 233, 235, 237, 249, 252
Christian Nationalism 49-65, 75-82, 100, 208-210. *Also see* Nationalism.
Church Discipline 14, 78, 158, 164-167, 169, 170, 171, 173-180, 182, 189, 240, 254, 259, 261, 262
Church State Separation 2, 3, 11, 12, 51-60, 62-67, 69-72, 75, 76, 81-83, 195, 205, 226, 240, 256. *See also* Religious Liberty
Clance, Wiley 141
Clayton County 8, 10
Cobb's Legion 100
Cohen, A. D. 128
Collins, Eugenius E. 149
Colonial Baptists 52, 55-57
Cold Harbor, Battle of 139, 141. *See also* Gaines Mill
Colportage 89, 96, 97, 100, 107, 127. *See also* Bibles and Newspapers and Tracts
Confederate Army 41, 48, 66-70, 74, 75, 77, 78, 96, 110, 117, 122, 124, 140, 145, 155, 157, 158, 169, 177, 192, 193, 195, 202, 206, 211, 213, 239. *See also* Army Camps
Confederate Baptist Banner 121
Confederate Navy 144
Confederate States of America 1-2, 4, 5, 11, 14, 16, 19, 20, 23, 26, 29-33, 36-41, 46, 48-51, 57, 58, 59, 62-65, 70, 71, 73-83, 88, 89, 93-97, 100, 101, 104, 106, 113-117, 119, 120, 128, 131, 134, 137, 138, 142, 145-147, 150, 154-156, 158, 161, 162, 164, 177-180, 183, 201, 203-209, 211-217, 219, 220-222, 224, 227, 229-236, 238-240
Congregationalists 188
County Line Baptist Church (Newton County) 218-220, 236, 237, 246
Covetousness 48
Crawford County 5, 8, 10, 27, 68, 121, 149, 221, 222, 245, 247
Crawford, Nathaniel M. 20
Crawford, William H. 20
Crowley, John 8, 226, 227, 251
Crumley, Rev. 155
Cumming, T. J. 45
Curry W. L. 120, 223
Dabney, Robert L. 132
Dagg, John L. 42, 43
Dallas, Edwin 135-137, 155
Dancing 170-172, 196, 197
Daniell, D. G. 95, 96
Davidson, D. L. 147
Davis, Edwin 13, 150, 151, 153, 155, 250
Davis, Jefferson 35, 60, 62, 63, 70, 81, 203, 204, 207, 209, 220, 221, 236
Dayton, A. C. 13, 73-75, 160, 161
Debauchery 34, 63
Defeat 12-14, 32, 35 38-40, 43, 44, 47-51, 64, 69, 79, 83, 96, 98, 105, 112, 115, 129-131, 145, 150, 154, 156, 161, 182, 208, 210, 214, 215, 220, 240, 254, 256
DeFore, Hiram 143
Denson, Elias J. 142-144
Denson, John 142
Dickinson, A. E. 109, 127
Dodd, J. S. 103
Dole, George B. 68
Dollar, Kent 155, 156
Domestic Mission Board, SBC 89, 99, 107, 127
Dooly County 5, 6, 10, 151
Drinking 29, 169, 170, 213. *See also* Alcohol and Drunkenness

Drunkenness 30, 34, 73, 74, 76, 77, 166, 169-171, 173, 175, 177, 178, 196, 200, 260-262
Duck River Baptists 6
Duggan, Ivy W. 102, 194
Early, Jubal A. 1
Ebenezer Baptist Association 7-10, 31, 35, 42, 43, 63-65, 84, 93, 94, 97, 105, 106, 114-116, 130, 131, 137-141, 223, 224, 229, 237, 245, 264
Ebenezer Baptist Church 103
Echeconnee Baptist Association 8
Economy 37, 53, 82, 111, 161, 215, 235
Edmonds, William 143
Electioneering 34
Eliot, E. S. 218-219
Elliott, George R. 219
Enlightenment 4, 28
Episcopalians 66, 188
Epps, Willis 142
Evangelicals 3-5, 14, 18, 27-29, 33, 38, 55, 78, 81, 104, 125, 132, 157, 171, 175, 176, 190, 200, 201, 253
Evergreen Baptist Church (Pulaski County) 114
Extortion 29, 34
Fasting and Prayer 11, 58, 93, 155, 203-210, 213-215, 217, 218, 220-222, 231-237
Faust, Drew Gilpin 4, 5, 12, 19, 79, 82, 105, 229, 252
Fayette County 8, 103
Finke, Roger 191, 192
First Baptist Church Atlanta 126, 210
First Baptist Church Augusta 22, 253
First Baptist Church Forsyth 80
First Baptist Church Milledgeville 80, 91, 254
First Baptist Church New Providence 149
First Baptist Church of Christ, Macon 9, 10, 17, 19, 22, 25, 57, 68, 88, 90, 91, 184, 186, 188, 189, 196, 208-211, 233, 235, 251

First Baptist Church Savannah 22, 23, 58, 59
Fletcher, Jesse C. 5, 133, 255
Flint River Baptist Association 8-10, 12, 26, 30, 35, 44, 45, 62, 63, 84, 85, 88, 92-94, 98, 99, 116, 130, 131, 213, 230, 232, 235, 246, 252, 264
Florida 108, 126
Folds, Thomas J. 213
Foreign Mission Board, SBC 85, 88, 89
Foreman, D. M. 92, 93
Forsyth, town of 9, 11, 21, 51, 80, 91, 122, 253
Fort Steadman, Virginia 143
Fort Sumter, South Carolina 20, 88, 158, 172, 178
Foster, J. T. 92
Fundamentalism 242
Free Will Baptists 6
Free will 44, 49, 242
Fredericksburg, Battle of 153
Fredericksburg, Virginia 100
Freedmen 129, 131, 179, 180, 183, 186, 188, 243
Freedom 22, 32, 33, 39, 49, 56, 132, 143, 158, 159, 162, 163, 165, 166, 176, 180, 185, 189, 193, 197, 242. *See also* Independence and Liberty
Friedman, Jean 3, 14, 166, 169-172, 190, 194, 230, 252
Furman, Richard 54, 163, 164, 250
Gaines Mill, Battle of 141. *See also* Cold Harbor
Galusha, Elon 83
Gambling 29, 76, 114, 166, 170, 173, 195, 196, 200, 213
Gardner, Robert G. 9, 78, 84, 85, 212, 234, 252
Genovese, Eugene D. 43, 44, 161, 252
Georgia Baptist Association 7-9, 88, 89, 122, 212, 250, 252, 254
Georgia Baptist Convention (GBC) 6, 10, 17, 20-24, 57-59, 73, 75, 84, 86-88, 90, 96, 120, 122, 125, 178, 183,

Index

203-209, 211-213, 231, 233-236, 239, 246, 253
Gettysburg, Battle of 12, 13, 16, 31-33, 35, 37, 38, 108, 121, 142, 153, 182, 191, 196, 215
Goen, C. C. 3, 18, 19, 55, 252
Gordon, John B. 111, 112; Georgia Brigade 111, 112
Grant, Ulysses S. 48, 110, 130, 144
Green, Thomas W. 146
Greene County 5, 9, 85, 120, 122-124, 151, 172, 173, 182, 185, 186, 210, 211, 222, 223, 225, 236, 237, 245, 246, 248, 249, 254
Greensboro Baptist Church (Greene County) 172, 185, 186, 225, 246
Guyatt, Nicholas 4, 28
Guyton, Cincinnatus S. 149
Hancock County Pierce Guards 118
Hardeman, Mrs. Thomas 57
Harmony Primitive Baptist (Pike County) 173, 223, 246
Hartsfield, H. H. 134, 135
Harvey, Paul 2-5, 252, 255
Henry County 8-10, 121, 223, 224, 247
Herring, James 143
Hill, Samuel 14, 15, 188, 212
High Shoals Primitive Baptist Church (Monroe County) 182, 183, 225, 246
Hinson, Elam, Jr. 143
Hinson, William 141
Hood, John Bell 125, 150, 153, 154
Honor 14, 28, 32, 39, 40, 42, 49, 59, 61, 104, 137, 139, 166, 255, 256
Houston County 5, 8, 10, 149, 180, 223, 246
Houston Factory Baptist Church 180, 223, 224, 246
Houston Female College 75
Hyman, John J. 102, 117, 118, 124
Independence 27, 39, 40, 48, 49, 58, 79, 148, 188
Independent Baptists 6

Indian Creek Baptist Church (Henry County) 121, 223, 224, 247
Irvin Militia 110
Jackson Baptist Church (Washington County) 170, 213, 214, 236, 247
Jackson County 219
Jackson, Thomas "Stonewall" 132, 254
Jackson, William T. 66, 72, 222
Jasper County 7, 9, 10, 25, 89, 119, 120, 145, 146-148, 171, 180, 182, 214-217, 221, 233, 245, 248, 250
Jasper Light Infantry 146
Jessup, William 143
Johnson, J. G. 65, 66
Johnson, Richard M. 71
Johnson, Sylvester 3, 4, 14, 160, 253
Johnson, William B. 56
Johnson, William C. 168
Jones, Archer 44, 251
Jones, Billy Walker 137, 138, 140, 141, 253, 255
Jones County 5, 7, 9, 10, 36, 220, 221, 233, 248
Jones, J. William 104, 105, 113
Jones, Stephen 141
Jones, William 104, 105, 113
Jonesboro, Battle of 139, 143
"Just Cause" 30, 36, 37, 38
Kansas Nebraska Act 87
Kentucky 53, 149, 150, 176
King, Peter C. 137
Kitchens, William 141
Ladies Relief Society 135
Land, John 144
Land, Newton 141
Landrum, Sylvanus 22, 23, 49, 100
Laurens County 8, 118, 170, 206, 207, 221, 224, 225, 237, 245, 247
Laurens County Volunteers 118
Lebanon Baptist Church (Crawford County) 26-28, 121, 222, 224, 247
Lee County 85, 248

269

Lee, Robert E. 31, 33, 74, 77, 105, 108, 112, 118, 121, 124, 144, 146, 151, 196, 197, 210, 251, 253, 254
Lee, William Henry Fitzgerald 121, 130, 142
Leland, John 52-55, 70, 71, 82, 255
Liberty 27, 32, 33, 39, 48, 162. *See also* Freedom and Independence
Liberty Baptist Church (Wilkinson County) 140, 223, 224, 247
Longenecker, Stephen L. 72, 78
"Lost Cause" 1, 45, 47, 83, 96, 132
Louisiana 149
Lowery, Joseph E. 218-220
Lowery, William J. 219
McAfee, A. J. 27, 28, 222
McAfee, Owen M. 27, 222
McClellan, George 72, 146
McCook, James W. 149
McInytyre Baptist Church 149
McKivigan, John R. 54, 55
McMahone, Martin 2, 3, 256
McPherson, James 13, 139, 176, 202, 203, 253, 256
Macon, Georgia 9, 11, 16-23, 25, 29, 46, 56, 57, 68, 88, 91, 107, 113, 126, 127, 141, 143, 162, 184, 186-189, 196, 208-211, 232, 233, 235
Macon County 10, 26, 36, 93
Macon Telegraph 20, 57, 151, 249, 253
Madison Baptist Church (Morgan County) 31, 80, 120, 183, 184, 186, 188, 212, 233, 247
Mallary, Charles D. 21-23
Malvern Hill, Battle of 139, 141, 146, 147
Manassas First, Battle of 21, 23, 24, 80, 205, 206
Manning, Kennedy 141
Marshall, A. M. 67-69, 120
Martin, Sandy 168, 176, 255
Maryland 136
Meadows, Caney S. 117, 118

Mell, Patrick 58, 59, 250
Mercer, Jesse 122
Mercer, Silas 122
Mercer University 13, 20-23, 42, 58, 122, 150, 151, 153, 155
Merrimac 153
Methodists 3, 18, 54, 65, 66, 68, 69, 78, 81, 96, 128, 132, 157, 166, 168, 175
Midway Baptist Church (Bibb County) 121, 185, 223, 224, 247
Milledgeville, Town of 16, 22, 49, 91, 187, 188, 251
Miller, Randall M. 3, 4, 79, 96, 104, 108, 132, 189, 255, 256
Millennialism 55
Mineral Springs Baptist Church (Washington County) 180, 223, 247
Missions, Missionaries 7-14, 36, 55, 83-95, 97-100, 107, 121, 130-133, 158, 167, 176, 189, 240-243; army 13, 66-70, 77, 94-103, 105-121, 124-132, 134, 195, 197, 205, 221-223, 237, 240
Mississippi 3, 86, 149, 166, 169-171, 174, 230, 254
Mitchell, Reid 4, 12, 18, 44, 54, 55, 79, 108, 255, 256
Mize, Mary 199-201
Monroe County 5, 7, 8, 10, 26, 80, 92, 173, 174, 183, 225, 246, 247, 253, 254
Montgomery County 149
Morality 13, 16, 30, 32, 37, 44, 53-55, 77, 78, 81, 99, 106, 130, 132, 156, 158, 159, 165, 166, 169, 174, 189, 193, 195-197, 200, 212
Morgan County 5, 9, 31, 80, 96, 97, 120, 121, 170, 172, 178-184, 207, 211, 212, 223, 229, 233, 245, 247, 248
Mormonism 104
Mount Calvary Baptist Church (Pulaski County) 180, 185, 247

Index

Mount Zion Baptist Church (Jones County) 36
Mt. Carmel Primitive Baptist Church (Crawford County), 221, 231
Mt. Vernon Baptist Association 205, 214, 232
Murrow, Benjamin 12, 92, 93, 97-99
"Myth of Ham" 3, 4, 13, 14, 37, 159, 160, 253
Nash, Edwin A. 144
National Baptist Convention 243
Nationalism 1-3, 14, 19, 38, 55, 57, 61, 62, 82, 130, 182, 228, 229, 233, 237, 239, 240, 252, 256
Native Americans (Indians) 12, 87, 88, 91-99, 101, 116, 121, 130, 131
New Baptist Covenant 243
New Bethel Baptist Church (Washington County) 80, 181, 205, 236, 237, 247
New Testament 19, 38, 101, 123, 128, 164. See also Bible, Scripture
New York 83, 96
New Hope Baptist Church (Greene County) 182, 210-212
Newspapers 42, 95, 96, 100, 106, 128, 249
Newton County 5, 7, 9, 181, 218-220, 223, 225, 236, 237, 245, 246, 248, 249
Noll, Mark 3, 4, 19, 28, 253
Norfolk, Virginia 153
North Carolina 152, 215
Northern Baptists 84, 25, 241
Northern Sins 47, 48, 60, 61. See also Southern Sins
Ocmulgee Primitive Baptist Association 7, 9, 36, 63
Oconee County 149
Old Testament 3, 24, 38, 41, 49, 60, 164. See also Bible, Scripture
Outer Banks, North Carolina 152
Palmer, Benjamin M. 132
Palmer, Rev. 49

Palmyra Baptist Church (Lee County) 85, 248
Parker, Gabriel 143
Patrick, David L. 213
Patriotism 14, 32, 33, 37, 40, 48, 59, 62, 81, 101, 105, 113, 209, 210, 227, 238
Peach County 149
Penfield, town of 23, 29
Peninsula Campaign 146
Pennsylvania 16, 142, 154
Perkin, James H. 211
Perry, Town of 74, 75
Petersburg, Siege of 48, 49, 113, 114, 117, 125, 127, 142, 143, 153, 154
Pettigrew, J. L. 111, 112
Phillips, William 144
Pierce, Franklin 143
Pike County 8, 10, 146, 173, 219, 223, 246
Pollard, Edward A. 1, 83
Poor Citizens 4, 12, 39, 41, 48, 89-91, 100, 157, 161, 199, 200, 215, 217, 227, 234-236, 254
Poplar Springs North Baptist Church (Laurens County) 206-209, 211, 232
Porter, R. K. 100
Potter, Rev. 155
Portsmouth, Virginia 152
Power, J. Tracy 151
Preaching 17, 19, 22, 23, 61, 67-69, 74, 77, 80, 90, 91, 93-95, 100, 101, 103, 111-115, 125, 127, 128, 131, 135, 138, 156, 158, 181, 182, 185, 189-191, 201, 212, 241. See also Sermons
Presbyterians 3, 18, 54, 65, 68, 69, 78, 81, 96, 132, 157, 166
Price, Lewis 126
Price, W. T. 118
Primitive Baptists 6-10, 26, 36, 37, 63, 64, 83, 132, 167, 170, 173, 174, 182, 183, 221, 223-227, 229, 231, 240, 242, 245-249, 251, 253, 256

Primitive Baptist Ebenezer
  Association 9, 10, 246
Profanity 29, 34, 74, 76, 79, 115, 166,
  170, 171, 175, 195, 197
Progressive National Baptist
  Convention 243
Providence 4, 11, 16, 18, 21, 24, 25, 27-
  39, 42-44, 46-50, 64, 100, 129, 130,
  195, 240, 242, 256
Providence Baptist Church (Baldwin
  County) 233, 234
Providence Baptist Church (Jasper
  County) 145-149, 180, 214-217, 248
Pulaski County 8, 10, 114, 118, 180,
  185, 225, 246, 247
Pulaski County Greys 118
Putnam County 7, 9, 202, 220, 221, 233,
  248
Quakers 54
Quitman Guards 138
Ramouth Baptist Church (Putnam
  County) 202, 220, 221, 233-235, 248
Read, Russell 142
Read, William 142, 143
Reconstruction 131-133, 165
Rehoboth Baptist Association 10, 12,
  26, 27, 93, 97-99, 121, 184, 186-188,
  192, 193, 221, 222, 224, 230, 232,
  235, 248, 264
Religious Liberty 52, 71. *See also*
  Church State Separation
Revivals, army 4, 11, 12, 38, 67, 69, 78,
  79, 96, 101-105, 108-114, 123, 124,
  131, 155; home front 91, 92, 158,
  190-192, 194, 197, 263, 264; pre-
  war 18, 22, 201
Revolutionary War 52, 56
Rice, Tullius 144
Rice, Ulysses 141
Richmond, Virginia 49, 84, 109, 135,
  139, 141, 143, 146, 249
Roanoke Island, North Carolina 152
Robertson, Thomas 144, 145
Rodgers, Joseph 142

Romero, Sydney 108, 157, 254
Ross, B. L. 61
Sabbath-breaking 29, 73-75, 77, 78, 195
Sabbath (Sunday) 11, 21, 28-31, 71-81,
  195, 200, 209, 210, 218, 238
Sabbath (Sunday) School 116, 187, 209
Salem Baptist Church (Jones County)
  220, 221, 233-235, 248
Sanders, Jeremiah 143
Sandy Creek Baptist Church (Morgan
  County) 96, 97, 117, 181, 223, 248
Savannah, Georgia 1, 6, 22, 23, 49, 58,
  59, 67, 69, 74, 100, 150, 162, 175
Savannah Republican 150, 151, 249
Scripture 3, 36, 46, 64, 83, 87, 154. *See
  also* Bible
Secession (of the South) 3, 10, 19, 20,
  56, 81, 88, 104, 135, 250, 252, 256
Second Baptist Church of Atlanta 126
Sermons 2, 10, 19, 20, 56, 57, 61, 77, 80,
  87, 93, 127, 155, 207, 209, 212, 251.
  See also Preaching
Sewell, Charles 185
Seven Days, Battle of 146, 147
Seven Pines, Battle of 141
Sharman, George 134, 135
Sharman, T. S. 134, 135
Sharpsburg, Battle of 136; *Also see*
  Antietam
Shattuck, Gardiner 69, 70, 104, 105,
  108, 110, 124, 202, 254
Sherman, William Tecumseh 41, 46,
  143, 154, 162, 177, 202-204, 207,
  210, 219, 224, 225
Sherwood, Adiel 21-23, 90, 91, 122, 251
Shiloh Baptist Church (Marion
  County) 73
Shiloh Primitive Baptist Church (Bibb
  County) 225, 248
Shinholser, John W. 149
Siloam Baptist Church (Greene
  County), 120, 222, 223, 248
Silver, James 1

Index

Slavery, Slaves 1, 3, 10, 13, 18-22, 25, 29, 34, 37, 42-44, 47, 48, 53-57, 60, 78, 82-87, 90, 98, 121, 129, 131, 145, 158-165, 167-176, 178-182, 186, 188, 189, 197, 202, 203, 207, 209, 210, 212, 215-217, 226, 232, 234, 236, 240, 251-253, 255, 256, 262. *See also* African-Americans
Slaveholders 43, 53, 54, 78, 84-87, 161, 162, 163, 167, 168, 172, 175, 176, 178, 179, 215-217, 234, 239
Smith, J. A. 149; Brigade 149
Smith, John 143
Smith, Joseph 119
Snay, Mitchell 18, 44, 54, 55
Soldiers Relief Societies 126
South America 137
South Carolina 7, 33, 54, 86, 128, 175, 217, 250
Southern Baptist Convention (SBC) 1, 19, 22, 52, 55, 56, 58, 59, 78, 83, 84, 87, 95, 107, 108, 133, 176, 209, 212, 234, 241, 242, 248, 252, 256
Southern Baptist Theological Seminary 242
Southern Baptists 2, 3, 19, 36, 42, 56, 70, 78, 83, 87, 88, 91, 95, 101, 116, 132, 133, 159, 239, 241-243, 252, 255
Southern Guilt 36, 42, 43, 44, 61, 77, 255
Southern Sins 24, 29, 30, 32, 34, 35, 37, 42, 43, 50, 73, 74, 76, 77, 99, 116, 129, 158, 161, 162, 166-175, 195, 197. *See also* Northern Sins
Sovereignty, God 44, 47-49, 50, 65, 104, 115, 154, 242
Spalding County 8, 10, 213, 232, 236, 249
Sparks, Randy 3, 14, 15, 165, 166, 169-172, 174, 179, 201, 230, 254
Sparta Baptist Church (Washington Association) 84, 85
Spencer, Alva 13, 118, 151-155, 251

Spivey, Charles 134, 135
Spivey, John 134, 135
Spivey, William 134
Stampp, Kenneth 43, 44, 254
Stanford, Julia 11, 21, 52, 80, 91-94, 138, 141, 247
Stansberry, J. M. 127
Stark, Rodney 191, 192
Stealing 170, 172, 178, 195
Stocks, Thomas 58
Stockton, J. H. 28
Stokes, J. M. 120
Stone Creek Baptist Church (Twiggs County) 137-145, 152, 180, 223, 224, 229, 248, 253
Stone Mountain Association 218, 232
Stout, Harry S. 4, 79, 108, 132
Stowell, Daniel 2, 3, 161, 239, 256
Taliaferro County Volunteers 118
Talmage, Samuel K. 164
Taylor County 8, 219
Taylor, James B., Jr. 121
Taylor, T. H. 149; Brigade 149
Teague, E. B. 159
Telfair County 5, 6, 8, 118
Telfair County Volunteers 118
Tennessee Baptist 61
Tennessee 113, 126, 149
Tharpe, Ivey 145
Tharpe, J. A. 145
Tharpe, Jefferson 143
Tharpe, Job 145
Tharpe, Judson 141
Tharpe, Marcellus 144
Tharpe, Max 145
Tharpe, Simeon 137-141, 248
Thigpen, Lucian B. 119
Theology 2, 4-7, 10, 18, 19, 21, 28, 31, 35, 42, 43, 46, 49, 51, 52, 55, 60, 65, 69, 82, 88, 104, 115, 125, 158, 160, 164, 165, 167, 180, 238, 240-242, 253

Thomaston Baptist Church (Upson
  County) 134-137, 145, 182, 183,
  187, 203, 221, 232, 235, 249
Thomaston, Georgia 137
Thompson, E. B. 137
Thornwell, James Henry 33-35, 132
Todd, John C. 149
Towaliga Primitive Baptist
  Association 10, 64, 249
Tracts 77, 98-101, 105
Traveler's Rest Baptist Church (Macon
  County) 25, 26, 93
Triennial Convention 83, 85, 86
Troup County 149
Tucker, Henry H. 122, 251
Tuggle, Edward B. 123, 124
Twiggs County 5, 8, 13, 137-139, 141-
  143, 180, 223, 229, 248
Twiggs County Volunteers 13, 138,
  139
Two Seed Baptists 6
Upson County 5, 8, 10, 134, 135, 182,
  183, 187, 203, 221, 225, 232, 246,
  249, 253
Upson County Guards 134
Vaughan, W. D. 119, 120
Van Hoose, Azor 68, 69, 126-128
Vann, Edmond 141
Vicksburg, Battle of 12, 13, 16, 31, 35,
  37, 149, 150, 153, 191
Virginia Baptist Historical Society 5
Virginia 17, 18, 22, 23, 33, 48, 49, 51,
  53, 74, 78, 86, 96, 100-103, 108-110,
  112-114, 117, 118, 121, 126, 127,
  135, 137, 139, 141-144, 146, 147,
  151, 152, 156, 175, 179, 194, 196,
  220, 222, 252-255
Walton, Edmund J. 215
Warren, Ebenezer W. 19, 28, 56, 68, 73,
  88-90, 196, 209, 232
Washington Baptist Association 71,
  84, 85, 117, 232, 238, 249

Washington County 5, 10, 80, 117, 118,
  170, 180, 181, 205, 214, 223, 236-
  238, 245, 247
Washington County Cold Steel
  Guards 118
Weaver, J. H. 135, 136
Weldon Railroad, Virginia 143
Wellborn, W. J. 164
Wetherington, Mark 4, 12, 91, 92, 254
Whalen, Daniel 149
White, George W. 68
Whitten, W. L. A. 120, 121
Whittle, O. 119
Wilcox County 6, 118
Wilcox County States' Rights Guards
  118
Wilderness Campaign 144
Wilkes County 110
Wilkinson County 8, 10, 118, 148-150,
  223, 247, 251
Wilkinson County Invincibles 118
Williams, G. F. 101
Williams, Roger 52, 75
Wilson, Charles Reagan 4, 29, 79, 108,
  132
Wingfield, John T. 109, 110
Wood, I. W. 144
Wood, John A. 117, 119
Wood, Thomas 117
Worship 31, 52, 71-74, 76, 77, 79, 95,
  109, 113, 119, 126, 130, 138, 176,
  181, 183, 184, 186, 201, 202
Woodworth, Steven 4, 103-105, 155,
  156
Wuthnow, Robert 191, 192
Wyatt-Brown, Bertram 14, 104, 166,
  176, 255, 256
Young, Pierce 51
Zion Baptist Church (Newton County)
  181, 223, 249
Zachry, William 144